OLD ENGLISH VERS

D1164249

English Literature
———————

Editor
JOHN LAWLOR
Professor of English Language and Literature
in the University of Keele

OLD ENGLISH VERSE

T. A. Shippey
Lecturer in English Language and Literature
University of Birmingham

HUTCHINSON UNIVERSITY LIBRARY
LONDON

HUTCHINSON & CO (*Publishers*) LTD
3 Fitzroy Square, London W1

London Melbourne Sydney Auckland
Wellington Johannesburg Cape Town
and agencies throughout the world

First published 1972

*This book has been set in Times type, printed in Great Britain
on smooth wove paper by Anchor Press, and
bound by Wm. Brendon, both of Tiptree, Essex*
ISBN 0 09 111030 0 (cased)
0 09 111031 9 (paper)

CONTENTS

ACKNOWLEDGEMENTS

I have intended to cover in this book as much of the Old English poetic tradition as is possible without allowing it to degenerate into a mere list of texts. As a result, I have had no choice but to use the six volumes of *The Anglo-Saxon Poetic Records,* the only editions to aim at a complete and uniform presentation, and have kept to the readings they offer in all but two cases (neither, I hope, of especial importance to my arguments). I have not preserved the diacritics used by the editors of these volumes to mark emendations, but have (in some six cases) used a diacritic of my own: a double diagonal line (//) marking abrupt and extreme changes of sense. For permission to quote from *The Anglo-Saxon Poetic Records* I am indebted to Routledge and Kegan Paul Ltd and Columbia University Press. The effect of using these at times old-fashioned editions has been in one respect salutary. Too often in the past critics of particular poems have moulded words, punctuations, and interpretations into whatever form best suits their own opinions. By accepting someone else's reading throughout I have been freed from this temptation (though I have often felt it), and so from the danger of making major lines of argument dependent on disputed matters of detail. It is right that such matters should be disputed; it is right also to broaden the field of enquiry in cases where, probably, certain knowledge can never again be reached. For similar reasons, the translations offered here, which are all my own, are *not* intended to reinforce my opinions silently, to extend the critical discussion, or to represent fully the stylistic force of the originals. They are there only to help students to follow the original, and in many instances reading the translation alone will prevent one from understanding criticism based on points of syntax, rhythm, or word-order. I have made a distinction throughout between Old

English (a language, or literature composed in that language) and Anglo-Saxon (a word I apply to men or to a society). In some few places this distinction is of importance.

My greatest debts in writing this book have been to Professor G. T. Shepherd of the University of Birmingham, whose common talk is aphorisms, and who has never failed to provide intellectual stimulus and encouragement; and to Professor John Lawlor, of Keele University, who has read successive typescripts with discriminating attention, and preserved me repeatedly from error and obscurity.

I

AN APOLOGY FOR VERSE:

INTRODUCTION

There was no light nonsense about Miss Blimber. She kept her hair
short and crisp, and wore spectacles. She was dry and sandy with
working in the graves of deceased languages. None of your live
languages for Miss Blimber. They must be dead—stone dead—and
then Miss Blimber dug them up like a Ghoul.

Dombey and Son, ch. XI

There is no evidence to show that Old English was one of Miss
Blimber's languages; but one might presume that it would have
suited her, for it is dead not only in the same sense as Ancient Greek
and Latin, which have no living native speakers, but also in the much
more restricted sense that for a long period of the world's history it
had no speakers at all, or writers, or readers. It was not used; it was
not taught. Only in the seventeenth century did this gap close, and
then, like a dinosaur, the language had to be laboriously re-articulated
through a process of comparison and analysis. The results are fairly
secure. But at any time the interpretation of a word or a phrase may
be challenged, and there is no definitive authority to appeal to,
except reason and context. Seemingly minor points are always important, because their solution has to precede any literary judgement.
There is no point in claiming that they do not matter. But, to the
average student of literature, can they ever matter enough? For most
people, is it worth resurrecting the language to read what is written
in it—especially as most of this is itself to some extent translated from
a language which may be more accessible, namely Latin?

This is a fair question, to which the usual answer is that some works
in Old English have enough intrinsic merit to be worth the linguistic
effort. Yet a sceptic could admit the merit, while still arguing that it is

insufficient compensation for the labour. Literature is after all a very wide field. Could the hours spent learning grammar not go more profitably into reading minor Victorian novels? or modern popular literature? or even major works in some other dead, or foreign, language? What needs to be proved is that Old English literature has a value different *in kind* from other types. And here the fact that the verse tradition is a dead one can, paradoxically, be an advantage. For in one way Old English poetry presents a challenge to any theory of literature based on our modern tradition from Spenser onwards. In another it can remind us of differences, affecting literature, in society and in human behaviour.

For the latter line of argument, moderns have help denied to even comparatively recent students of Old English—the rediscovery of living epic poetry produced orally for listening audiences in the half-civilised cultures on the fringe of the Western world, and luckily preserved just until the coming of the tape-recorder.[1]* Though the problems concerned with this discovery are many and complex, it gives at least a chance of putting flesh on dead bones; and the reanimated poetry can startle those for whom ancient epic has hitherto been a matter of silence, dictionaries, and a printed text. For one common element in the descriptions of barbarian narrative verse is the violence of audience response. In *Oral Epics of Central Asia,* for instance, Mrs N. K. Chadwick quotes the Hungarian traveller Vambéry on heroic recitation among the Turkmens. To the European the singing sounds dull and forced. But: 'The hotter the battle, the fiercer grew the ardour of the singer and the enthusiasm of his youthful listeners; and really the scene assumed the appearance of a romance, when the young nomads, uttering deep groans, hurled their caps to the ground and dashed their hands in a passion through the curls of their hair, just as if they were furious to combat with themselves.'[2] With this, as Mrs Chadwick points out, one could connect the very similar scene of nearly 1500 years before, in the nomadic encampment of Attila's Huns, when, as the Byzantine historian Priscus tells us, his fierce and stoical enemies were moved to joy, to excitement, or to tears, at the song of the deeds of Attila.[3]

Modern Turkmens, it may be objected, are not Anglo-Saxons, and no more are ancient Huns. But their similarity becomes more credible if we look at the fifth-century Gallo-Roman Sidonius Apollinaris writing to his friend, senator Catullinus, and complaining again of the ubiquity of poetry among the Burgundians, and the passion with which it was pursued:

* Superior figures refer to Notes, pp. 193–211.

Quid me, etsi valeam, parare carmen
Fescenninicolae iubes Diones
inter crinigeras situm catervas
et Germanica verba sustinentem,
laudantem tetrico subinde vultu
quod Burgundio cantat esculentus,
infundens acido comam butyro?
vis dicam tibi, quid poema frangat?
ex hoc barbaricis abacta plectris
spernit senipedem stilum Thalia,
ex quo septipedes videt patronos.
felices oculos tuos et aures
felicemque libet vocare nasum . . .

[Even if I could, why ask me to prepare a song of Dione, fond of Fescen-
nine verses, placed as I am among these hairy troops, putting up with German
words, often praising with a sour face what the gluttonous Burgundian
sings, who smears his hair with rancid butter? Do you want me to tell you
what destroys a poem? Frightened away from it by barbaric harps, Thalia
spurns her six-foot style, for she sees seven-foot devotees! Happy your eyes
and ears, happy I am glad to call your nose . . .][4]

For, as R. W. Chambers pointed out,[5] the subject of the songs to
which Sidonius reacted so superciliously can hardly have been other
than the destruction of the Burgundians by the Huns a generation
before, the kernel of the whole Nibelung legend; while the Burgundian king Gundahari who fell in that battle has to be identified with
the 'Guthhere' of the Old English epic fragment *Waldere*. Maybe
the links between such descriptions and Old English manuscripts
are still tenuous; but the situation exists within the poetry itself. In
Sidonius or Priscus we can recognise a perverted and hostile view of
the scene of Hrothgar's hall in *Beowulf*:

Þær wæs sang ond sweg   samod ætgædere
fore Healfdenes   hildewisan,
gomenwudu greted,   gid oft wrecen   (1063–5)

[There together was song and music before the battle-leader of Healfdene,
wooden harp touched, a tale often made],

or of the richly rewarded singing before Eormanric in *Widsith*:

Ðonne wit Scilling   sciran reorde
for uncrum sigedryhtne   song ahofan,
hlude bi hearpan   hleoþor swinsade   (103–5)

[When Scilling and I with clear voice lifted up song before our victorious
leader, and sound was sweet, loud to the harp]

The excitement in such scenes puts any 'participation' of modern poetry to shame. Like the precious Roman or the scheming Byzantine, or even like Hamlet watching the player, we may look on and wonder, 'What would he do, Had he the motive and the cue for passion That I have?'

Yet the death of the Old English poetic tradition must give us pause. We do not after all know whether the surviving poems were intended for singing, recitation, or even private reading, and though the latter seems unlikely, it is no more so than the connection of poems like *Christ* or *Juliana* with scenes like the ones described above. The texts are all we have; reading through them to a simpler but imaginary situation in their past is the temptation of ignorance. Since it is impossible to revive a dead tradition by power of imagination alone, a modern's response must, no matter what desiccation it involves, be based on the sobriety of a printed text. But even on this level there are differences from a similar reading of a later work. For if it is granted that a modern response, though weak, may still be favourable—and some of the shorter pieces have attracted poets as diverse as Tennyson, Pound, and Robert Graves[6]—*if* this is so, then one must still admit that the grounds for praise or imitation are curiously hard to define. Unlike, say, Virgil or Horace, but like the products of oral epic, Old English poetry stubbornly resists the current of modern criticism. It does not try to reach what we would recognise as a goal; though consistent and regular, it is, by any of our standards, odd.

If one considers the widely varying remarks on poetry of respected modern writers, one can see that in spite of all arguments there is a substantial body of agreement. As a first principle it is assumed that in poetry all words are weighed. The poet's job is essentially to combine (one thinks of Eliot's famous remark about Spinoza-and-the-typewriter-and-the-dinner-cooking);[7] but the reader is assured that whatever has been put in is relevant, even if by association rather than strict logic. On the one hand, words have to be used with the utmost care; on the other, their combined effect may be such as to outdistance completely the range of prosaic criticism. As W. K. Wimsatt puts it, poetry is 'like the square root of 2, or like pi, which cannot be expressed by rational numbers, but only as their *limit*. Criticism of poetry is like 1·414 . . . or like 3·1416 . . ., not all it would be, yet all that can be had and very useful.'[8] It is some such welling from the unconscious that, for Northrop Frye also, distinguishes the true production from verse, or doggerel.[9] The principles, to sum up, are unity, relevance, ambiguity, individuality; principles which can be seen and have been demonstrated everywhere in English literature from Shakespeare to Pope, from Donne to Yeats.

To this Hamlet-like subtlety Old English poetry returns the blank stare of the player without a personality. For one thing, almost all the poems we have are quite anonymous. Four are 'signed' internally by one Cynewulf, but even with this guide many scholars have felt quite unable to determine with certainty where his work begins and ends, still less to decide whether any of the other poems can be grouped as the work of one author. In Old English, style is not the man. Moreover, the anonymity is only part of a general carelessness about words which leaves no trace of 'creative ambiguity'. It is only too clear, for example, that the many synonyms for 'man' or 'sea' or 'warfare' are used not because they have faint but distinct shades of meaning, but because they provide easy variety for alliteration—an excuse ('because it rhymes')—applicable nowadays only to the most shameless poetaster. As Gavin Bone rather acidly wrote of one phrase in *Beowulf, wonna leg* [black? flame], 'the Anglo-Saxon poet is using *wann* in a careless emotive sense—he is thinking of nothing but the eeriness and horror of the scene. The next minute he will be talking of the "icy flame" if he does not keep himself under control.'[10] Still, the determination with which the eye is taken off the object, the utter lack of concern about visible unity, these prove only that Anglo-Saxon poets were not interested in externals. It does not lose them all hope of good effects, as indeed some critics are aware. In his chapter on 'Elegant Variation' in *The Verbal Icon* Wimsatt appears to feel almost irritation from the clash between admitted excellence and theoretical failure; discussing the sea-voyage of *Beowulf* 210–28, with its peculiar concentration of repetitions and synonyms, he makes of it an expression of almost naïve enthusiasm: 'He was delighted with the boat. He was eager to tell about it, as much about it as possible while telling what it did.'[11] Yet in fact the poet repeats this passage quite closely later on in lines 1905–13, by which time the enthusiasm has surely worn off, and he is by and large uninterested in objects except when they have some representative significance, as with Hygelac's torque (line 1202) or Wiglaf's sword (line 2611). So the attempt at explanation fails, and the failure is caused by the assumption that archaic writers set themselves to keep the bargain of modern poetry—that nothing vital will be left out and nothing unnecessary put in, that every word counts. But in Old English they do not. If, then, successful poetry can be written against the grain of general modern acceptance, it would seem essential for every student of poetry to know about it, and about the ways it works. The death of Old English poetry therefore has one positive value, as well, no doubt, as inescapable drawbacks. Since it means that our modern tradition is totally alien to it, in learning Old English one gains not just some modifications of insight but a second eye and a discovery of perspective.

The area which this 'perspective' encloses is largely that of language and its relation to literature. Old English verse depends very heavily on a learnt technique amounting almost to a separate poetic language, something which, as has been said, quite overrides the individual personality of the author. In some ways this learnt technique also seems to override at times the qualities of the subject-matter it is applied to. We can accept nowadays that several Old English poems owe a debt to the ideas of Boethius or someone like him;[12] and yet the Old English *translation* of Boethius is itself a highly original work, while the poems which borrow his ideas still show a characteristic and consistent bias, deep-rooted in their mode of expression. The realisation that meaning depends in the last analysis on how it is expressed is not of course a new one. In Old English, however, because of the comparative fixity of the poetic technique, it has to be raised to a higher power and kept in mind the whole time. The poems which have come down to us are almost all deeply conventional; but each separate 'convention' has a meaning and a purpose—or so at any rate one must imagine from their sheer persistence. To elucidate their rationale and to show how each part relates to the others is of course another effort at archaeology if not sheer resurrection, but only in this way is it possible to grasp such a poem as the Old English *Andreas,* which though a direct translation from Latin is still in its poetic effect much more like the rest of Old English verse than it is like anything else, including its original.

Old English poetry gains from being read in large blocks; the most valuable commentary on one poem may well be another poem. That this view has not recently found much favour among critics is largely the result of arguments drawn from what we know of Anglo-Saxon life. It has been pointed out often and vigorously that the Anglo-Saxons were enthusiastic converts to Western Christendom, that they were surprisingly well-read and even learned in Latin, and that they were therefore much more probably affected by Latin Christian prose and poetry (which still exists) than by oral, native, and possibly pagan productions (which do not).[13] 'Nothing could be more mistaken than the usual notion that Old English literature exists in a kind of peculiar Germanic isolation from the rest of medieval literature', urges D. W. Robertson, adding that on the contrary 'it is in Old English poetry that the grand themes and the poetic techniques of medieval literature are first established in a vernacular'.[14] In many ways this is impossible to dispute since, as has been said, the bulk of the literature is translation or paraphrase of one kind or another. Nevertheless it is possible to have two reactions to this situation—one, to try to ascertain what is derivative even in that part of the literature *not* obviously translated; two, to examine what is original even in the derivative parts, and, more important, to try to find out how and why it was introduced there. This second method returns us to the interrelation of language and subject-matter, an area too much neglected. Attempts to explore it, especially when dealing with a dead language, are always open to the objection that they must be subjective and circular, relying on no external authority. But this may be outweighed by the discovery of unexpected consistencies and parallels between one work and another, often between translations and poems which must be original. At any rate, this second method, of searching for perhaps a concealed individuality, is not open to the objection that might be raised against the first—that in the end it discovers only ideas that might more easily be found elsewhere, and in the process very much reduces the status of Old English as a separate literature.

As a final point, one might add that every now and then Old English poetry does *not* seem to mirror Anglo-Saxon life, so that any amount of 'background information' need not be conclusive. On one occasion in *Beowulf* King Hrothgar suggests that if the Geatish king Hygelac is killed (as we know he will be) and Beowulf himself survives, then:

> 'þe Sægeatas   selran næbben
> to geceosenne   cyning ænigne,
> hordweard hæleþa,   gyf þu healdan wylt
> maga rice'   (1850–3)

['the Sea-Geats will not have any better king to choose than you as treasure-guardian for heroes, if you will wish to hold your kinsmen's kingdom']

The elementary principle behind the phrase *'to geceosenne cyning ænigne'* may not startle a modern reader, but is quite anachronistic in historical Anglo-Saxon kingdoms, in which as far as we know the theory of kingship *Dei gratia* was established fairly early, and the people at least in theory excluded from direct control.[15] The casual nature of the remark gives *Beowulf* a ring of archaic truth, which could not have been a unique import, but must have lasted, in poetry, for some generations.[16] From it one can deduce a little of the independence of Old English verse. To return to D. W. Robertson's remarks: any reading of this literature shows that it *is* peculiar and isolated in many respects; perhaps it is only the 'Germanism' that should go out of fashion.[17]

No poet creates entirely individually. So what this book attempts to do is to explore the hidden and probably unconscious principles of composition behind Old English verse. But equally no critic writes without a background: his temptation is always to make the subject fit what he happens to know. What I hope to avoid is the urge to make the unfamiliar conform to the accepted, to label genres and mark transitions. It is worth remembering that no Old English poem has a title in the manuscripts, and that many have only slight indications of where they begin and end. Nor are they arranged as we see them printed, half-line by half-line, but are written out simply as rhythmic prose. Indeed the terms 'prose' and 'poetry' are not Old English ones at all and in this case may not represent the most important distinction; 'song' and 'speech' might be better. It is one more reminder that since so many modern assumptions are wrong it will be as well, so far as one can, to do without them—to seek comparison as well as pursue analysis, and so to see not many individual parts but one body.

2

THE ARGUMENT OF COURAGE:
BEOWULF AND OTHER HEROIC POETRY

> Rightly to be great
> Is not to stir without great argument,
> But greatly to find quarrel in a straw
> When honour's at the stake.
>
> *Hamlet*, IV, iv

If Old English poetry has any distinctive subject, it is that of courage,
of honour or the heroic life. Yet while Hamlet's apparent paradox
is only a part of the debate about honour conducted, in Shakespeare,
by Iago and Falstaff as well as by Fortinbras and Hotspur, one
defect of Old English poems seems to be that in them no such debate
is possible. In *Maldon* there are good retainers and bad retainers;
the only choice open is to die honourably or live shamefully.
In *Beowulf* those who have made the wrong choice are rebuked
simply by *'Deað bið sella eorla gehwylcum þonne edwitlif!'* ['for any
nobleman death is better than a life of shame']—and to this there is
no answer. Not even those who run away are allowed to disagree
with the ethic of honour; so, though the Old English philosophy
may be admirable, it hardly seems in any way complex.

Are matters really so simple? At one extreme the historian Arnold
Toynbee could call *Beowulf* a poem of 'barbarism on the warpath'.[1]
But at the other, the considerable literature of explanation which
has grown up around the poem over the last fifty years is in almost
total agreement about the work's extraordinary delicacy and
sophistication; it is seen as allusive, elegiac, ironic. Nor is this merely
critical over-refinement. The highly educated response to the poem
which most scholars would now accept has become established
because external facts give it firm support—for one, the identification

of Beowulf's king and uncle Hygelac with the historical pirate
'Chochilaicus', for another, the later Latin and Norse references to
the Scylding family and King Hrothgar, at whose court Beowulf
carries out his first adventures.[2] The conclusions drawn need not be
set out here. What is important is that the *Beowulf*-poet seems to rely
consistently on allusions to (presumably well-known) legends, and
that he uses this material in what is almost an anti-heroic way, to
prove that 'the wages of heroism is death'.[3] He is not satirising, and
maybe not even criticising; the emotions aroused are intricate. But
clearly something which could be called a philosophy of the honourable life is present.

Still, firmly as one may believe in such views, they have not so far
been extracted from the text of the poem alone, but rely on a very
large body of background information and speculation. The only
way to prove the 'educated' and ironic opinion right would be to set
up an experiment involving children who would be taught Old
English and given every scrap of Northern prehistory we possess
before being permitted to read, or even hear of, *Beowulf*. Their
reactions to the poem might then be both pure and competent.
Even so, it is to be doubted whether any but the brightest would
grasp immediately the dark significances of the hall of the Scyldings!
Scholarly opinion may be in agreement about *Beowulf*, but it has
come a long way from the simple reactions of most people's first
readings.

One is forced to consider the limits of response of the original,
Anglo-Saxon audience. Given the help of established scholarship and
criticism, a modern reader can see irony in *Beowulf* practically
everywhere. But is that likely to have been intended under Dark
Age conditions, when such a poem could hardly be studied, and
when most people would never read it, but only hear it, and perhaps
only once? If it was, we must conclude either that Anglo-Saxons
were abnormally intelligent, or that they had some assistance in
responding which is denied to us, but which compensated for the
modern reader's learned apparatus. The first possibility must regret-
fully be ruled out. Indeed Kenneth Sisam, the most notable sceptic
among modern critics, has expressed justifiable doubt about the
sensitivity or simple knowledge to be expected from the men who
might listen to heroic poetry, the military nobility and their companions, the 'hearth-band' (*heorðwerod*), the 'shield-companions'
(*bordgeneatas*)—men, as he drily reminds us, 'not chosen primarily
for their intellectual qualities'.[4] This is a fair remark, and should
warn us off from the too-facile modern assumption that *Beowulf* has
been from its origins a matter for the learned and subtle (whose
numbers are always few and whose interests, in the Anglo-Saxon

period, might well have been elsewhere). But the second possibility, that the original audiences had some guide to response which we do not, remains, and is almost certainly to some extent valid.

The limits of subtlety commonly reached by traditional literatures are after all not as narrow as has sometimes been assumed. Icelandic saga-writing is a case in point. At an early stage these works were often taken to be naïve reproductions of historical fact, whose quality came directly from the Icelandic way of life. But when attention became fixed on them more closely, it was seen that many were quite unreliable historically, and that they contained only kernels of fact, deliberately reshaped for a greater moral or artistic force.[5] The effects are powerful, the subtlety demonstrable. Yet the sagas were also produced under Dark Age conditions, for people little more advanced than early Anglo-Saxons, if at all. What made such achievements possible, one feels, was a certain community of interest between authors and audiences, an agreement to aim at familiar goals, and to use familiar methods, even if these were developed to a greater extent than usual or in a novel way. For this agreement we have only the weak words 'literary convention', with their implications of artifice and restriction. But what one gains from reading *Beowulf* in conjunction with other heroic material (and vice versa) is an awareness that this exploitation of familiarity can act as an almost irreplaceable guide for audiences of all types; not only the heroic vocabulary, but also the scenes, the characters, and the stories may all be seen as deeply 'conventional', without being thoughtless or repetitive. Behind them, powerfully felt, if never exactly codified, stand the controlling interests and natural ironies of the Old English heroic ethic.

The heroic foreground

To appreciate what an Anglo-Saxon poet could do, and what his audience might expect, it helps to look at the *account* of a poem given by the author of *Beowulf* in lines 1068–1159, the so-called *Finnsburg Episode*. This incident is told at the first moment of rest in *Beowulf*, during the great banquet which celebrates the hero's defeat of Grendel. As we soon realise, the feast is to end in a further, unexpected attack; but for the moment there is a trough between peaks of action. In it a Danish minstrel sings his song of the fighting between Finn, king of the Frisians, and the Danish heroes Hnæf and Hengest—a feud ending in Pyrrhic victory for the Danes. The song's position may be a significant commentary on the main action, or it may be inserted purely for variety. But it is at any rate complete and self-contained. We ought to be able to understand its point (if not all its details) from what is there. And as it happens, we have a little

further corroboration in the shape of the *Finnsburg Fragment,* a
short, fifty-line piece of an independent poem on the same subject.
Yet for moderns the intention of both pieces seems to be essentially
obscure, made so by the mode of narration.

In the *Fragment,* for example, battle-piece though it is, there is
virtually no description of action. *Hig fuhton fif dagas,* we are told,
swa hyra nan ne feol [they fought for five days, still not one of them
fell]. The major part of the battle is passed over in two apparently
colourless lines to reach a conversation, between Finn, the *folces hyrde*
[guardian of the people], and one of his wounded men. Presumably
their talk might have led up to some change of tactics, but we can feel
sure that whatever that change might have been, it would not be
narrated for itself alone, but to reflect the determination (or otherwise) of Finn. For though the poem is only fragmentary, the incidents
picked out for the fifty lines we have are all mental rather than physical, and they lead as a rule to direct or indirect speech. So, a young
Frisian is urged to hold back; is challenged laconically by one of the
Danish party; goes on and is killed—without us being told how, or
why the event is important. Similarly, action is introduced at the
start only through a fierce but cryptic speech from the Danish chief-
tain, presumably Hnæf, as he realises he is under attack:

> 'Ne ðis ne dagað eastan,   ne her draca ne fleogeð,
> ne her ðisse healle   hornas ne byrnað.
> Ac her forþ berað;   fugelas singað,
> gylleð græghama,   guðwudu hlynneð,
> scyld scefte oncwyð.   Nu scyneð þes mona
> waðol under wolcnum.   Nu arisað weadæda
> ðe ðisne folces nið   fremman willað.
> Ac onwacnigeað nu,   wigend mine,
> habbað eowre linda,   hicgeaþ on ellen,
> winnað on orde,   wesað onmode!'   (3–12)

['This is not day from the east, nor is a dragon flying here, nor are the
gables of this hall burning; but here they are advancing(?), birds sing,
the grey-coat howls, the spear clashes, shield speaks to shaft. Now the
moon shines, wandering under the clouds. Now woeful deeds arise, which
will carry out this enmity of the people. But wake now, my warriors, grasp
your shields, think of courage, fight in the front, be resolute!']

The phrases themselves are utterly simple, mere strings of facts or
orders, a different verb or subject almost every half-line. But they
cover a strange mixture of emotions, prophecy, melancholy, resolution, even humour. Why is Hnæf so certain? How is the moon
linked with the *weadæda* [woeful deeds]? Why is there the apparent
touch of mirth in the solutions put forward and discarded before the

true one? No doubt answers could be found for all these questions, and there is no denying that the speech produces a chilling effect overall. But Hnæf's train of thought is not an obvious one; nor is the poet's selection of material for the whole of the *Fragment* at all clear.

Difficulty is further increased when one moves from the independent *Fragment* to the merely reported *Episode,* for the *Beowulf*-poet seems to have felt here that it was unnecessary for him to explain matters at all fully, while he refrains entirely from direct speech. Moreover, as with the poet of the *Fragment,* his idea of what is important in a story hardly corresponds at all to ours. His 'principles' seem to be, once again: avoid action, seek the abstract, allow central facts to be inferred from those on the periphery.

So, he begins by totally ignoring the first attack in which Hnæf and Finn's son are killed (with all the immediately exciting material of the *Fragment*), giving instead three rather ambiguous lines observing that Hnæf was to fall in Frisia. These are followed by a sudden switch to someone looking on *after the fighting is over*—Hildeburh, the Danish wife of Finn and sister of Hnæf, the only person who cannot act for either side but must suffer with both. At the end, too, the poet very markedly avoids any description of central events, when Hengest decides to renew the fighting and take vengeance for his dead lord in spite of the agreement he has made with Finn. There the decision, *ne meahte wæfre mod forhabban in hreþre* [the restless spirit could not hold back in his heart], changes immediately into what it causes, *Ða wæs heal roden feonda feorum, swilce Fin slægen* [then the hall was reddened with enemies' lives, Finn killed too]. In both cases past becomes future in a breath, moving from happiness to despair (with Hildeburh), or from intention to result (with Hengest), without any recognition of a present time at all. The method is of course highly dramatic; but, as we find quite often in Old English poetry, it does not even pretend to gratify any simple taste for the description of adventure.

Human emotions occupy the foreground. Even these, though, are presented at least superficially in a curiously abstract way, with no impulse towards individuality or precision, as we can see from the poet's all but totally restrained picture of Hildeburh in her first despair, when she knows her son and her brother to be dead:

> Nalles holinga   Hoces dohtor
> meotodsceaft bemearn,   syþðan morgen com,
> ða heo under swegle   geseon meahte
> morþorbealo maga,   þær heo ær mæste heold
> worolde wynne   (1076–80)

[Not without reason did Hoc's daughter lament fate, once morning came, when under the sky she could see the deadly killing of kinsmen, where before she had held greatest joy in the world]

The suddenness of change, the contrast between previous joy and present sorrow, make the strength of her emotions plain. Still, she does not mourn for the dead, but for fate, *meotodsceaft*; she sees not corpses but *morþorbealo,* killing. As in the speech of Hnæf, the style here is powerful and compressed, but ruthlessly selective, and not closely visualised.

The poet's reticence in describing the two main battle-scenes, however, contrasts oddly with his readiness to expand on relatively minor topics. After the appearance of Hildeburh, he spends a few lines in telling us what the situation at that moment is: that both sides, attacking Frisians and defending Danes, are fought out and have settled for a draw.[6] But he then goes on to describe, with considerable detail, first the terms of the contract between the two sides (lines 1085–1106), and second the cremation of the slain (lines 1107–24). These sudden expansions are not wayward; rather, they provide a clue to the real interests of the *Beowulf*-poet and other writers in Old English. Both sections imply, though they do not state, a terrible turmoil in the minds of the main characters. The contract consists solely of propitiatory offers to the Danes, but also contains more than a hint that their position is shameful, with its stipulation that no-one is to taunt them,

> ðeah hie hira beaggyfan   banan folgedon
> ðeodenlease,   þa him swa geþearfod wæs   (1102–3)

[although they followed the killer of their ring-giver, as they were then compelled to, without a lord]

Similarly, the agonising stress on Hildeburh is suggested at the burning.

> Het ða Hildeburh   æt Hnæfes ade
> hire selfre sunu   sweoloðe befæstan,
> banfatu bærnan   ond on bæl don
> eame on eaxle   (1114–17)

[Then Hildeburh commanded her own son to be given to the flame at Hnæf's pyre, the body to be burnt, put on the fire by his uncle's side]

The last phrase, with its suggestions of a fitting closeness, only emphasises the fact that uncle and sister's son have been killed fighting each other.

Poetry of this kind, though peripheral and working indirectly, is by no means clumsy. It forces the reader, or listener, to think for a moment of what lies at the story's unexpressed centre. What can the survivors, Hengest or Finn or Hildeburh, be thinking and suffering behind their outward actions? More than that, if even the peace which follows can be so painful, how much more powerful must the active agent itself be, the undescribed force of *wig* and *morþorbealo*, warfare and killing! It is these two considerations, mightily evoked, which clash and form the centre of the *Finnsburg Episode*, the so-called 'tragedy of Hengest'.

For in the pause after the cremations, the poet turns for the first time to presenting a mind.[7] Several direct comments are made on the emotions of Hengest, now leader of the surviving Danes—*Eard gemunde* [he thought of his homeland], *Fundode wrecca, gist of geardum* [the exile longed to go, the guest from the courts]. Nevertheless, his state is still turbulent, for the second remark is immediately followed, without link or preparation, by the near-contradiction,

> he to gyrnwræce
> swiðor þohte   þonne to sælade,
> gif he torngemot   þurhteon mihte
> þæt he Eotena bearn   inne gemunde   (1138–41)

[he thought more of desired revenge than of the sea-journey, if he could carry out a bitter meeting, so that he might take account inwardly of the sons of the Jutes]

The clash of motives, though, is not inexplicable; indeed, the reader gets a strong sense of the violence of Hengest's thoughts by this piling-up of opposed desires. The hero's state is mirrored further by another peripheral and 'reflective' device, the description of the *wælfagne winter* [death-stained winter] which frustrates Hengest's thoughts of revenge—for a time:

> holm storme weol,
> won wið winde,   winter yþe beleac
> isgebinde,   oþðæt oþer com
> gear in geardas,   swa nu gyt deð,
> þa ðe syngales   sele bewitiað,
> wuldortorhtan weder.   Ða wæs winter scacen
> fæger foldan bearm.   Fundode wrecca . . .   (1131–7)

[the sea surged with storm, fought the wind, winter locked the waves with an icy band, until another year entered the courts, as it does now, those which always observe their times, the glorious weather. Winter had gone, the earth's lap was fair. The exile longed to go . . .]

These clashes of storm and ice, of change in the year set against an unchanging purpose, brilliantly express a contorted state of mind, built up from Hengest's opposing desires and from the unexpressed implications of the contract and the burning. But violent confusion is only half of what the poet wants to achieve; the other half appears in the laconic four lines which follow—sudden decision, action, and release:

> Swa he ne forwyrnde   woroldrædenne,
> þonne him Hunlafing   hildeleoman,
> billa selest,   on bearm dyde,
> þæs wæron mid Eotenum   ecge cuðe   (1142–5)

[So he did not deny his worldly duty, when Hunlaf's son put in his lap the battle-light, best of blades, whose edges were known among the Jutes]

The exact force of 'Hunlafing's' gesture is obscure, as are the motives behind the retrospective *swa,* but the upshot is clear.[8] The Danes break out, attack their enemies, and kill Finn, the slayer of their lord; Hengest's dilemma is presented at length, its solution in a moment.

Clearly this is a satisfying ending, and one which should draw our attention to the daring but effective changes of pace within the narrative. It also presents a pattern, one might note, rather similar to the speech of Hnæf quoted earlier from the *Finnsburg Fragment.* Clear-sighted recognition of what has happened leads to an indeterminate period of suspense, which is then broken by the decision to fight on, regardless—a dual or triple movement of some importance in Old English heroic verse. This pattern should tell us something about what the Anglo-Saxons might expect from a hero: and that is not always, or not only, the inflexible bravery of the retainers in *Maldon.* What Hengest displays is rather a mixture of two almost opposing qualities—one, the ability to feel powerfully emotions of different types; two, the ability to escape from that inner maelstrom, breaking the *stasis* by decision and action. These qualities are signalled by the different speeds of the narrative.

Such a reading is adequate in so far as it refers to the single figure of Hengest. Most readers of the *Episode,* however, feel that it is meant to make some wider affirmation of the heroic ethic, though it is not at all clear what. One might wonder, for example, whether the final revenge is intended as an exaltation of the claims of duty to one's lord, or as a half-ironic statement of the greedy power of *guþ, wig, morþorbealo,* that which breaks the strictest of oaths and leads always to final misery—for at the end the focus is once more on Hildeburh, now bereft not only of son and brother, but also of husband. This is only one of the questions raised by the *Episode* as a whole. Some of the others, especially if one is thinking of the simplest versions of the '*comitatus*-ethic', prove more embarrassing. Finn after all makes an attack which seems simply treacherous, at night, against men who must be his guests since they sleep in his hall. Can he be excused? If he cannot, then how should we take Hengest's surrender, whatever the conditions he exacts? For he follows his lord's *bana,* accepting the offer rejected by Cynewulf's men in the *Chronicle,* ignoring the spirit which animates Byrhtnoth's men in *Maldon:*

> 'Ne mæg na wandian   se þe wrecan þenceð
> frean on folce,   ne for feore murnan'   (258–9)

['He who means to avenge his lord on the people cannot waver nor care for his life']

In any case, after giving a *fæste frioðuwære* [firm pledge of peace], Hengest goes back on it by attacking Finn as treacherously as Finn attacked Hnæf. Finn ambushes sleeping men; Hengest first surrenders, then breaks his word. No sign here of 'Germanic loyalty'!

It may be that some of these vices are more prominent to modern Englishmen than to Anglo-Saxons, for genuine Heroic Ages often throw up a streak of cunning and ruthlessness disliked in gentler eras.[9] Still, the *Episode* has proved so disturbing that many commentators have tried to re-arrange it into a decorous contempt for death or subterfuge. Of these the most subtle, and the most widely-accepted, has been R. W. Chambers, who goes to great lengths, in his *Introduction* to *Beowulf,* to remove blame from Finn.[10] Briefly, his argument is that here (as in the poem *Widsith*) Finn is ruler of the Frisians (*Frysan*) but not the Jutes (*Eotan*). Now, though the *Eotan,* or some of the *Eotan,* are linked with him in the *Episode*, it is possible to imagine a situation in which they (apparently traditional enemies of the Danes) might get out of hand and precipitate events Finn neither wanted nor intended. The truth of this argument must rest on whether the *Episode* is felt to make a clear distinction between the two tribes; and here there is room for genuine disagreement. But though Chambers' re-arrangement may solve the problems at the start of the *Episode,* and possibly those in the middle—since Hengest's surrender is more tolerable if to a man he still respects—it has precisely the opposite effect at the end, when Hengest kills (the now largely blameless) Finn. Professor Chambers here has to argue that the actual deed may not have been performed by Hengest himself but by his rasher confederates (Guthlaf and Oslaf?).

To all this there must be several objections, of which the most important is that the whole interpretation exists only to excuse characters from the demands of a quite hypothetical 'code'. Professor Chambers' last argument before his 'reconstruction' of the story is a flat refusal to consider dishonourable behaviour: 'if Finn had, as is usually supposed, invited Hnæf to his fort and then deliberately slain him by treachery, the whole atmosphere would have been different. Hengest could not then be the hero, but the foil: the example of a man whose spirit fails at the crisis.' Earlier on he claims: 'Had Hengest been a man of that sort [a traitor] he would not have been a hero of Old English heroic song.' But we do not know. Perhaps there *was* a heroic song about that other Hengest—the one who kidnapped Vortigern and massacred the British in another hall, a man still treated with great respect in Layamon's *Brut* in the twelfth century, where he is *cnihten alre hændest* [most courteous of men].[11] It is impossible to be dogmatic when there are so few texts of this nature. Besides, as explanation of the *Episode* creeps towards conformity with the ethic of the 'gentleman', it abandons individuals. To accept Professor Chambers' view is to shift the main burden of responsibility from Finn and Hengest to either the shadowy *Eotan* in the background (men without a named leader, a motive, or a separate fate) or to the hardly less obscure Danish companions—a dehumanising process most unlike the *Beowulf*-poet elsewhere. Chambers' scruples are natural but unjustified; to modern readers they may no longer be necessary.

In some ways, late twentieth-century literature, with its moral ambiguities and uncertainties, is a better preparation for ancient heroic poetry than nineteenth-century literature ever was. To see how, one should consider, for a space, the curious similarities in the Old English hero-stories left to us, similarities probably not founded on literary borrowing so much as on the circumstance that only certain human situations could be counted on to stir most violently the restricted, but responsive imaginations of Anglo-Saxon poets and audiences. One may list these stories as follows: the *Finnsburg Episode,* and part of the feud of Hrothgar and Ingeld told in a later part of *Beowulf; The Battle of Maldon;* the fragments of *Waldere* (supplemented by the Latin poem *Waltharius*); the prose story of 'Cynewulf and Cyneheard' in the *Anglo-Saxon Chronicle*; and perhaps, without being too eclectic, the Old High German *Hildebrand-slied*—not a great many, but enough to raise a few points and to cast some light back on the problems of the *Episode* already stated.[12]

One immediate and distinctive feature of all these stories (except the Ingeld one) is that heroes fight on the defensive. Hengest guards the hall-doors, Waldere his defile in the rock, Byrhtnoth the *bricg* over the river Panta. Of course the defence of a tight place is a common motif in both life and literature (witness Rorke's Drift and the Alamo, both adapted easily to film), but in Old English poetry it is further combined with less usual elements. For one thing, in all the stories (except this time *Maldon*) the opposition is not simply one of good and evil; instead the hero will almost always have a friend or near relation on the other side—Hnæf fights his sister's son, Ingeld his wife's father, Hildebrand his son. Waldere faces his friend Hagena; and when Hagena becomes the hero of a later epic, the German *Nibelungenlied* of about 1200, he too is given a friend to fight, the Markgraf Rüedeger. Even in the *Finnsburg Fragment* (though this may be coincidence), Ordlaf and Guthlaf are attacked by one Garulf, *Guðlafes sunu*. In the end this habitual pattern can lead to the virtual identity of the two sides, as at the most dramatic moment of 'Cynewulf and Cyneheard', when the two bodies of retainers meet. Cyneheard and his men, having killed King Cynewulf, are besieged by a larger body of avengers. They ask the besiegers not to attack, with the reminder that (as we might expect) there are kinsmen on both sides, who will not stay out of any fighting. The avengers refuse so to betray the dead Cynewulf, and counter with an almost identical proposal, that perhaps their kinsmen with Cyneheard would rather desert *him*. But this is rejected too. Clearly the narrator approves of both parties and sees a parallel between them, for their motives are indistinguishable, even if they have to kill each other.[13] We must ask what significance lies in this habitual similarity of two opposing sides—for it is so consistent as to preclude any accidental rather than aesthetic basis.

One insight which emerges most clearly from the *Episode* itself is that the relationship of enemies makes the aftermath of fighting by so much the more bitter, a fact stressed by what seems to be a real literary invention on the *Beowulf*-poet's part, his use of otherwise unimportant female figures to link the two sides of a feud and reflect the injury done to both. These are Hildeburh the wife of Finn, and later on Freawaru the wife of Ingeld, two characters who have no future but to suffer. Still, a preliminary recoil from the killing of men is present in even the sternest figures of Old English epic, giving rise to the *invariable* feature in such stories, hesitation and delay. The real climax of the 'Cynewulf' story is the pause in the morning while both sides seek an (impossible) compromise; for Hagena in *Waldere,* nothing at all happens except the increase of tension, presumably to the breaking-point; and the whole of the *Hildebrandslied,* apart from the first six lines, consists of Hildebrand's attempts to avoid a fight without backing down. Even in *Maldon* Byrhtnoth suffers

repeated delays from the tide and the river, which give him a chance
to consider his decisions, to minimise the effects of battle with the
Danes.[14] Of course, all the hesitations end the same way. But their
appearance testifies to a thoughtful streak in Old English heroes.
What we are asked to admire in them is never bull-headed bravery
or Marlovian grandiloquence, but deliberate decision, taken in full
awareness of the terrible possibilities both for themselves and the
equally honourable men who may be on the other side.

Linked with these hesitations, and with the characteristic similarity-
in-opposition, is a further general feature of Old English epic—a
quality which we may call 'moral neutrality'. As a rule it is impossible, in these stories, to *blame* anyone for the tragic events which
occur. Who is responsible for the outbreak of the feud between
Ingeld and Hrothgar? Beowulf himself offers no opinion as to
whether it is Dane or Heathobard, and it may all depend on the
actions of some anonymous ancestor, or the *eald æscwiga* [old
spear-fighter] who utters the immediately decisive taunts. In the same
way, no one can decide whether it would be better for Hagena in
Waldere to betray his lord or kill his friend (that being the only choice
available). Such situations are not meant to be resolvable; if they
have any moral, it is Hardy's, that 'neither Chance nor Purpose
governs the universe, but Necessity'. But it is this 'moral neutrality'
to which the modern reader can most easily respond. Since *Animal
Farm* it has been easy for us to imagine situations in which there are
two sides increasingly indistinguishable—though of course in the
modern fable one's reaction is to sympathise with neither, while in
heroic story one is compelled to sympathise with both. It is interesting to note that in Old English the quality of a hero can even be
verbally ambiguous. Byrhtnoth allows the Danes to cross the river
for his ofermode [out of his high heart], and is condemned for it by
the poet; but the word used, *ofermod,* obviously relates to *mod*
[courage, spirit], so that in a way the poet recognises the virtuous
beginnings of vice. In the same way Hygelac's fatal raid in *Beowulf*
is caused

> sypðan he for wlenco   wean ahsode,
> fæhðe to Frysum   (1206–7)

[when he sought out woe, feud from the Frisians, out of recklessness]

But the word *wlenco* can be used both in decisively praiseworthy
senses (see *Beowulf* 338–9), and as strong condemnation (*Beowulf*
508), so that once again Hygelac, like Byrhtnoth, is detached from
an easy criticism.[15] Old English heroes are not presented to be
judged. They inculcate rather an uneasy awareness that good

intentions can lead to evil results, that the same mental quality (*wlenco*) may bring success or misery, depending on circumstance. It is with some such uneasy awareness that Waldere, Ingeld, Hildebrand, the retainers of Cynewulf and Cyneheard, and especially Hengest, do their best to procrastinate and avoid conflict—not fear of death, but fear of an unknown future. Duty triumphs, but not supported by simple hatred. Nor is a merely dutiful hero to be admired, if he has no foresight or sense of the probable results of his actions; the audience is moved in proportion to the hero's reluctance.[16]

Bearing these habitual patterns in mind, it may be possible to return to the *Finnsburg Episode* and find that some of its difficulties have become less puzzling. To begin with, the decision to omit the whole source of the action is proper, if daring. It parallels the vague *unryhtum dædum* [wrong actions] of Sigebryht which are the real, but unimportant, reason for the Cynewulf–Cyneheard feud, or the quite forgotten cause of Ingeld's enmity to the Danes. Similarly, though the instinct not to blame Finn must be right, there is no need for Professor Chambers to drag in the *Eotan* as accessaries, direct blame of anyone being foreign to most Old English heroic situations. The question as to whether Hengest's final revenge exalts or erodes the ideal of honour also becomes irrelevant, for although there is an element of irony in the increased grief of Hildeburh at the end, that is ascribable not so much to Hengest as to 'Necessity'. Indeed, possibly the most valuable insight gained by such comparative study is the half-ironic one that grief is a necessary part of the higher reaches of heroism itself, and helps to measure it. A clear path with no restraints would not make a man a figure of song; that quality is conferred only by a dilemma and a choice.

From the half-dozen stories mentioned it would be possible to make up something like a 'composite' hero—a process that perhaps does not recommend itself very readily. But the relative unanimity of these stories remains striking, and one might think that an audience which half-knew what to expect would be the quicker to grasp any new features the poet chose to stress. We might then decide rightly to praise the *Beowulf*-poet for the several uncommon elements in his handling of the *Episode*—for instance his use of Hildeburh; his half-symbolic mention of the changing seasons; his marked variations of speed during the narrative. At the same time we could still see that his hero does not challenge the patterns of 'literary convention', but fulfils them. Like his fellows, Hengest is not valued for what he does (as is Marlowe's Tamburlaine), or what he is (Shakespeare's Antony), but for what he understands and resolves. He is the 'man in the middle', torn between the impulse to act and the restraint that comes

from an awareness of results, continually looking back to the past and
forward to the future, wondering how, in the present, he can alter
the chain of events. Like a saga-hero, we might think that his greatest
quality is to be touched by no illusions of honour or easy success,
því at hann sá allt eptir því sem var [because he saw everything the way
it was].[17] In all of this presentation, the *Episode* is typical, if superior.

It has, however, one possible flaw, stemming from the fact that it is
only the *account* of a poem and so must avoid direct speech. For
what Old English epic seems elsewhere to look for are the mental
acts which precede physical ones, the moments of insight in which a
hero sees past and future, appreciates his situation of impossible
stress and, we may say, boils over into action. We can see the expression of one such moment in Hnæf's speech from the *Fragment*,
with its irresistibly clear-sighted recognition *'nu arisað weadæda'*
['now woeful deeds arise']. There is another in the *Hildebrandslied*
when the hero, reviewing his life, cries out *'wewurt skihit'* ['a woeful
fate works itself out'] because he has been allowed to survive for so
long, and then prepares to kill his son. Potentially the greatest
speech of all lies hidden behind the *Beowulf*-poet's laconic *ne meahte
wæfre mod forhabban in hreþre* [the restless spirit could not hold
back in his heart]; but it is kept unexpressed.

The ironic background

The *Finnsburg Episode* centres on a painful 'moment of truth'.
Outside it, though, in the rest of *Beowulf,* is the more normal side of
the *eorla lif* [life of nobles], a happy immersion in the present. To
this the poet returns with the triumph of Hengest's men and the
resumption of the banquet in Heorot:

> Leoð wæs asungen,
> gleomannes gyd.   Gamen eft astah,
> beorhtode bencsweg;   byrelas sealdon
> win of wunderfatum   (1159–62)

[The song was sung, the minstrel's melody. Mirth rose again, talk brightened
along the benches, the chamberlains gave out wine from wondrous bowls]

But is it possible for any reader or listener to return without suspicion
to such a state? Very soon after this the poet, preparing for the
sudden attack of Grendel's mother, will be inviting us to see the
pleasure of the Danes as dangerous, vulnerable:

> Wyrd ne cuþon,
> geosceaft grimme,   swa hit agangen wearð
> eorla manegum,   syþðan æfen cwom   (1233–5)

[They did not know their fate, grim destiny, as it had happened to many men, once evening came]

Yet has this change not already been made by the pain and sacrifice of the *Episode,* accepted by its Danish audience as *entertainment*? Many would argue for an even closer connection than that, suggesting that even while the Danes applaud heroism and Hengest, we are meant to see that some of those present are already cast in the roles of Finn, Hnæf, or Hildeburh.

For as the *Episode* ends with the recapture of Hildeburh, another queen is moved into the foreground with six most ominous lines, put in a longer measure, one might imagine, to give them more emphasis:

> þa cwom Wealhþeo forð
> gan under gyldnum beage,   þær þa godan twegen
> sæton suhtergefæderan;   þa gyt wæs hiera sib ætgædere,
> æghwylc oðrum trywe.   Swylce þær Unferþ þyle
> æt fotum sæt frean Scyldinga;   gehwylc hiora his ferhþe
>   treowde,
> þæt he hæfde mod micel,   þeah þe he his magum nære
> arfæst æt ecga gelacum.   Spræc ða ides Scyldinga . . .   (1162-8)

[Then Wealhtheow came out, going under her golden coronet to where the two good men sat, uncle and nephew. Then their kinship was still together, each true to the other. There as well sat Unferth the '*þyle*', at the feet of the lord of the Scyldings. Each of them trusted his spirit, that he had great courage, though he was not faithful to his kin in the play of swords. Then the woman of the Scyldings spoke . . .]

Nowadays the interpretation of this passage is all but universally agreed. Present at that moment in the hall are the *suhtergefæderan* [uncle and nephew], Hrothgar and Hrothulf, with the former's sons and latter's cousins, Hrethric and Hrothmund. The last name is unknown to Scandinavian legend, and the fate of King Hrothgar is at least dubious. But the twelfth-century Latin historian Saxo Grammaticus tells quite clearly of the killing, by Rolvo, son of Helgo, son of Haldanus (= O.E. Hrothulf, son of Halga, son of Healfdene), of a certain Røricus (= O.E. Hrethric); and the assertion is supported to some extent by other sources. Furthermore, in Saxo again the eventual killer of Rolvo himself is given as one Hiarwarthus, paralleling yet another character mentioned in *Beowulf* but notably not present at this time, Heoroweard, son of Heorogar, son of Healfdene, again a cousin involved in the internecine Scylding feud.[18] It sounds as if, in history or legend, the family present in Heorot was known to dissolve in treachery, murder, and final extinction; to such knowledge the six longer lines presumably refer. Still, since all this comes from outside the text, one can never be sure how far to take the theory. Would a shudder have gone down the spines of an Anglo-Saxon audience as soon as it heard of this gathering of father and sons, uncle and nephew, posed (one might think) in almost symbolic groupings? Would Anglo-Saxons have seen immediately that Wealhtheow was like Hildeburh in that she too would wake one morning to *morþorbealo maga* [the killing of kinsmen] and the loss of all her hopes? The answer from most quarters is unhesitatingly 'Yes!' But if this is true, it causes some revaluation of Old English poetic technique.

It has to be admitted that if these complex and reverberating ironies have in fact been created, then the job has been done with exceptional economy. The poet after all tells us nothing whatever of the Scyldings' future. Nearly all his remarks could be taken as observations of the peace and joy of that evening in the hall. He writes earlier:

> Heorot innan wæs
> freondum afylled;   nalles facenstafas
> Þeodscyldingas   þenden fremedon   (1017–19)

[Heorot was filled inside with friends; the Scylding people did not then by any means carry out treacherous deeds]

We may feel that he protests too much; a great deal depends on the stress on *þenden* [then], as it does on *þa gyt* [still] in the passage introducing Wealhtheow.[19] But on the face of it the remark is thoroughly approving, meaning no more in its typically negative form than the praise of Beowulf himself:

> nealles druncne slog
> heorðgeneatas;   næs him hreoh sefa   (2179–80)

[not at all did he strike his hearth-companions drunkenly; his mind was not fierce]

One could be forgiven for thinking that if Saxo Grammaticus had not survived, then this interpretation of *Beowulf* would never have been considered. So, is the poem self-contained, an artistic success? Is there anything present in the text that should sensitise us—and also an Anglo-Saxon audience without libraries or cross-references—to the possibilities of this scene, with its thoughtful opposition of insight (in Hengest) and ignorance (in the feasters)?

Something can indeed be gained if one makes the further assumption that Old English poetry can express a state of mind delicately through speech, and (as in the *Episode*) by what is left out as well as by what is put in. For the next speech by Wealhtheow seems to be amazingly precise. It conveys hesitation, worry, suspicion against everyone on behalf of her sons; but it does so within the conventions of a speech of encouragement. Speaking to Hrothgar, Wealhtheow begins with a series of cheerful imperatives; *'Onfoh þissum fulle'*, she says, *'Þu on sælum wes . . . to Geatum spræc mildum wordum . . . Beo wið Geatas glæd'* ['Take this cup . . . be happy . . . speak to the Geats with kind words . . . be gracious to the Geats']. But then one sentence changes the mood. She refers back (some 250 lines) to Hrothgar's joyful praise of Beowulf after the death of Grendel:

> 'Nu ic, Beowulf, þec,
> secg betsta,   me for sunu wylle
> freogan on ferhþe'   (946–8)

['Now, Beowulf, best of men, I will take you for my son and cherish you in my heart']

It was accepted then, perhaps, as hyperbole, and forgotten. Wealhtheow takes it literally, and comments on it in one sentence with cautious indirection:

> 'Me man sægde   þæt þu ðe for sunu wolde
> hererinc habban'   (1175–6)

['Someone told me that you wished to have the warrior for your son']

And though that subject is immediately dropped, the next two imperatives are not outgoing, but restrictive:

> 'bruc þenden þu mote
> manigra medo,   ond þinum magum læf
> folc ond rice   þonne ðu forð scyle'   (1177–9)

['enjoy while you may the praise of many, and leave to your kin the people and kingdom, when you must go forth']

The 'and' in that sentence cries out to be replaced by 'but', for she is making several distinctions at once: 'Give away what you like but not the succession, reward the Geats as a whole but do not exalt one of them, live while you can but leave a chance for others'. Still, it is typical that any overt sign is avoided. Though the two imperative series oppose each other over the vital words *for sunu* [for your son], the audience is left to make out what it can. A further startling leap

B

marks the rest of the speech. Turning from the possible adoption of
Beowulf and the risks involved, Wealhtheow addresses Hrothulf.
Twice she makes assertions about past and future:

> 'Ic minne can
> glædne Hroþulf,   þæt he þa geogoðe wile
> arum healdan,   gyf þu ær þonne he,
> wine Scildinga,   worold oflætest;
> wene ic þæt he mid gode   gyldan wille
> uncran eaferan,   gif he þæt eal gemon,
> hwæt wit to willan   ond to worðmyndum
> umborwesendum ær   arna gefremedon'   (1180–7)

['I know my gracious Hrothulf, that he will maintain the young ones in
honour if you, friend of the Scyldings, leave the world before him; I
expect that he will repay our sons with good, if he remembers all the
honours we did him as a child, for his desire and his glory']

'I *know* . . . I *expect,* that he *will* help our sons, *if* . . .' The pattern
itself implies vulnerability. Wealhtheow's connection of Hrothulf
with Beowulf, her unexpected vision of the latter as a rival—these
reveal movingly a state of mind, without any necessity of statement.
The absence of connections is characteristic, but in no sense vague.

Though this speech has admittedly been considered with every
advantage of outside knowledge, it still looks as if it might, on its
own, provide good reason for thinking twice about the joyful scene
of the banquet. To do so is to add a new dimension to *Beowulf*—
especially if one assumes that the poet is in full control of these
subtleties. His next four or five sentences open up the history of the
Geats even more clearly than has been done for the Danes, as he
mentions the giving of a great torque to Beowulf, and then suddenly
flashes years into the future to remark:

> Þone hring hæfde   Higelac Geata,
> nefa Swertinges,   nyhstan siðe,
> siðþan he under segne   sinc ealgode   (1202–4)

[Hygelac of the Geats, Swerting's grandson, had that ring on his last
journey, when he defended treasure under his banner]

Up to this moment, Beowulf has been presented consistently as
reliant on his uncle;[20] now in the midst of Beowulf's triumph the
reader is forced to glimpse an unhappy future, though he does not
know exactly how it will come about. Possibly in the circumstances
there is something additionally pathetic in Wealhtheow's second
speech, this time to Beowulf, with mingled and twice-repeated
appeal and blandishment:

'cen þec mid cræfte,   ond þyssum cnyhtum wes
lara liðe;   ic þe þæs lean geman . . .
. . . Beo þu suna minum
dædum gedefe,   dreamhealdende'   (1219–27)

['know your strength, and be good in your counsel to these boys; I will remember a reward for you for that . . . Be gracious in your deeds to my son, you who possess joy']

As we can now see, it is only one character doomed to unhappiness calling on another. Her hopeful summary of the situation in the hall is followed immediately by the poet's pitying one:

Þær wæs symbla cyst;
druncon win weras.   Wyrd ne cuþon,
geosceaft grimme . . .   (1232–4)

[There was the best of feasts, men drank wine. They did not know their fate, grim destiny . . .]

He makes the careless sleep of the thanes, from which one of them will never awake, seem representative of the life of man.

The poetic results are unmistakable. They cannot be fortuitous. But are we to think that the poet, casually introducing nine or ten references to Hygelac before this point, did it all in full knowledge of the effect he was going to produce in this scene and nowhere else? That the *Finnsburg Episode* was chosen from all other legends precisely to create the right kind of ironic gap between its audience and that of *Beowulf*? These things are possible; the difficulty with this poem is, always, knowing where to stop. But to agree with such a reading is to declare *Beowulf* a work at least as subtly handled as, say, the *Aeneid*—a poem from a much higher level of culture. Nor is the Old English poem at all *like* any Classical one in these effects, having apparently no visible model.[21] But could any poet have invented a whole ironic technique, involving contrast, allusion, interpolation and the use of 'authorial voices', all by himself? If he did, who could have understood him without prolonged study? Once again, we are driven back to considering the credible limits of an Anglo-Saxon audience's responses. And once again—since the ironic intention is (almost) undeniable—we must conclude that in his background of irony as in his foreground of incident, the *Beowulf*-poet was able to rely on that community of author and audience we have discussed on p. 19, developing methods and concepts already familiar, at least in their essentials.

We cannot expect much of this presumed tradition of story-telling to survive in any very obvious form, there being no other secular

poem in Old English or any related language on anything like the
same ambitious scale as *Beowulf*. What can still be seen is something
of the state of mind, the habitual turns of thought which may have
contributed to the *Beowulf*-poet's ironic development. We can see
these in the smallest and best-preserved units of Old English verse,
the characteristic syntax and even the individual words which do
so much to signalise and define this type of narrative. It does not do to
underestimate the importance of words and word-orders, though
they may evade the nets of scholarly method. Considerable evidence
now exists to suggest that even something as natural and apparently
physiological as the apprehension of colour is affected by the words
that exist, in any particular language, to describe it, and of course
abstract concepts must be even more readily affected.[22] A rather
similar study of the specialised vocabulary of Homer has led one
scholar to declare: 'Since Homer also gave to the Greeks their
lingua franca of literature, we must acknowledge that it was Homer
—using his name in the broad sense which scholarly practice has
sanctioned—who *created* [my italics] the intellectual world of the
Greeks, their beliefs and their thoughts.'[23] The claim may seem
ambitious, but is justified. Words codify men's understanding of
events.

To turn from the general to the particular, one essentially ironic
device can be seen in several of the passages already quoted. It is the
use of the conjunction *siþþan*, a word varying its meaning between
'since', 'when', 'after' and 'because'.[24] We have met it at three
important moments—Hildeburh's awakening:

> Nalles holinga   Hoces dohtor
> meotodsceaft bemearn,   syþðan morgen com   (1076–7)

[Not without reason did Hoc's daughter lament fate, once morning
came]

Hygelac's raid:

> Þone hring hæfde   Higelac Geata,
> nefa Swertinges,   nyhstan siðe,
> siðþan he under segne   sinc ealgode,
> wælreaf werede;   hyne wyrd fornam,
> syþðan he for wlenco   wean ahsode   (1202–6)

[Hygelac of the Geats, Swerting's grandson, had that ring on his last
journey, when he defended treasure under his banner; fate took him, when
he sought out woe, out of recklessness]

and the Danes asleep in Heorot:

            Wyrd ne cuþon,
      geosceaft grimme,   swa hit agangen wearð
      eorla manegum,   syþðan æfen cwom   (1233-5)

[They did not know their fate, grim destiny, as it had happened to many men, once evening came]

Each of these passages centres on human ignorance, and each expresses it in a similar way. Which came first, the thought or the expression? That question is hardly answerable, but we should note here one of *Beowulf*'s marked grammatical peculiarities. Subordinate clauses beginning with *siþþan* can naturally come before or after their main clauses, and there is no reason to expect one order to be more common than the other. But, in fact, of the 57 *siþþan*-clauses in the poem, all but one follow the pattern, main clause first, subordinate clause second.[25] It may appear a conclusion of interest only to pedants, but the poetic effect of many of these passages is very strong. The fact comes first, the explanation, cause, or time-indication trailing loosely behind. As a result the reader is often left momentarily in a condition of surprise or ignorance parallel to that of the characters inside the poem. Consider, for example, this brilliant transition in a 'digression' towards the end of the poem, when a beaten Geatish army is trapped in 'Raven's Wood', the fierce old Swedish king Ongentheow drawing his forces round them in the darkness, promising the survivors a painful death in the morning:

            cwæð, he on mergenne   meces ecgum
      getan wolde,   sum on galgtreowum
      fuglum to gamene. // Frofor eft gelamp
      sarigmodum   somod ærdæge,
      syððan hie Hygelaces   horn ond byman,
      gealdor ongeaton,   þa se goda com
      leoda dugoðe   on last faran   (2939-45)

[he said that in the morning he would cut them with the edge of the sword, some on gallow-trees as sport for the birds. // Relief then came to the dispirited, with the dawn, once they heard the sound of Hygelac's horn and trumpets, when the good man came on the track of his people's army]

How much of the effect depends, not on vocabulary, but on word-order! In that situation *frofor* [relief] is for a moment inconceivable; dawn seemed to promise only death. Then, in the subordinate clause, the trumpets of Hygelac explain it. Clearly the sound is simultaneous with the relief, but its postponement creates a momentary shock for the reader, paralleling that of the dispirited Geats. Naturally, the meaning of *siþþan* then varies between a time-word 'once', and a cause-word 'since'; but what is important is the change from despair to triumph within a single line, *frofor* alliterating with *fuglum,* the birds of death. In all, the reader or listener experiences similar effects 56 times in *Beowulf.* The *siþþan*-clauses finely exemplify what Coleridge called 'quick reciprocations of curiosity still gratified and still re-excited . . . too slight indeed to be at any one moment objects of distinct consciousness, yet . . . considerable in their aggregate influence'.[26] Implicit in the type of pleasure they provide is a sense of irony, of the sudden reversals of time. Though this sense might never, for most Anglo-Saxon listeners or poets, have attained to 'distinct consciousness', the familiarity of constructions expressing it cannot but have strengthened their sensitivity to the ironic possibilities of history. The grammar of *siþþan* is part of the same continuum as the hints and prophetic glimpses of the banquet in Heorot, whether or not it helped to form them.

Similar examples are not hard to find in the syntax of *Beowulf.* Clauses beginning with *gif* [if] follow much the same pattern as *siþþan* ones, reaching for effects of afterthought and menace. More interestingly, *oþðæt* clauses produce what has been called the 'pattern of until',[27] in a way the reverse of the *siþþan* pattern in that it deals with the long periods between and leading up to moments of sudden insight. Twice the *Beowulf*-poet (or scribe) uses this conjunction to begin a section in the manuscript, and it starts off both main adventures.[28] The warriors live happily in Heorot *oððæt an ongan fyrene fremman feond on helle* [until a hell-fiend began to commit crimes], while after Grendel's destruction Beowulf reigns happily for fifty years *oððæt an ongan deorcum nihtum draca ricsian* [until on dark nights a dragon began to rule]. Probably the parallelism is not deliberate. For poets of this type it is natural to see joy growing into sorrow, and to pull the two opposites together, carefully linked within a sentence.

Only subsidiary to these syntactic habits is the question of vocabulary. Did Anglo-Saxons have words for the specialised concepts of the heroic life which this chapter is trying to isolate? Without any Old English 'philosophical tractate' it is impossible to say for sure. But some words, in poetry, do stand out. The 'moments of reversal' which bring sudden insight to heroes appear to be expressed, in *Beowulf* and elsewhere, by the word *edwenden* [a change back], or by similar forms such as *edcyr, edhwyrft, edsceaft.*[29] *Edwenden* is used forcefully and dramatically in several places, but has overall a curious neutrality. It can be seen as a good, for Beowulf assumes that Hrothgar's unhappy subjection to Grendel would be saved,

'gyf him edwenden   æfre scolde,
bealuwa bisigu   bot eft cuman'   (280–1)

['if a change should ever again come to him, a cure for the turmoil of evils'][30]

But later Hrothgar is to use the same word, not for his deliverance, but for the shock of Grendel's first attack:

'Hwæt, me þæs on eþle   edwenden cwom,
gyrn æfter gomene'   (1774–5)

['From this indeed a change came on me in my home, sorrow after pleasure']

Edwenden is again a consolation when the poet remarks on Beowulf's recovery of a bad early reputation; but a similar word is applied to the killing of Æschere:

þa ðær sona wearð
edhwyrft eorlum,   siþðan inne fealh
Grendles modor   (1280–2)

[Then soon there was a change for men, once Grendel's mother forced a way in]

Clearly the idea of surprise and reversal is present for this Old English poet in *any* situation; the only places where there is no change are Heaven and Hell. The concept's neutrality is reminiscent of that other neutral word already mentioned (on p. 28), *wlenco,* the quality of a hero—or of a meddler? Perhaps this should be translated, at least in heroic verse,[31] neither as 'arrogance' nor as 'courage', but as 'a man's readiness to risk *edwenden*' (which he knows may be a change for the better or for the worse). This is something which Beowulf does share with Hygelac and Saint Guthlac[32]—he goes outside his own boundaries (and he succeeds while his uncle fails). It is also notably a quality he does not share with his thanes, even if to a modern mind their courage is equal to his own. They stay in Heorot, though 'none of them thought that he would ever go from there to seek his loved home again' (lines 691–2); still, though brave, they are not heroes, since they are not ultimately responsible for their own presence in the hall. The Old English attitude is the reverse of fatalistic. It exalts individual decision.

Other words could be drawn into this discussion. The qualities of the hero are pre-eminently *andgit* and *foreþanc* [sense and forethought], for it is these virtues which help the hero to perceive the inevitable changes of time and to prepare for them. One might look especially at the total *non sequitur* of lines 1057–62, where the poet curiously relates Christian trust in God's power with a suspicious awareness of change rather similar to the advice of the Old Norse *Hávamál*! Another word loaded with a sense of ultimate responsibility is *bana*, meaning not always 'the physical killer' (since Hygelac is named as the *bona Ongenþeowes* in line 1968, whereas the man who struck the actual blow was Eofor son of Wonred), but more generally 'the causer, the man responsible'. But the most obviously significant word peculiar to Old English philosophy is that ancient stumbling-block of translators, *wyrd* or Fate.

The ubiquity of this concept in Old English verse may seem to refute the earlier suggestion that a passive and fatalistic attitude was by and large not admired by Anglo-Saxons. Yet though the word was used on occasion to translate Latin *Fata* or *fortuna*, it still seems probable that most of the time a modern reader would be misled by the 'false friend', the easy translation by 'fate' or 'destiny' (used so far in this book to avoid premature explanation). *Wyrd* is at least remotely related to *weorþan*, 'to become', and an acceptable translation is often 'what becomes, what comes to pass, the course of events', not a supernatural and wilful Power, but more simply, the flow of Time.[33] Only some such rendering avoids giving an oddly (and wrongly) pagan turn to what might be fairly unpretentious statements, as when Beowulf observes cheerfully *'Wyrd oft nereð unfægne eorl, þonne his ellen deah'* ['often *events turn out to* save the undoomed man, as long as his courage holds'], or when the poet explains that Grendel would have killed more men *nefne him witig god wyrd forstode ond ðæs mannes mod* [if God's wisdom and the man's courage had not prevented *that turn of events*]. In both cases the more impersonal translation saves one from strange conflicts between Fate and Doom, or God and Fate. The question is, how can what is to us a relatively weak concept have gathered its obvious associations, in Old English, with death, fear, the ultimate challenge? Perhaps the answer lies in the connection of 'events' with 'change'. As so many characters in *Beowulf* find out, men cannot predict their lives, and often in the midst of success come upon disaster. To know this is to be aware of *wyrd*, 'the way things turn out', the way results do not follow intentions. Still, though it is foolish not to recognise the possibility of disaster—like Hygelac attacking the Frisians, or the Danes asleep in Heorot who *wyrd ne cuþon*—the true hero is nevertheless not prevented from trying to force his personality on events when they are amenable to human will.[34] Indeed, this is his glory. The concept of *wyrd*, then, more chaotic and less irresistible than the Classical one of Fate, exists, like many other Old English words, in intimate relation with the idea of the ironies brought about by Time.

To take it no further, it could be claimed that a strong and consistent outlook on life, honour, and courage lurks in the very syntax and vocabulary of the epic style; and that this attitude acts as a preparation for the great contrasts underlying that banquet in Heorot, where the heroes' achievements are simultaneously acknowledged, and shown to be impermanent by hints and allusions. It goes with the frequent rhythms of *wop æfter wiste, gyrn æfter gomene* [lament after feasting, sorrow after joy]; it underlies the repeated metaphors of debt and payment (*lean, gyldan, forgyldan*); above all it explains how a delicate irony could be created and recognised without any overly subtle context. One speech may finally be taken as a coherent, if partial statement of this philosophy.

The speech is, of course, Hrothgar's 'sermon' of lines 1700–84, delivered to Beowulf at the poem's second point of rest, in the trough between the action-peaks of Grendel's mother and the dragon. The time is long gone when anyone would venture to call it irrelevant. But it certainly has no point in the story; Beowulf needs the old king's speech neither as warning for the future nor reprimand for the past.[35] The analysis of the *monnes modgeþonc mæran cynnes* [mentality of a man of famous race] is a detailed, but general, rounding-off of themes till then present, but submerged.

The speech is given one immediate motive—Beowulf's recovery of a sword-hilt with curiously appropriate carvings from the submarine hall:

> on ðæm wæs or writen
> fyrngewinnes,   syðþan flod ofsloh,
> gifen geotende,   giganta cyn   (1688–90)

[on it was written the origin of that far-off fight, when the Flood, the pouring ocean, killed the giants' race]

He presents this to Hrothgar, and the king speaks from it as from a text. Professor Irving has acutely pointed out that both the capture of the hilt and what was written on it express the theme of 'the sudden and extreme shift of power, a lesson implicit both in the frequency with which the hilt has changed hands and in the calamitously sudden overthrow of the arrogant giants. To warn Beowulf now of such a change is precisely the chief purpose of Hrothgar's sermon'.[36] It is not just a warning, though, but also an explanation of how this change occurs.

The utterly typical feature of what Hrothgar has to say is his grounding of all evils in ignorance, short sight, over-confidence.

Heremod is picked as an example, one feels, because he fell from a situation in which *everyone's* opinion was in his favour; but popularity leads through complacence to disaster. Generalising, and also making a striking attempt to penetrate to inner psychology, Hrothgar forces on us the insight that both the immediate causes of disaster, pride and avarice [*oferhygd, gytsung*], come from the fool's idea (and desire) that things will last for ever, without change. The mind of the stupid, or sinful, man—Hrothgar makes no distinction between the two—dwells on present happiness,

> 'þæt he his selfa ne mæg
> for his unsnyttrum   ende geþencean.
> Wunað he on wiste;   no hine wiht dweleð
> adl ne yldo . . .
>   (he þæt wyrse ne con),
> oðþæt him on innan   oferhygda dæl
> weaxeð ond wridað.   Þonne se weard swefeð,
> sawele hyrde;   bið se slæp to fæst,
> bisgum gebunden,   bona swiðe neah'   (1733–43)

['so that he himself, in his unwisdom, cannot think of ending. He lives in joy; sickness and age do not disturb him at all . . . (he does not know the worse side), until within him a measure of pride grows and spreads. Then the watcher sleeps, the soul's guard; the sleep is too firm, bound with cares, the killer very close']

No doubt the attempt to analyse the soul owes something to the developments of theology.[37] But the stress on ignorance, lack of experience, the dangers that mere lapse of time must bring, are all part of the attitude expressed in *Beowulf* at least from the *Finnsburg Episode*. Like the Danes asleep in Heorot, the soul is proud not from malice, but because it lacks foresight; it suffers from what one might call the 'young man's disease'. It is this failure in philosophy of which Hrothgar accuses himself and warns Beowulf, not the crude and (for them) unbelievable temptations of *Superbia* and *Avaritia*. Grendel was not called up by sin; yet Hrothgar rebukes himself for somehow not expecting something like it, twelve years before:

> 'Hwæt, me þæs on eþle   edwenden cwom,
> gyrn æfter gomene,   seoþðan Grendel wearð,
> ealdgewinna,   ingenga min'   (1774–6)

['From this indeed a change came on me in my home, sorrow after pleasure, once Grendel became, that old enemy, my invader']

Great labour has been spent on relating this speech to homiletic commonplace. It is not commonplace; it is in some ways a masterpiece of abstract thought. Yet it grows out of an attitude one can, and must, see everywhere in Old English heroic verse, from vocabulary to narrative structure. No one should be surprised to find less impressive analogues of it in half a dozen other poems, not only in *Christ* and *Daniel* (the ones most commonly cited), but also in *Guthlac, The Gifts of Men, Judgement Day I*, and the Proem to King Alfred's verse *Boethius*.[38] Not that the authors of all these had necessarily read *Beowulf*. The sense of time's ironies and human insecurity must have been familiar enough to Anglo-Saxons for many of them independently to recognise it, express it, and develop it artistically.

The good and the bad

After Hrothgar's speech, many readers feel a sense of anti-climax. Beowulf's report to Hygelac on his return home consists largely, though not entirely, of material already used; and though the hero's old age, dragonfight and death are essential for a sense of balance, there is little about them that is not predictable. Moreover the mode of narrative changes, becoming plainer, slower, with fewer subsidiary figures (indeed, only one). There is a high proportion of 'digressive' material dealing with the wars of Geats, Swedes, and Franks; but it leaves few questions unanswered, and even those one would like to ask—Why is Beowulf's ancestry so strangely mixed? What was he doing when his king was killed, and the son of his king?—offer no promise of enhancing the subject. Yet the difference from earlier sections seems deliberate. What can the last part add to, or change in, our view of *Beowulf*?

One fact that emerges very strongly is that the poet has abandoned suspense. He begins the last section (lines 2200–3182) by devouring large amounts of potentially fascinating and hitherto unexplained material, moving in one stride from Hygelac at the height of his power to the extinction of that dynasty's male line:

> Eft þæt geiode   ufaran dogrum
> hildehlæmmum,   syððan Hygelac læg
> ond Heardrede   hildemeceas
> under bordhreoðan   to bonan wurdon,
> ða hyne gesohton   on sigeþeode
> hearde hildfrecan,   Heaðoscilfingas,
> niða genægdan   nefan Hererices,
> syððan Beowulfe   brade rice
> on hand gehwearf   (2200–8)

[Later it came about in future days through the strokes of battle, once Hygelac lay and the war-swords became Heardred's killers under the

shield-rim, when those hard fighters, the warlike Scilfings (i.e. Swedes)
sought him out among his victorious people, oppressed Hereric's kinsman with hostility, (that) then the broad kingdom turned to Beowulf's
hand]

The breathless sentence ends by saying that Beowulf ruled well for
fifty years, until a dragon began to prowl. Interest shifts to the
dragon and its treasure, but within a hundred lines we are told that it
is Beowulf's doom, and twelve lines later that the dragon has no hope
itself. No rag of doubt is left for the dullest reader:

> Sceolde lændaga
> æþeling ærgod   ende gebidan,
> worulde lifes,   ond se wyrm somod   (2341–3)

[The excellent prince was to experience an end of short days, life in this
world, and the dragon with him]

There is none of the misty menace of Grendel's introduction here.
But if suspense, even tension, have become inappropriate, what is to
replace them?

Fortuitously, a contrast with the more famous 'primary epics' of
Homer can bring out something of *Beowulf*'s special quality in this
last part. In a fine essay Erich Auerbach has shown just how peculiar
the narrative mode of the *Odyssey* is;[39] there, too, suspense vanishes.
Even at the moment when Odysseus returns home and is first
recognised after his twenty years' wandering, action can stop dead
for an alive and interested résumé of a side-issue—how he got his
distinguishing scar. One might easily think of that very similar moment
in *Beowulf,* when the old hero advances into the dragon's den, but
breaks his sword on the monster and is almost overcome by fire.
What can he do now? The poet answers by taking us outside again,
to introduce with leisurely detail (over sixty lines) a character
previously unknown, Beowulf's young kinsman Wiglaf. The Greek
and the Old English passages both ignore most of the conventions of
modern narrative, but they still differ from one another. The
difference centres on ideas of *time*.

Auerbach's conclusion about the *Odyssey* is that its 'digression' is
deliberately disconnected from the scene of potential discovery.
The reason—or is it a failing?—is that Homer 'knows no background.
What he narrates is for the time being the only present, and fills
both the stage and the reader's mind completely'. Though it would be
easy to relate the scar to Odysseus's awareness of danger 'any such
subjectivistic-perspectivistic procedure, creating a foreground and
background, resulting in the present lying open to the depths of

the past, is entirely foreign to the Homeric style; the Homeric style knows only a foreground, only a uniformly illuminated, uniformly objective present'. How easily we can see in *Beowulf* all that Auerbach denies to Homer! The only point the long discussion of Wiglaf *has* is to show, in one moment, a nexus of emotions leading back to 'the depths of the past', and forward to several conceivable futures. The moment is one when the individual can force his own interpretation on scenes already experienced and others to come, making an assertion of value in the face of all possible *wyrde,* all outcomes. The way the 'digression' moves can help us to understand this— though no doubt any modern and necessarily subjective analysis is an inadequate replacement for the quicker and more assured responses (in such scenes) of the original audience.

In spite of the pause's length—it occupies lines 2596–660—one can still see that the poet was concerned to stress speed as he made the transition from the old hero suffering,

> nearo ðrowode,
> fyre befongen,   se þe ær folce weold   (2594–5)

[he who once ruled the people suffered great straits, surrounded by fire],

to the young one impulsively reacting,

> Ne mihte ða forhabban;   hond rond gefeng,
> geolwe linde,   gomel swyrd geteah   (2608–9)

[then he could not hold back; his hand seized the shield, the yellow linden, drew his ancient sword]

Between these there is only a little delay. The flight of the other retainers is passed over in three and a half lines. The struggle in Wiglaf's mind takes only seven words, *Hiora in anum weoll sefa wið sorgum* [in one of them the mind boiled with sorrows], to be instantly resolved by the approving and confident generalisation, perhaps the heart of the whole adventure,[40]

> sibb æfre ne mæg
> wiht onwendan   þam ðe wel þenceð   (2600–1)

[nothing can ever change kinship, for the man who thinks properly]

Wiglaf's very brief naming and description present hints of difficulty to come with the phrase *leod Scylfinga* [Swede], but without developing this, the poet returns to the main point:

geseah his mondryhten
under heregriman   hat þrowian   (2604–5)

[he saw his lord suffering heat, under the battle-mask]

Surely Wiglaf must start to the attack? As he does, though, we
should notice that his declared motive is not purely devotion, or
sympathy for his lord's present pain. In what one might even call a
slightly materialistic way, the sight of Beowulf suffering makes him
think of the past.

Gemunde ða ða are   þe he him ær forgeaf,
wicstede weligne   Wægmundinga,
folcrihta gehwylc,   swa his fæder ahte   (2606–8)

[He remembered the honour given him before, the fine homestead of the
Wægmundings, each customary right, as his father had possessed them]

Only then 'could he not hold back'. He remembers what is in fact an
implicit 'contract', and clearly the poet sees this as a powerful
stimulus. As has been said, the transition from sight to response is
spare, praising the automatic reaction and the natural force of *sibb*
[kinship]. But for a modern, Wiglaf's thinking is not entirely straightforward.

The carrying-out of his response is, furthermore, then hindered
twice, though still with the aim of explaining *why* Wiglaf responds.
First, we have the description of an object, the 'ancient sword'
Wiglaf has just drawn, and then (as with Hrothgar and the giants'
sword-hilt) a speech drawing appropriate conclusions from that
object. With both Hrothgar and Wiglaf, the speech is the more
important; we should note that there is no visual description of the
sword at all, since it matters only through its relevance to Wiglaf's will.
In any case the sword is in itself downright paradoxical. For it is the
laf [relic] of Eanmund, son of Ohthere, robbed from his dead body
by his killer, Wiglaf's father Weohstan. Both Eanmund and Weohstan
were foreigners, Swedes. But the events surrounding that killing
have been referred to twice before[41]—the deadly onslaught of the
Swedes on the Geats, when they dared to shelter King Onela's
rebellious nephews, Eanmund and Eadgils. In that invasion both
Eanmund, son of Ohthere, and Heardred, son of Hygelac, were
killed. It is one of Beowulf's glories to have avenged them. Yet now
behind him stands the killer's son, with the sword he took as booty.
Far from supporting Wiglaf, one might wonder, how did Beowulf
refrain from murdering him? The young man has committed the
same error as the Dane of the Ingeld story. *'Meaht þu, min wine,
mece gecnawan?'* ['Do you, my friend, *recognise* that sword?'].

The passage has filled the hearts of all commentators with discord and dismay; no attempt to find in it further triumphant irony has had much success.[42] All one can do, for the moment, is leave it, noting only the approving re-affirmation of Weohstan's virtuous life and death, which ends with his legacy to Wiglaf and now leads to his son's good use of that legacy:

> Ne gemealt him se modsefa,   ne his mæges laf
> gewac æt wige;   þæt se wyrm onfand,
> syððan hie togædre   gegan hæfdon   (2628–30)

[his mind did not melt, nor his father's relic weaken in battle; that the dragon found, once they had closed together]

Wiglaf's speech follows. Considering it realistically, he speaks to no one, since the other ten retainers, having already fled, can make no answer. But he uses the first person plural nearly all the time, returning to the singular only at significant moments:

> 'Ic ðæt mæl geman,   ðær we medu þegun . . .'   (2633)

['I remember the time, when *we* accepted mead . . .']

For he is continually making a distinction between himself and the others, not that he is brave and they are cowards, but, at a higher level, that he remembers and they do not. The root of the others' flight is seen to be in the past. Then they 'promised to pay for their benefits', and they did not lie deliberately. But their imagination was not strong enough; they had no *foreþanc* [forethought]; *edwenden* [change] to them was only a word. Wiglaf controls the past, for he makes visible *now* a distinction present *then,* but unknowable—that he meant his promise and they could not. He also controls the future, for he envisages and chooses between two possible (bad) endings:

> 'me is micle leofre   þæt minne lichaman
> mid minne goldgyfan   gled fæðmie.
> Ne þynceð me gerysne   þæt we rondas beren
> eft to earde,   nemne we æror mægen
> fane gefyllan'   (2651–5)

['it is much better to me that the fire should swallow my body with my benefactor. To me it does not seem right that we should carry our shields home again, unless we could *earlier* destroy our foe']

Even the future, for him, is apprehended in terms of himself looking back on what could have happened. The speech is full of references to time:

'Ic ðæt mæl geman,   ðær we medu þegun,
þonne we geheton   ussum hlaforde . . .
þæt we him ða guðgetawa   gyldan woldon
gif him þyslicu   þearf gelumpe . . .
        . . . Nu is se dæg cumen!'   (2633–46)

['I remember the time when we accepted mead, when we promised our lord
that we would repay him the war-weapons, if this kind of necessity
happened . . . Now that day *has* come!']

The conclusion is inescapable, the response inevitable, *if* one has the
sort of mind that can conquer time.

Wiglaf's speech is not by any means unparalleled in Old English
verse. *'Nu is se dæg cumen'* forms a climax in *Waldere* as well, while in
Maldon Ælfwine makes almost exactly the same contrast of past and
present, vow and proof, as in the few lines above.[43] Clearly Wiglaf
epitomises heroic propriety. But what can one make of his sword, with
its damning history, a feature so bizarre and unexpected as to make
several commentators urge that it must all have been true (since no
one would want to invent such a tangle)? It helps to observe that the
sword has two functions. On the one hand it works quasi-symbolically
as a further proof of the power of *sibb* [kinship]—as Professor
Irving puts it: 'Wiglaf's courage *is* his *mæges laf* . . . the sword is only
a tangible aspect of it.' In this respect the weapon, like the speech,
shows the better and more normal side of the *eorla lif* [life of nobles].
That symbolic function could however have been carried out by any
inherited weapon, not necessarily one passed on in such peculiar
circumstances; and so the arguments of Professor Irving (and others),
though true, go only part-way. The decision to describe the sword's
history casts a darker shadow on the responses of heroes—one that
could perhaps be ignored on its own, were it not part of a theme
presented fairly insistently in the later parts of *Beowulf,* and related
ultimately to the change in narrative-mode noted at the start of this
section.

To see a part of this theme quickly one need do no more than glance
at that other protagonist in the scene—the dragon. It too has a quasi-
symbolic quality. As Professor Tolkien wrote, 'the conception
approaches *draconitas* rather than *draco*: a personification of
malice, greed, destruction (the evil side of heroic life), and of the
undiscriminating cruelty of fortune that distinguishes not good or
bad (the evil aspect of all life)'.[44] The dragon is like Revenge. It
sleeps, but can be woken; it is monstrously sensitive to the slightest
of injuries. An Anglo-Saxon might not have seen quite such abstract
connections, but he might well have been able to feel powerfully the
ramifications of feud or vendetta; and this theme grows increasingly

prominent in *Beowulf* after Hrothgar's speech, reaching a first climax in Beowulf's account of Freawaru and Ingeld, with his own conclusion:

> 'Oft seldan hwær
> æfter leodhryre   lytle hwile
> bongar bugeð,   þeah seo bryd duge!'   (2029–31)

['As a rule the deadly spear seldom rests anywhere after the fall of a prince, except for a little while, even though the bride is good!']

Though the proof of his remark seems to be skipped over in the connecting 'breathless' sentence of 2200–14, it is only postponed. Furthermore the poet, by his economy here, juxtaposes the dragon closely with the deaths of Hygelac and Heardred and the story of Ingeld, with all the wars of Swedes and Geats, Danes and Heatho-bards. It takes little skill after that to see that the robbing of the dragon, its revenge and Beowulf's own counter-attack, form only another example of the feud. The change of mode is that this feud, unlike the *Finnsburg Episode,* the Scylding civil war, and the other human conflicts, all entered *in mediis rebus* and then told by prophecy or allusion, is set out in a plain, clear, linear fashion from outbreak to conclusion, with nothing omitted and nothing merely hinted. Every reader or listener feels this change, even if he cannot name it. Its effect—a vital one—is to reduce irony and increase explanation.

The moral most obviously conveyed is the paradoxical and profit-less nature of feud and malice. The dragon after all gains nothing from its treasure, *ne byð him wihte ðy sel* [he is no way the better for it]. Nor does Beowulf profit. We are told explicitly that the gold he wins is buried with him *eldum swa unnyt swa hit æror wæs* [as useless to men as it was before]. The thief indeed seems to gain something from stealing the dragon's cup, but it is explained carefully and repeated twice that his motive is to allay a feud or avoid punishment by offering this as *frioðowære* [pledge of peace]:

> Nealles mid gewealdum   wyrmhord abræc
> sylfes willum,   se ðe him sare gesceod,
> ac for þreanedlan   þeow nathwylces
> hæleða bearna   heteswengeas fleah   (2221–4)

[Not deliberately, not by his own wish did he who injured it grievously disturb the dragon-hoard, but out of misery some slave of the children of men fled hostile blows]

So the entire conflict is an accident from the start, swinging from one frightened or vengeful reaction to another.

The same futility marks even more strongly three rather incidental *tableaux* carefully inserted into the story-line. In the first the treasure's previous owner merely laments the (violent?) extinction of his race, making an obvious statement of a general rule:

> 'Bealocwealm hafað
> fela feorhcynna   forð onsended!'   (2265–6)

['Hateful death has dismissed many living races!']

But in two others Beowulf himself more interestingly presents type-figures, in heroic *exempla* of profitless and unrevenged death.[45] First he recalls how his grandfather, King Hrethel, died of grief from the death of one son, shot by another; then he compares the old king to a man who sees his son hanged. The connection between the cases is that in both the father is prevented, legally or naturally, from taking any action. These memories of futility reflect Beowulf's own sombre state of mind, as he sees himself in a situation where he must act, but with little more hope of gain than the hanged man's father or King Hrethel. His foresight and understanding—totally unlike the ironic ignorance of Wealhtheow and his own younger self at the banquet in Heorot—complement the new, clear, straightforward style of narrative.

The ultimately profitless nature of the revenge-ethic is presented, then, on several levels in this last third of *Beowulf,* if never with perfect clarity. The historical world from which Wiglaf emerges is especially packed with the paradoxes of feud and its bitter repayments, from Ongentheow's *wyrsan wrixle* [worse exchange] with the sons of Wonred to Hæthcyn's purchase of victory *heardan ceape* [with a hard bargain]—his life. In this world it can be assumed that a Swedish king who apparently owes his throne to the Geats will nevertheless not forget their killing of his grandfather, while on the other hand Onela does not trouble to avenge his nephew on Weohstan, Wiglaf's father:

> no ymbe ða fæhðe spræc,
> þeah ðe he his broðor bearn   abredwade   (2618–19)

[(Onela) did not speak of the feud, though (Weohstan) had killed his brother's child]

It is hard not to see an expression of such 'logic' in Wiglaf's appearance behind Beowulf, drawing the sword *Eanmundes laf* in full knowledge of its history, unconcerned that it has now 'changed sides' for yet another time.

An adept critic could easily extract further layers of significance

from the scenes with Wiglaf, perhaps turning it into a kind of allegory, as representatives from two sides of a bitter war join to fight
an embodiment of their own instincts, like Error in *The Faerie
Queene*; or presenting the last section as a satire on 'escalation' in
warfare; or arguing that Beowulf's failure stems from the corruptions
of power.[46] All these views have some slight foundation in the text;
but they would involve the mistake of pressing too firm and sharp a
conclusion on what is essentially a balance, a series of contrasts.
Much of the complexity of the end of *Beowulf* stems from the
existence in it of two possible and valid attitudes to the heroic life—
one admiring its strength and beauty (in places like the speech of
Wiglaf), the other considering its disastrous long-term effects on
nations and individuals.[47] Accepting one does not mean denying the
other. Indeed, true heroism is enhanced by an awareness of eventual
defeat, true criticism by a sense of the worth of what is lost. The
Beowulf-poet never gives any final decision about the two attitudes,
which remain powerfully combined in the poem's last lines of praise
and mourning. The way in which both points of view are present in
the hero himself at different stages in his life—the young, confident
Beowulf warned by Hrothgar; the old, sombre Beowulf helped by
Wiglaf—suggests that the poet had in mind no sharp dichotomy, but
rather an inevitable progress. If the duality of good and bad in
heroism was familiar, at least in its essentials, to Anglo-Saxon
audiences, they might also have been the readier to appreciate the
faint tones of symbolism in Wiglaf's sword and the dragon, or the
effects of the radical change of narrative-mode over the last thousand
lines.

Beowulf's distinctive quality is one of respect—respect for enemies
as well as friends, for those who, like Hrothgar, try to prevent violence, as well as for those who exist to cause it, like Hygelac and
Hæthcyn. It is this which gives heroic propriety its peculiar charm.
It is this, too, which makes subtlety of the kind I have invoked even
momentarily credible for an Anglo-Saxon poet and audience. Irony,
thought, and fairness are built into the smallest units of the epic
style and the epic situation. To distil them and make them as
clear and economical as they are in *Beowulf* is an achievement
worthy of the highest admiration; but it is not quite unbelievable.
Some of the work had been done before. The poet did not need to
invent his diction or his story or even his attitude to it. What he
did, we must think, was to scheme, to connect, to re-arrange allusion
and incident and speech. As a result, the folk-tale basis of his story,
with its fantasy and brutality, has all but disappeared.[48] It is replaced by a gravity and a respect for the human spirit which is

amazingly consistent, found in every scene and every few lines, and shared, also, with what other Old English epic fragments we possess. The poem's success is not one of story and not one of style, but stems from a 'genius of attitude'[49] which is common to both, a distinctive fusion of irony and praise.

3

WISDOM AND EXPERIENCE:
THE OLD ENGLISH 'ELEGIES'

What is the price of Experience? do men buy it for a song?
Or wisdom for a dance in the street? No, it is bought with the
    price
Of all that a man hath, his house, his wife, his children.
Wisdom is sold in the desolate market where none come to buy,
And in the wither'd field where the farmer plows for bread in vain.
BLAKE, Vala or The Four Zoas

The problems of experience

Apart from *Beowulf* and *Maldon* the only Old English poems to achieve any great modern popularity are a small group from the *Exeter Book* usually known as 'the elegies', a term vague enough to be inoffensive if unhelpful.[1] Seven poems are most frequently cited in discussions of this group, *The Wanderer, The Seafarer, Deor, Wulf and Eadwacer, The Wife's Lament, The Husband's Message,* and *The Ruin.* All the titles are modern ones, with no particular authority, and, more important than that, the very selection of these seven poems from the *Exeter Book,* with its implied rejection of eight or nine comparable ones, displays a certain arbitrariness which might usefully be challenged. Nevertheless, there is a reason for the modern impression that these poems form a group, and one no doubt connected with their popularity: all seven are urgent and passionate poems. Unlike the great bulk of Old English verse, with its anonymous and hortatory tones, several of these claim insistently to be personal, the products of individual experience. *Mæg ic be me sylfum soðgied wrecan* [I can make a true song about myself], declares the 'seafarer'; the 'wife' begins her outcry, *Ic þis giedd wrece bi me ful geomorre, minre sylfre sið* [I make this song about my unhappy self, my own

experience]; the poet 'Deor' turns from mythical examples to his
own state with the application *Þæt ic bi me sylfum secgan wille*
[I can say that about myself (as well)]. Most comprehensively, the
poet of *Resignation* or *The Penitent's Prayer*—a marginal member
of the 'elegy' group—combines several of the others' motifs with:

> Ic bi me tylgust
> secge þis sarspel   ond ymb siþ spræce,
> longunge fus,   ond on lagu þence   (96–8)

[I tell this painful story most aptly about myself, speak of my experience
(journey?), eagerly yearning, and think of the sea][2]

Grief, desire, and personal emotion are expressed with a characteristic power—and obscurity, for it is quite uncertain, in the passage
quoted, whether the speaker means his *siþ* mentally or physically,
realistically or symbolically.

No doubt as a result of this generally confused attraction, scores of
critics have been driven to write on one or several of these poems
together, looking in them for signs of a mental structure or an
external source which would make it easier to understand what they
are about. Some genuine information has emerged. Unfortunately,
by the same process many controversies have been generated which
now seem to have a life of their own apart from the texts, a prominent
one being the 'mingling of Christian and heathen material' suggested
by Lawrence in 1902, and rejected or re-discovered all too frequently
since.[3] It should now be possible to say with some confidence that
there is no explicitly heathen material anywhere in the poems, but of
course that they were not created to express any limitedly pietistic
concept of Christianity. In the same way the old speculation that
some of the poems, particularly *The Wanderer* and *The Seafarer,*
might be easier to read if they were dialogues has probably been
effectively spoilt by the inability of any two readers to agree where the
dividing lines between one speaker and another might be.[4] As
hypotheses multiply (and cancel each other out) it becomes more
obvious that the 'elegies' contain some essential obscurity not to be
solved by the discovery of any single key. What is wanted is not
further offensives over the various scholarly Passchendaeles already
marked out, but some broadening (and perhaps some blurring) of
the area to be investigated. As Mrs. I. L. Gordon put it nearly twenty
years ago, we need 'a thorough investigation into the poetic environment of these poems—the background of thought from which they
drew their ideas, the nature of their poetic pattern, and the meaning
and association (to a contemporary audience) of their terms'.[5]
Environment, thought, associations—these, rather than pure

reason, are what must serve. The need for a study of that kind is only emphasised by the number of features unique to these poems and obscure to us, yet repeated and held in common by several poets and, we must expect, at least a certain number of listeners.

One avenue of approach is opened up by an antithesis present in the several 'declarations of personal involvement' already quoted. The speakers insist on the immediacy of what they have to say; yet at the same time the repetition of this feature in similar terms argues a certain formality in the claim. There is a related opposition between the (occasionally incoherent) impulsiveness of speech in several poems, notably *The Wife's Lament* and *Wulf and Eadwacer,* and the invariable stress on generalisation and the extraction of a moral from circumstance. *Stieran mon sceal strongum mode* [a man must control with strong mind], insists the 'seafarer', and he is echoed verbally by the author of *Maxims I* a few pages later in the manuscript, and in spirit by all speakers in this group of poems. Even the 'wife' ends with a firm, if mournful, definitive statement. How is one to explain this typical alternation between spontaneity and the imposition of categories? An answer emerges from the ambiguities, not calculated but exploited, of the word *siþ,* used twice in quotations already.

The normal meaning of this word is 'journey' or possibly 'exploit', a sense it may bear in the 'declaration of involvement' from *Resignation.* However, by a process analogous to that in modern German *Erfahrung* (= 'experience', but related to *fahren* = 'to travel'), *siþ* must also have come to mean 'experience', something one 'travels through' on the path of life. In its double meaning the Old English word has a connection with poetry. *Widsið* [widely travelled *or* widely experienced] is the name given to a typical poet; and in his compilation *The Fates of the Apostles* Cynewulf claims:

> Hwæt! Ic þysne sang   siðgeomor fand
> on seocum sefan   (1–2)

[Lo! I found this song in my sick heart, saddened by experience]

There is clearly no basis for this assertion, since personal experience can have had little to do with listing the martyrdoms of the twelve apostles, and their fates could not in any case be considered, by a devout Christian like Cynewulf, as genuinely depressing. To be *siðgeomor* [saddened by experience] is rather the proper stance for a poet in Anglo-Saxon minds. But the *effect* of his poetry should be the opposite. The thoroughly conventional *Maxims* of the *Exeter Book* assert that to know songs is a road out of grief:

Longað þonne þy læs   þe him con leoþa worn,
oþþe mid hondum con   hearpan gretan;
hafaþ him his gliwes giefe,   þe him god sealde   (169-71)

[He grieves the less who knows many songs, or who can play the harp with his hands; he has the gift of his mirth, which God gave him]

The poet gains experience, and is saddened by it; expresses himself, and gives cheer. Something like this alternation is present in most of the Old English 'elegies', accounting for their use of both spontaneous reaction and conscious control. In one sense they are 'consolation-poems'. But part of the consolation offered is poetry itself, the expression and formalisation of raw experience.[6] The poems can therefore present grief tumultuously and immediately, without necessarily remaining in that state, moving instead to the greater certainty that is a delayed result of experience, and to the relief that comes from speech. If one realises that these poems describe a process rather than a fixed point, much of their ambiguity becomes at least less confusing.

The Wanderer, most vexed but also fullest of the 'elegiac' group, provides a good starting-point for an analysis of their subtle and self-reflective techniques. For most readers its most memorable part—the part that has led to the modern title—must be the long speech from lines 8-57, by the 'wanderer' himself, introduced by the words *Swa cwæð eardstapa, earfeþa gemyndig* [So spoke the wanderer, remembering hardships]. Its distinctive combination of emotional, physical and social stress produces a vivid and pathetic picture of the Anglo-Saxon exile. Yet simple description is unlikely to be its purpose; most readers feel vaguely that there is something larger and more symbolic about the figures introduced, though there is nothing explicit, and the generally gloomy tone of that speech in particular contrasts with the firm and confident statements at beginning and end of the poem. Possibly the introductory phrase *eardstapa earfeþa gemyndig* provides a clue to the source of this feeling. Like Wiglaf's speech in *Beowulf*, the 'wanderer's' is permeated by a sense of time, and of memory. The source of his misery is the death of his lord *geara iu* [in years long ago], while its culmination, neither physical nor social, is the remembrance of time past. The friendless man 'remembers retainers and taking treasure'. In sleep his dreams betray him:

þinceð him on mode   þæt he his mondryhten
clyppe ond cysse,   ond on cneo lecge
honda ond heafod,   swa he hwilum ær
in geardagum   giefstolas breac.

> Đonne onwæcneð eft   wineleas guma,
> gesihð him biforan   fealwe wegas . . .   (41–6)

[It seems to him in his mind that he embraces and kisses his lord, laying hands and head on his knees, as often before when he took gifts from the throne in days gone by. Then the friendless man awakes, sees the grey waves before him . . .]

It is not the death of his lord which most moves the 'wanderer', but the contrast between past and present, dream and awakening; it is this which 'renews sorrow', *þonne maga gemynd mod geondhweorfeð* [when the mind passes through the memory of kinsmen].[7]

Sudden oppositions between joy and sorrow are of course the particular delight of Old English poets, but there are also elements to suggest that this one was not aiming at the simple goal of a luxuriant self-pity. The contrast between times is only one of several contrasts set up in this early part of the poem, and with some of them the *Wanderer*-poet displays curious ambiguity. Besides memory, one of the major torments of the *eardstapa* is his compelled silence. He can speak freely to no one now alive (lines 8–11); he must do without *his winedryhtnes leofes larcwidum* [the advice of his dear and friendly lord]; breaking out of his dream the sea-birds seem to mock him with their lack of *cuðra cwidegiedda* [familiar speeches].[8] Silence, a restriction by mental fetters, as he imagines it, is the greatest sign of his isolation. But is it an unmitigated evil? Outside the speech of lines 8–57 the poet praises silence and restraint several times, ending the poem indeed with the very firm triple statement;

> Til biþ se þe his treowe gehealdeþ,   ne sceal næfre his torn
>   to rycene
> beorn of his breostum acyþan,   nemþe he ær þa bote cunne,
> eorl mid elne gefremman.   Wel bið þam þe him are seceð,
> frofre to fæder on heofonum,   þær us eal seo fæstnung
>   stondeð   (112–15)

[He who keeps his trust is good; a man must never make his grief known too quickly from his heart, unless he knows first, the nobleman, how to perform the cure gloriously; well for him who seeks favour and consolation from the Father in Heaven, where a complete security stands for us]

There is no possibility of irony in these lines. Yet in them restraint is put on a level with loyalty and trust in God as a virtue. How can one relate this to the enforced misery of the *eardstapa's* speech?

Behind this ambiguity lies the poem's central contrast. The first half, the 'wanderer's' long speech, has a double motive. On the one hand the poet wishes to stir up passion, and does it through the powerful contrasts of memory and the interrupted dream; on the other, he wishes, not to diminish, but to bridle passion, through the stress on restraint. The result, as these two forces collide, is a sense of anguished struggle in the mind between outburst and repression, fact and illusion, present and past, an opposition put memorably enough in the speech's last few lines:

> Cearo bið geniwad
> þam þe sendan sceal   swiþe geneahhe
> ofer waþema gebind // werigne sefan   (55–7)

[Care is renewed for him who must send, very often, his weary mind // across the frozen waves]

The mind and the sea confront each other in the attempt to find mental rest. This situation, of increasing disturbance increasingly kept down, bears some resemblance to that of Hengest in the *Finnsburg Episode* in *Beowulf*: and the use of the phrase *waþema gebind* to reflect the 'wanderer's' frozen mind reminds one also of Hengest's *wælfagne winter* [death-stained winter].[9] But no spring comes for the 'wanderer', nor can he escape from his dilemma by actions.

Yet an escape of some kind has virtually been promised in the poem's first few lines:

> Oft him anhaga   are gebideð,
> metudes miltse,   þeah þe he modcearig
> geond lagulade   longe sceolde
> hreran mid hondum   hrimcealde sæ,
> wadan wræclastas.   Wyrd bið ful aræd!   (1–5)

[Often the solitary man experiences favour, God's mercy, although unhappily he has long had to strike the ice-cold sea with his hands, tread the paths of exile across the ocean. Events are fully determined!]

Inability to see where 'God's mercy' appears in the rest of the poem has led many to translate *are gebideð* as 'waits (unavailingly) for favour'. But the appearance of the phrase in other poems leaves little doubt that the sentence really is a promise, and that it turns on the word 'although'.[10] As we should perhaps expect, the favour that God grants is not, however, a physical one; after all, even if the *eardstapa* were to find a new lord and happiness, that would hardly solve his problem of painful memory. His dilemma, as we have seen, is an internal one, to be solved only by a change of attitude resulting from control of the mind—a change increasingly evident in the latter part of the poem, though marked by no firm dividing line. Essentially it

consists of the abandonment of personality for a general historical
perspective; along with this goes a concern, not for the past alone,
but for the past as a guide to future events. The speaker draws an
insistent deduction from the sight of ruins—'as they were, so are we:
as they are, so will we be'—and urges it on his listeners, *Ongietan
sceal gleaw hæle hu gæstlic bið* [the wise man must perceive how
terrifying it will be . . .]. The tone remains melancholy, but it has
become prescriptive rather than descriptive; escaped from his inner
turmoil, the speaker can see truth, offer advice, decide what is best
for men to think and do. If one gives full weight to the apparently
inescapable introversion experienced earlier, this change of viewpoint
alone becomes a satisfactory mark of *metudes miltse*. It is mirrored,
we might note, by a general shift from the first person to the third,
linked by the neat transitional sentence of lines 58–62, where the
speaker, still using the 'I' form, begins to consider the *eorla lif*
[life of noblemen] in general rather than himself, and then moves
into the third person with *þes middangeard* [this earth] as his next
grammatical subject.

The two voices of *eardstapa* [wanderer] and *snottor on mode*
[the man wise in mind] may seem dissimilar enough to belong to
separate people.[11] But to think this is not to allow enough weight to
the Anglo-Saxon interest in *how* wisdom is gained. In both *The
Wanderer* and *The Seafarer* (and in several places elsewhere), the
speakers insist that experience of one's own is a necessary prologue
to wisdom. *Wat se þe cunnað* [he knows who makes trial of it],
observes *The Wanderer*; in a more negative way, *The Seafarer*
presents three times the figure of 'the man who does not know, who
little believes' what others have gone through, because he has only
lifes wyn gebiden in burgum [experienced the joys of life in human
dwellings]. Both halves of *The Wanderer* are necessary. One stage has
to be lived through to provide, not only the knowledge but, one feels,
the mental fire necessary for attaining the next. Most Anglo-Saxon
poets would probably agree with the short explanation of 'Widsith',
their archetype:

> Godes ond yfles
> þær ic cunnade   cnosle bidæled,
> freomægum feor   folgade wide.
> Forþon ic mæg singan   ond secgan spell . . .   (51–4)

[There I made trial of good and evil, deprived of my nation, far from my
friends, I took service widely. *Therefore* I can sing and tell a story . . .]

The alternating styles of *The Wanderer* reflect the two traditional
duties of the poet, to endure bitter experience, and to give men
relief through the expression of its lessons.

The two 'halves' of the poem of course gain from each other, the first seeming somehow more typical for what follows, the second being pulled back from cold detachment. The changes of narrative mode also point to what may be the poem's imaginative kernel, the theme of *mens absentia cogitans,* 'the mind brooding intensely over distant things'. Professor P. Clemoes has suggested convincingly that this idea, very prominent in both *The Wanderer* and *The Seafarer,* owes something to the arguments of Alcuin in his treatise *De Animae Ratione,* and behind him the greater figures of Ambrose and Augustine.[12] These Latin writers all dwell on the mind's power of instantaneous movement. But where they see this as an argument for the power of the Divine Mind, the Old English authors more fully understand the mind's limitations. It can indeed travel, can call up visions even of the dead. But having done that, can it preserve them, touch them, alter the external world? The 'wanderer's' awakening proves that it cannot. It is this sense of human desire thwarted which gives the Old English melancholy its power, as the mind remembers but cannot create. *Swa heo no wære* [as if it had never been] is a culminating phrase in both *The Wanderer* and *The Wife's Lament,* combining in itself the external reality of absence and the internal one of painful memory, both powerful but not quite equally so. Still, a balance is kept. Though a man's mind cannot change the world outside, it can control itself and so lead in the end to victory of a sort. The 'exaltation of undefeated will' was a theme congenial to other Old English poets, as one can see from Byrhtwold's famous opposition of mental and physical strength at the end of *The Battle of Maldon:*

> 'Hige sceal þe heardra,   heorte þe cenre,
> mod sceal þe mare,   þe ure mægen lytlað'   (312–13)

['Thought shall be the harder, heart the keener, mind the greater, as our strength decreases']

A sense of similarly paradoxical victory is even stronger as *The Wanderer* records its more universal struggle of the mind against the outside world.[13]

The Wanderer is obviously not a neat poem. Its arbitrary transitions are not the result of artistic failure, nor was it probably ever intended to be, in our terms, an artistic success. Perhaps the best adjective to use of it is to say that it is a 'performative' poem, one which, for full effect, demands a certain involvement from reader or listener, and repays him not with abstract knowledge but with a strengthening of the mind, an awareness of human limitations and of the way in which they are conquered.[14] This, to Anglo-Saxon minds, is one of the fruits of wisdom.

The answers of the wise

Regrettably, wisdom is not always recognised. Mrs N. K. Chadwick tells an amusing story of a Russian traveller in Central Asia during the last century who, finding that his host had begun to speak in cryptic rhyming couplets, concluded that the man was insane— whereas 'in reality it seems clear that the chief was merely entertaining his guest with the most formal and polite kind of conversation with which he was familiar', that is, compressed, proverbial verse.[15] Many readers of Old English jump to the same wrong conclusion as the Russian traveller when they first encounter the dialogues of *Solomon and Saturn,* the charm and medicine anthologies, the two collections of 'gnomic verse', or the many poems which exist to give advice and make general statements on the human condition. These no longer appeal to modern taste, or fall into any recognisable verse-category. In their way, though, all of them enshrine a type of traditional lore which (from the existence of the manuscripts) must have been dear to many Anglo-Saxons, and which crops up indestructibly even in the religious epics. It may be no accident that several of the heroes selected from Christian history for treatment in Old English verse are prophets, wise men and soothsayers, or that Christian doctrine in these poems is consistently and delightedly reported as *gæstgeryno* [spiritual mystery]. A native liking for the figure of the 'ancient sage' may well have been reinforced, in poems like *Daniel, Elene* or *Exodus,* by Christian learning, while a love of mysterious obscurity appears also in the *Riddles,* learned compositions themselves, but appealing to a taste fairly widespread in Old English and Old Norse. Poems like the *Precepts* and *Maxims* of the *Exeter Book* and other manuscripts may seem to us cryptic or pointless, and they are certainly not designed to be easy. But it is important to try to pick out the drift of meaning behind them, if only because of their at times surprising resemblances to (parts of) the Old English 'elegies'.

To take one example, it gives any reader of *The Wanderer* a jolt to find, in the Exeter *Maxims,* first the lines already quoted (on p. 56) about the relieving effects of poetry, and then, immediately following, the remark:

> Earm biþ se þe sceal　ana lifgan,
> wineleas wunian　hafaþ him wyrd geteod　　　　(172–3)

[Wretched is he who has to live alone, events have dictated that he lives without joy]

The observations are unconnected grammatically, but present exactly the contrast of solitude and expression found in *Deor* or

The Wanderer. One suspects that the contrast is not the invention of some individual poet, but is latent in Anglo-Saxon habits of thought. In the same way, thinking of *The Seafarer,* one might see a concealed relevance in lines like:

> Styran sceal mon strongum mode.   Storm oft holm gebringeþ,
> geofen in grimmum sælum;   onginnað grome fundian
> fealwe on feorran to londe,   hwæþer he fæste stonde.
> Weallas him wiþre healdað . . .   (*Maxims* 50–3)

[A man must control with strong mind. The sea often brings a storm, the ocean in grim times; the fierce grey waves begin to strive from afar to the land, whether it may stand fast. The walls hold them back . . .]

Here human control and the chaos of the sea are brought into a startling but quite undeveloped juxtaposition, and, oddly associated with both, the image of the walls resisting, found in similar contexts in *Juliana* and *The Wanderer.* Verse like the *Maxims* is bald and not immediately purposeful. But in its curt oppositions, one might say, many poems lie in embryo; from this unformed state some are developed, even though they never shake off entirely the tone of mystery and reliance on association. To understand the 'elegies', it helps to find out what linkages are consistent in Old English proverbial verse, and to see what implications about human existence lie behind them. No doubt any modern mind will be over-systematic; but once again, system is our only possible replacement for what to an Anglo-Saxon audience may have been obvious and automatic.

In these respects the poem known as *Solomon and Saturn II* is unusually valuable, if challenging. These two disputants appear in several Old English prose and verse dialogues, almost certainly by different hands,[16] and with widely varying subjects. The first poetic dialogue, for instance, consists very largely of Solomon's exposition of the supernatural powers of the separate *letters* of the *gepalm-twigede* [palm-twigged] Pater Noster—a witness to the eclectic nature of Anglo-Saxon learning, but unapproachable in present terms. The second poem, however, is more genuinely a dialogue, a real contest between the two sages, Solomon standing generally for a Christian world-view, Saturn not for paganism exactly, but for doubt. In the end Saturn is overcome, but like the heathen English priest Coifi, in Bede,[17] is still treated with respect. He rejoices at losing the debates, having gained new knowledge; *næfre ær his ferhð ahlog* [never before did his mind exult].[18] The nature of the contest, too, is curious. At times the sages merely ask each other riddles to be solved by ingenuity, or offer each other mysterious knowledge; but as the poem continues, Saturn especially begins to ask, not riddles, but questions about human life and death, drawing from Solomon not plain answers but half-agreements and cryptic modifications. In this section particularly something of the deeper reaches of Anglo-Saxon philosophy can be glimpsed. Typically, the results are not to be measured simply in terms of knowledge, but rather according to the difference they make to Saturn's (and the reader's) mental state. Both wise men, towards the start of the dialogue, agree firmly on the importance of literature, but only because of its strength and utility:

> Salomon cuæð: 'Bec sindon breme,   bodiað geneahhe
> weotodne willan   ðam ðe wiht hygeð.
> Gestrangað hie and gestaðeliað   staðolfæstne
> geðoht,
> amyrgað modsefan   manna gehwylces
> of ðreamedlan   ðisses lifes'   (238–42)

[Solomon said: 'It is books which are famous; they preach the ordained purpose often to anyone who considers at all. They strengthen and confirm the resolute thought, they cheer the mind of every man, out of the means of compulsion (harsh restraints?) of this life']

This is perhaps the intention of *Solomon and Saturn* itself; not to console (since no calamity has occurred) but to explain and reassure, cheering the mind with a promise of order.

Nevertheless, the general attitude of both debaters no doubt strikes the modern reader, to begin with, as essentially gloomy, Saturn in particular creating an early impression of *fear*. He asks Solomon what it is that can be resisted by nothing in the world, sea or sky, and gets the answer *yldo* [old age], characteristically expanded with further force and directness by his antagonist. Then to a lost question from Solomon he replies laconically (with an echo of *The Wanderer's* dream-sequence):

> 'Nieht bið wedera ðiestrost,   ned bið wyrda heardost,
> sorg bið swarost byrðen,   slæp bið deaðe gelicost.'   (312–13)

['Night is darkest of weathers, necessity hardest of conditions, sorrow the heaviest burden, sleep most like death.']

A little later he begins a linked series of questions with the enigmatic *'hwæt beoð ða feowere fægæs rapas?'* ['what are the four ropes of the doomed man?'] to be answered, chillingly:

> 'Gewurdene wyrda,
> ðæt beoð ða feowere   fæges rapas'   (334–5)

['Transpired events; those are the four doomed man's ropes']

The alliteration here of *wyrd* and *gewurden* is traditional. But why they are ropes, and why there are four of them, we do not know. Possibly the poet did not know either. As it is, his curtness and precision give an air of final certainty to human bondage, not decreased by the surrounding references to Doomsday, and perhaps in any case playing on the peculiar terror of binding and paralysis occasionally present elsewhere in Germanic literature.[19] For a time, at least, both speakers point deliberately to that sense of human weakness and isolation so prominent in Old English literature generally.

Saturn's next five questions (lines 336–63) narrow the issue considerably. In succession, he asks Solomon: (1) who is it that will judge Christ on Doomsday? (2) why does the sun cast shadows, instead of shining on all creation? (3) why are those companions lament and laughter always together? (4) why can we not all go to Heaven? (5) why does the evil man live longer? Diverse though these queries are, their drift is obvious. Saturn is concerned essentially with justice—to him the existence of shadows (the success of sin) demands an explanation. He is also aware of human weakness—the vulnerability of joy, the seemingly universal dualism that sends some to Heaven and some to Hell. What he wants to know is whether Solomon, as proponent of Christian wisdom, has any cogent answer to the problems of evil and suffering. Naturally, there can be no brief answer; and indeed Solomon often seems to confirm Saturn's doubts rather than disperse them, occasionally adding a veiled threat of divine justice to come. He reacts violently only to the first question —who will judge Christ?—giving the harsh reply:

> 'Hwa dear ðonne dryhtne deman, ðe us of duste geworhte,
> nergend of niehtes wunde?'   (338–9)

['Who will dare then to judge the Lord who created us from dust, the Saviour from the wound (womb?) of night?']

Christ is above judgement; with that there may be a suggestion that He is above injustice too, outside the restricted and failing natural universe. Saturn's reassurance, perhaps, is not that what he fears is not true, but that there is a Power to which this truth does not apply. Solomon cooperates and agrees with his opponent's gloomy world-view, reserving only the fact that it is not final. One could see here something like that 'mixture of Christian and pagan' thought so often discovered confusingly in the 'elegies'; but it is not so much a mixture as a demarcation of different areas.

In fact it is Solomon who then goes on to give a fine and moving statement of an 'elegiac' situation, the mother who rears her children,

ignorant of how they may grow up, and powerless to intervene if
they turn out badly. He is answering a question from Saturn as to
why two twins, outwardly alike, may lead totally different lives—a
question again implying some kind of hidden compulsion beneath
the surface of human lives:

'Modor ne ræðeð,   ðonne heo magan cenneð,
hu him weorðe geond worold   widsið sceapen.
Oft heo to bealwe   bearn afedeð,
seolfre to sorge,   siððan dreogeð
his earfoðu   orlegstunde.
Heo ðæs afran sceall   oft and gelome
grimme greotan,   ðonne he geong færeð,
hafað wilde mod,   werige heortan,
sefan sorgfullne . . .
Forðan nah seo modor geweald,   ðonne heo magan cenneð,
bearnes blædes,   ac sceall on gebyrd faran
an æfter anum; ðæt is eald gesceaft'   (372–86)

['A mother has no control, when she bears a son, over how his wide
journey through the world will be formed. Often she brings up a child to
woe, to her own sorrow, and then endures his hardships and destined
hour. Often and again she must weep painfully for the child, when he goes
about as a youth, has a wild spirit, a despairing heart, a sorrowful mind . . .
So the mother has no power over her child's prosperity, when she bears a
son, but one thing must follow another as fated; that is ancient destiny
(the way things are made?)']

Both the passive suffering of the mother and the desperate restless-
ness of the young man have their parallels in the 'elegiac' group and in
heroic story;[20] Solomon fuses the two stock situations into a powerful *tableau* of human weakness and ignorance in the face of time.
But he also begins to open up a fuller answer to this problem than
could be contained in his earlier blunt assertions.

To Saturn's further query as to why young men will not 'struggle for
wisdom' [*winnan æfter snytro*] (and so presumably escape the fate he
has described), Solomon answers that men after all have a choice.
The hint that men can do something to save themselves is followed
when Saturn asks which of the two conflicting powers, *wyrd* and
warnung, is the stronger, suggesting that he himself can find no
difference—a passage which has been thought to show the Boethian
and Augustinian doubt as to whether free-will [*warnung?*] is stronger
than predestination [*wyrd?*]. But that antithesis does not seem to be
thoroughly expressed in Old English anywhere,[21] and it is more
likely that Saturn simply wants to know whether human beings can
control their own lives and alter circumstance [*wyrd*] by taking

thought and receiving warning [*warnung*] in advance. His own opinion—not surprisingly, in view of Solomon's story of the mother and child—is that they cannot. But rigid determinism is rejected by Solomon's answer:

> 'Wyrd bið wended hearde,   wealleð swiðe geneahhe . . .
> and hwæðre him mæg wissefa   wyrda gehwylce
> gemetigian,   gif he bið modes gleaw
> and to his freondum wile   fultum secan,
> ðeh hwæðre godcundes   gæstes brucan'   (437–43)

['The course of events is changed with difficulty, it swells very often . . . and yet the man wise in mind can moderate every event, if he is sage in spirit, and wishes to seek help from his friends, moreover to make use of the divine spirit']

The reassurance is limited, for Solomon does not deny the world's indifference to men's wishes; yet he does offer two possible escapes— first, the power of wisdom; second, the turning to God (vaguely expressed though it is). Religious consolation indeed seems to be contingent on wisdom. As Solomon has said before (lines 391–3), men can make a choice *if they wish to*. Making the *right* choice is, however, a product of wisdom and foresight. A few lines later Solomon explains how each man is accompanied by two spirits, an angel and a devil, both of whom teach and prompt him in their different ways. Men are left free to choose, and decide according to their strength of mind; on their death-day they will know the result of that choice (when it will be too late to change). The ultimate source of this situation, and of all human evils, seems to be not so much Original Sin as the Fall of the Angels, the event which raised up all opposition to the divine order. Solomon describes the devils' rebellion in answer to Saturn's further queries about *wyrd seo swiðe* [mighty fate], and says plainly:

> 'Ðæt sindon ða usic feohtað on.
> Forðon is witena gehwam   wopes eaca'   (460–1)

['That (i.e. the devil bound in Hell) is what fights against us. That is why there is increased lament for every wise man.]

In short, Solomon presents a picture of intense struggle in the universe and in every man's mind, a struggle which produces suffering of all kinds, never entirely to be avoided. The reassurance he offers is that the struggle can be won—when suffering will presumably cease to matter. The road to victory is strength of mind, wisdom, making the right decision.

In many respects the end of this debate reflects points made earlier and in different contexts. The stress on insight and decision has been seen in Anglo-Saxon military heroes; the idea that the mind changes reality by changing itself, in the structure of *The Wanderer*. Several other motifs appear elsewhere in Old English verse, for example the warring spirits in *Guthlac A*, the feeling that childbirth is ironic and mysterious in *The Fortunes of Men*. *Solomon and Saturn* is not presenting particularly original ideas, nor expressing them with any special clarity. What one can learn from the poem is how traditional ideas might associate with each other to produce a philosophy, even a religion, which if not exactly heretical had at least a distinct bias and great consistency. The dialogue does something to explain the curious popularity of the Fall of the Angels as a theme of Old English poetry—it crops up half-a-dozen times[22]—as well as re-inforcing the often incomplete, if urgent statements of the many Old English 'poems of advice', such as *Resignation, Precepts, Vainglory, The Order of the World,* and the various *Homiletic Fragments*. It points out, too, the immensely high value that might be set on traditional expressions of wisdom, a virtue not to be confused with the accidental attribute of intelligence or the purely acquired state of knowledge, but instead a condition of mind inseparable from such concepts as resolution, power, and foresight. When a poem like *The Wanderer* breaks into passages of gnomic reflection and generalisation, the modern reader may see them as banal and uninteresting; but when wisdom was the greatest virtue and the key to salvation, such passages could easily have been felt as climactic.

There is some justification for treating much Old English poetry, and especially the 'elegiac' group, as 'wisdom literature', nowadays an unfamiliar literary category, but in its day a large and successful one.[23] Many poems in the *Exeter Book* qualify for such treatment in two ways, first by offering advice, the fruit of wisdom, second by describing the process of acquiring wisdom. Recognition of this fact has been held up by the natural difficulty that in any epoch 'common sense' is a 'complex agglomeration of highly sophisticated half-truths',[24] and so easy to lose sight of, and by the further compli-cations of Anglo-Saxon eclecticism and delight in dramatic obscurity. However, any examination of the *Exeter Book* as a whole makes the point quite easily. Not many of the poems collected in it are narrative or even descriptive. Instead the compiler has brought together a very considerable block of admonitory, reflective verse, in which the 'elegies' are planted without any mark of distinction, and from which they differ only through their deliberate illusions of person-ality. Criticism of poems like *The Seafarer, The Wife's Lament, Deor* and the rest, has been merely hindered by the tendency to consider them in isolation, away from the manuscript context.

Individual poems

The 'wise men's reflections' of the *Exeter Book* spiral repetitively round many themes—the dangers of pride, drink and boasting; the need for decision and endurance; the devil's archery, and the power of God; man's ignorance at his birth; the powers of poetry and experience. By modern standards they are shapeless, dropping into familiar scenes without preamble, as if confident of their automatic acceptability to an Anglo-Saxon audience. Their corresponding virtue is to maintain in tension disparate but loosely-related elements of thought and emotion, forcing the reader or listener to supply his own interpretation, if he feels the need. *The Seafarer* is a good example of the powerful but superficially irritating nature of this technique.

In many ways *The Seafarer* resembles *The Wanderer* closely, and has often been attached to it as a companion-piece. The poems are of similar length; both begin with a section in the first person taking up about half the poem, and describing the pains of exile; both then shift to a more generalised exhortation and end firmly with statements in the form *Wel bið . . . Eadig bið . . .* [it is well for . . . he is noble who . . .] etc. They both change, in other words, from personal experience to the expression of wisdom. What they have to recommend is also similar, *The Wanderer* urging the wise man to 'perceive how terrible it will be when the good of all this world stands desolate', the 'seafarer'-figure asserting personally that he believes just that:

> Ic gelyfe no
> þæt him eorðwelan   ece stondað   (66–7)

[I do not believe that the goods of the earth will stand for ever]

Both poems centre on the image of the mind opposed by harsh reality, as expressed by the sea and the screaming sea-birds.[25] Yet *The Seafarer* contains several problems from which *The Wanderer* is relatively free. All of them contribute, some might think deliberately, to make it a poem of considerable ambiguity.

The most obvious example of this is the notorious reversal of line 33. Up till then, the speaker has been dwelling forcefully on the physical and mental miseries of seafaring. Then, in the middle of a line and without pretence of warning, he expresses sudden desire for what he has been given every reason to loathe:

Nap nihtscua,   norþan sniwde,
hrim hrusan bond,   hægl feol on eorþan
corna caldast.   // Forþon cnyssað nu
heortan geþohtas,   þæt ic hean streamas,
sealtyþa gelac   sylf cunnige   (31–5)

[The shadow of night grew dark, it snowed from the north, frost bound
the earth, hail fell to ground, coldest of grains. // So the heart's
thoughts impel me to make trial myself of the deep currents, the salt waves'
tumult]

The juxtaposition is a shock for the wariest of readers. No wonder
that a dialogue theory sprang into being! or that the loose connective
forþon has been racked with scrutiny in an attempt to make it seem
something firmer. Still, similar and only slightly less shocking
reversals of expectation take place later on. The cuckoo, though
sumeres weard [watchman of summer], offers only sorrow instead of
pleasure; the beauty of spring is summed up with an ominous urgency
in the phrase *woruld onetteð* [the world hastens on],[26] and is then
rejected for the dangers of the sea. The speaker's emotions seem
incompatible, and we are not given any obvious reason for the
contrast (as we are by the 'wanderer's' sequence of dream and
awakening). Why should any man flee from all that is pleasant to
those traditional enemies, *sorg* and *longung* [sorrow, grief], 'heaviest
of burdens'?

To this question there may indeed be a simple and literal answer.
In an important article Professor Dorothy Whitelock reminded
scholars of the well-attested existence, in Anglo-Saxon times, of the
peregrinus pro amore Dei, the man who went on pilgrimage for the
love of God.[27] Three such came to King Alfred from Ireland in 891,
having travelled in a boat without oars, 'because they wished to be
on pilgrimage for the love of God, they cared not where'; and many
other cases of equal or lesser piety are on record. Such men might
naturally fear the sea and be aware of the pleasures of the land, while
still determined to venture out again, increasing their sacrifice indeed
by memories of what they left behind. This fierce asceticism was
especially prevalent among Celtic Christians—whose influence on the
Anglo-Saxons is increasingly clear—and several Welsh and Irish
poems record mixtures of emotion astonishingly like those of
The Seafarer.[28] But while there need be no dispute that the poem
has a background in the facts of religious experience at that time,
a literal reading does not solve all the problems. For one thing, the
sea itself, and the sea-land opposition, give a strong impression of
having more than merely literal importance, more even than the
vaguely typical force of the frozen ocean in *The Wanderer.* At times

the poem sways towards allegory, most noticeably towards the end of
the first-person section. The speaker describes his mind ranging
over sea and land and returning to him

> gifre ond grædig; gielleð anfloga,
> hweteð on hwælweg hreþer unwearnum
> ofer holma gelagu, forþon me hatran sind
> Dryhtnes dreamas þonne þis deade lif,
> læne on londe   (62–6)

[eager and greedy; the solitary flyer cries, urging the mind irresistibly to
sea, over the expanse of oceans, because the joys of the Lord are hotter to
me than this dead and transient life on land][29]

Here the land is linked closely with impermanence and mortality;
by opposition one might think the sea to represent immortality,
the *Dryhtnes dreamas* being the joys of Heaven—an idea taken further
by Professor G. V. Smithers, who retains the manuscript reading of
wælweg for *hwælweg* and translates it not as 'the whale's way, the
sea' but as 'the path of the dead'.[30] In this view—and it has some
basis in the poem's tone—the speaker's fierce longings are for death
and his eternal homeland far away, the whole life of man being
seen as a pilgrimage, under the image of seafaring.

Yet like the 'literal' view which sees the poem as the monologue of
a *peregrinus,* the 'allegorical' view has also to be rejected, both for
much the same reason. The success of *The Seafarer* as a whole
(that is, including the gnomic and hortatory second half) depends
on the establishment of moral authority for the speaker. This is the
purpose of the first half and its personal description. It would be
weakened either by restricting the ocean-scenes to the accidental
viewpoint of a single individual, or by diffusing them to a mere
image of some other reality. Wisdom grows out of experience alone.
So, as with *The Wanderer, The Seafarer* begins by presenting its
speaker's 'credentials' for having attained authority, and then goes
on to give (in a less direct form) the conclusions drawn. In achieving
this purpose, the poet can rely on the very looseness of much Old
English verse.[31] He does not need to declare who his 'I' may be.
He can allow the sea to suggest at one time cold, sorrow, the whole
chaos of the external world, and at another (as in the Exeter *Maxims*
already quoted) all that resists chaos, the obstinate self-control of
human minds. If one of the results of this vagueness is a sense of
struggle and obscurity, quite probably the poet would regard that
only as a further excellence.

It would be wrong to decry the poem's wavering between literal
and symbolic modes, since this produces much of its aura of urgent

significance. But it is possible to be perturbed in some ways by the *order* in which attitudes are presented. Both *The Wanderer* and *The Seafarer* rest on the paradox that there are two responses to experience. Some experiences are so painful that few care to undergo them; at the same time no one becomes wise through an easy life. Where the 'wanderer's' wisdom is a by-product of compelled exile, however, 'the seafarer' actively chooses his wanderings, and speaks of those who do not make the same choice with a hint of disapproval, not only as 'men who do not know', but also as men who are *esteadig* (or perhaps *sefteadig*), 'favoured' (or even 'comfortable') men. Implied by this attitude is a double response not just to experience, but to misery itself. The 'seafarer' actually seeks this as a stimulus. He goes to sea, he says, because there is no one so strong or lucky

> þæt he a his sæfore   sorge næbbe . . .
> ac a hafað longunge   se þe on lagu fundað   (42, 47)

[that he does not always have sorrow over his sea-journey . . . but he who is eager to go to sea always has grief]

The traditional enemies become goals, not deterrents. The fault—if it is one—is not that the 'seafarer' seems masochistic, but that the moral strength which enables him to pick good out of evil is given him too early. The suddenness of the change from complaint to desire in line 33 is suspicious not because of its totality—total discrepancy between the views of youth and age being rather the rule in Old English poetry,[32] and sometimes found in the same man at different periods—but because it has not been built up in any way. Explanation (lines 39–66) follows decision (lines 33–8) in a way perturbing to the modern reader, and possibly to some Anglo-Saxons as well.

In *The Seafarer,* the poet's aim seems to have been to exploit attitudes already familiar and to stretch them into new shapes and confrontations. Even his vocabulary shows signs of deliberate ambiguity,[33] while neither the emotions presented nor the mode of presentation is ever perfectly homogeneous. The result is powerful, but it is only precariously in balance. Still, the existence of other poems in the 'elegiac' group, notably *The Wife's Lament, The Husband's Message* and *Wulf and Eadwacer,* reminds us that Anglo-Saxon audiences must have had a high tolerance of enigma—or else some extra information, now completely lost, about these poems. Especially in the cases of *The Wife's Lament* and *Wulf and Ead-*

wacer, modern scholars have been quick to assume the latter possibility, and have tried to make up for the hypothetical loss by fitting the poems into contexts of folk-tale, animal story or forgotten epic, meanwhile disputing over the speakers' sexes.[34] But such approaches are inherently difficult to prove. In view of the general shapelessness of many Old English poems, it is at least as likely that these two poems—if not *The Husband's Message*—are substantially as complete as they were meant to be. The best approach is perhaps to describe the limited but undeniable success they do have even for modern readers, and to see them also in connection with the repeated themes of poems already discussed.

Both *Wulf and Eadwacer* and *The Wife's Lament* are love-poems, consisting of a single, unintroduced speech by a woman—as is proved in the latter case by feminine forms in the first two lines, and clear in the former from the situation. Interest in the woman's point of view is not uncharacteristic of Old English verse, if one remembers the prominence of Hildeburh, Wealhtheow and Freawaru in *Beowulf,* or the several poems dedicated to female saints. But the lack of introduction or conclusion outside these single speeches shows a distinct change of emphasis away from other 'wisdom' poems. In *The Wanderer* or *The Seafarer* painful situations are finally resolved; by contrast, the endings of the love-poems are summary but without hope, observations by characters who have attained clear sight but not been able to use it to reconcile themselves to their fate. Possibly this emotional arrest is connected with the sex of the speakers, women, in heroic societies, being as liable to suffer as men, but being also naturally unable to act, to decide, to escape from suffering by violence—like Hengest—or by giving expression to wisdom—like the 'wanderer'. Female characters are well suited to being final embodiments of the 'frozen mind', poised between breakdown and control; it may be that in these two poems we have pure distillations of experience which could be suited to many epic situations, but were specifically intended for none.[35] Whether that is true or not, both poems present with great force the image of a mind circling over past events, unable to find any position of rest.

In *Wulf and Eadwacer* the speaker's despair is summed up by her last two (completely paradoxical) lines:

> 'Þæt mon eaþe tosliteð   þætte næfre gesomnad wæs,
> uncer giedd geador'   (18–19)

['It is easy to dismember what was never joined—our song together']

For, as Alain Renoir aptly pointed out,[36] if two things have *never* been joined, there can be no question of tearing them apart again!

Yet what may not be true on a physical level can make sense emotionally. In her understated generalisation the speaker here is expressing,
once more, the 'elegiac' sense of the mingled strength and weakness
of the mind. The woman and her lover (?) Wulf are parted physically.
Her imagination yearning after him brings about a powerful re-
creation; yet, like *The Wanderer*'s dream, its strength leads only to a
concomitant failure as she is returned to reality once more—a reality
of separation stressed by the refrain *'Ungelic is us'* ['our two conditions are different'], and by the very baldness of the statements in
the early lines:

> 'Wulf is on iege,   ic on oþerre.
> Fæst is þæt eglond,   fenne biworpen.
> Sindon wælreowe   weras þær on ige;
> willað hy hine aþecgan,   gif he on þreat cymeð.
> Ungelice is us'   (4–8)

['Wulf is on an island, I on another; that island is a fastness, surrounded
by fen; cruel men are there on the island; they will take him if he comes to
that band; our fates are different']

The repetition of the verb 'to be' shows her awareness of what
exists physically—separation and danger—while elsewhere her
memory struggles towards a happier state, only to admit its non-
existence at the end. There seems to be no way for her to change her
mental state; the circle is perfect, unbreakable, paralysing—a
concept filled with terror. Even without any clear knowledge of the
situation, the poem makes some impression, through the contrasts of
its style and its characteristic bias towards mental rather than
physical facts.

Interestingly, though *The Wife's Lament* does not have a refrain, it
too is based deliberately on contrasts and verbal repetitions, ranging
from single words such as *geomor* [sad] in lines, 1, 17 and 42, to
phrases such as *bliþe gebæro* [a cheerful bearing] in lines 21 and 44,
and the complete lines *under actreo in þam eorðscræfe* (28), *under
actreo geond þas eorþscrafu* (36) [under the oak-tree in the cave /
throughout these caves]. Scenes also recur as the 'wife' speculates
on her lord's whereabouts (lines 8 and 46), or suddenly recalls her
own hateful surroundings.[37] Like a thread through the poem run
her outbursts of grief and yearning, *'ond mec longade . . . eal ic eom
oflongad . . . ealles þæs longaþes'* ['and I longed . . . I am full of
longing . . . all the longing'], personal statements which link firmly
with the general conclusion, *'Wa bið þam þe sceal of langoþe leofes
abidan'* ['Woe to him who must wait in longing for a dear one'].
The number of recurrences prevents their being accidental. The poet

is trying deliberately to show the alternations of a grief-stricken mind between past and present, escape and renewed recapture, and doing it through a series of overlapping, repeated contrasts.

At the start the 'wife' is relatively controlled, explaining what has been happening with only momentary references to her own present condition, the interjections *'ond mec longade'* ['and I longed'] or *'Forþon is min hyge geomor'* ['So my mind is sad']. Then, in sudden awareness of the ironies of time, her feelings escape in a longer passage, where memory gives way to the present as suddenly as in *The Wanderer,* and in similar terms:

> 'ful oft wit beotedan
> þæt unc ne gedælde   nemne deað ana
> owiht elles;   eft is þæt onhworfen;
> is nu [fornumen]   swa hit no wære,
> freondscipe uncer'   (21–5)

['Often enough we promised that nothing would divide us but death alone, nothing else. That is reversed since; now our love is taken away as if it had never been']

Recovering, she repeats the cycle of narrative followed by emotional outburst, this time ending on a comparison, not with her own past, but with more fortunate lovers in the present. Then, for a moment, we seem to reach a kind of stability with a gnomic section once more recommending restraint and endurance. But this too passes only to a remembrance of her lover's own sorrowful memory, *'he gemon to oft wynlicran wic'* ['too often he remembers a happier place'], and to the gloomy generalisation of the end. Many problems remain within this outline—the reason for the separation, the curious phrase *morþor hycgendne* [intending murder], the precise but seemingly unnecessary localisation 'under the oaktree'—all of which whet the appetite for a precise explanation. But it is hard to see what even a well-attested explanation in narrative terms could add to the picture of the speaker's restless mind. Though one may be reluctant to credit an Old English poet with the sophistication necessary to invent a 'dramatic monologue', with no purpose other than the revelation of character, that is what seems to fit the poem's obvious preoccupation with a present state in which the past serves *only* as material for dramatic contrasts. Nor need we see this as too anachronistically modern a goal. As with *The Ruin,* or in a different form with the 'awakening of Hildeburh' in the *Finnsburg Episode,* we can see that this poet's main aim is not to delineate an individual so much as to create a familiar mood; the elements of an 'exile' or 'retainer' figure present in the 'wife's' vocabulary[38] show only the

Old English poet's characteristic opportunism, or perhaps his inability even to frame a situation without drawing on already familiar patterns. Whatever the facts or motives behind it, *The Wife's Lament* still centres once again on the struggle between separation and memory, a struggle in this case decisively won by the power of physical reality.

To this situation the poem of *The Husband's Message,* some pages away in the *Exeter Book,* is largely irrelevant. Verbally it parallels *The Wife's Lament,* and it could easily be taken as a later stage in that 'story', when the 'husband', now come into prosperity, reminds his 'wife' of their *wordbeotunga* [words of promise] and asks her to rejoin him across the sea 'once you have heard the sad cuckoo singing in the wood'. But in this poem the speaker's emotional problems are shelved, not solved, by lucky physical interventions. To see a more valid solution of the conflict between the human spirit and its surroundings, it is better to look at that most perfect of Old English poems, on a small scale, *Deor.*

Its contents can be described fairly quickly. Five loose stanzas of two to six lines, plus a refrain, mention legendary situations of difficulty. The refrain, *Þæs ofereode, þisses swa mæg* [as for that, it passed, so can this],[39] makes a dismissive comment on the far-off grief of ancient heroes, but also leaves one uncertain as to what *þisses,* the present trouble of the speaker, may be. Then, in two longer sentences, the situation is extended to that of any mournful man, and a consoling general reflection is offered. The speaker then asserts its efficacy by applying it to himself, saying that his name is Deor, poet of the Heodenings, and that his place and rights have now been given to another *leoðcræftig monn* [man skilled in songs], one Heorrenda. In four lines similar to those of the first five stanzas he describes his present position, and observes again *Þæs ofereode, þisses swa mæg.* Only in this, its sixth repetition, do we grasp the full point of the refrain and understand what 'this' refers to. The poem, then, reminds one of grief; asserts that it can be cured; and proves it, the existence of the poem and the 'Deor'-persona being itself the proof. It is a perfect example of self-reflective poetry, and of the truth of the line in *Maxims:*

> Longað þonne þy læs   þe him con leoþa worn

[He grieves the less who knows many songs]

The epic material is not only stated, but used; and in other ways as well *Deor* relies heavily on the habitual associations of other Old English poetry.

The first stanza, for instance, carries a heavy load of words which should by now be familiar:

> Welund him be wurman   wræces cunnade,
> anhydig eorl   earfoþa dreag,
> hæfde him to gesiþþe   sorge ond longaþ,
> wintercealde wræce;   wean oft onfond,
> siþþan hine Niðhad on   nede legde,
> swoncre seonobende   on syllan monn.
>   þæs ofereode,   þisses swa mæg   (1–7)

[Among the Wermas(?)[40] Weland made trial of exile, the determined nobleman suffered hardships. He had sorrow and yearning as his companions, a winter-cold exile; often he discovered woe, once Nithhad laid fetters on him, supple sinew-bonds on the better man. As for that, it passed, so can this]

The words *wræc, cunnian, winterceald* are frequent in other 'elegies', as is the almost physical idea of *sorg* and *longaþ* as the companions of the solitary man. Weland, the Northern Daedalus, indeed appears as another example of the 'wanderer / seafarer / mourner' figure, the man, once happy, who comes to know grief at first hand. The poem's delicate periphrases, and carefully understudied postponement of the central facts to the last two lines, also remind one of the agonising truth behind poetic formalisation—for the *seonubende* do not refer to mere 'sinewy bonds'; they mean also that Nithhad hamstrung his captive (as we are told by other sources).[41] Nevertheless, Weland escaped physically from his time of despair. He killed Nithhad's sons, raped his daughter, and flew off on the wings he had manufactured. That too, of course, caused grief. In the next stanza 'Deor' takes for his figure of agony Nithhad's daughter Beadohild, to whom her brothers' death was not as painful as *hyre sylfre þing . . . þæt heo eacen wæs* [her own state . . . that she was pregnant]. Again, the point is that when one experiences grief personally it seems too immediate and overmastering to be controlled, outweighing even the deaths of brothers. Beadohild could see no hope; yet her son was the hero Widia. In similar ways the poet works through the *sorglufu* [sorrowful love] of Mæthhild, the exile of Theodric(?),[42] the *wylfenne geþoht* [wolvish mind] of Eormenric the tyrant, which caused many men to sit *sorgum gebunden* [bound by sorrows], wishing for the kingdom's downfall—as indeed was to happen before the onslaught of the Huns. Each stanza makes its point: the injustice of defeat, the strength of passion, the feeling that nothing can overpower sorrow once it is there. Yet against each case, presented always at its worst and most hopeless moment, stands the memory that things changed, the promise of the refrain.

To move from physical solutions to mental ones is a long step. Obviously, if every person afflicted by depression could disgrace his enemy, overthrow a kingdom, or give birth to a hero, grief would never last long. But no poet is in a position to guarantee happy issues of that sort. Instead, 'Deor' moves to a relatively gentle generalisation, which nevertheless begins to close the gap between the physical woes of ancient heroes and the purely internal control advocated in poetry:

> Siteð sorgcearig, sælum bidæled,
> on sefan sweorceð, sylfum þinceð
> þæt sy endeleas earfoða dæl.
> Mæg þonne geþencan, þæt geond þas woruld
> witig dryhten wendeþ geneahhe,
> eorle monegum are gesceawað,
> wislicne blæd, sumum weana dæl (28–34)

[The sorrowful man, deprived of joy, sits and grows gloomy in his heart, thinks to himself that his share of hardships is endless. Then he can reflect, that throughout this world the wise Lord makes many changes, shows honour and sure fame to many a man, to others a share of woes]

The statement is so light as to be hardly disputable. It opposes only passive reflection to the miseries that have been skilfully evoked. Yet it is an assertion backed by more than just 'Christian resignation' or 'devil-may-care recklessness', though these choices have been rather ungenerously foisted on it.[43] Perhaps the key words are *endeleas* and *wendeþ*; behind them lie the ideas, so strongly present in Old English poetry, of *edwenden* [reversal] and the inevitable changes of time. Everyone knows that grief is irresistible while there, not to be banished by resolve alone. But wise men also know that everything is temporary, that grief is *endeleas* only in Hell (and that, perhaps, is a definition of Hell). Paradoxically, if one is aware of this, feeling it as more than a simple truism, one can step out of personal experience altogether, and see it as something distanced, like the far-off trials of ancient heroes. This, at least, is what 'Deor' is to assert, giving us yet another example of the mind that conquers time, and the power of expressed wisdom.

In the last eight lines the speaker moves from his indefinite *we* to a personal introduction:

> Þæt ic bi me sylfum secgan wille,
> þæt ic hwile wæs Heodeninga scop,
> dryhtne dyre. Me wæs Deor noma.
> Ahte ic fela wintra folgað tilne,
> holdne hlaford, oþþæt Heorrenda nu,

leoðcræftig monn   londryht geþah,
þæt me eorla hleo   ær gesealde.
            þæs ofereode,   þisses swa mæg!   (35–42)

[I will say this about myself, that once I was the poet of the Heodenings,
dear to my lord. My name was Deor. For many winters I had good service
and a kind lord, until now Heorrenda, a man skilled in songs, received a
right to the lands that the guardian of nobles gave me before. As for that,
it passed, so can this!]

The point is made by a contrast of style and subject. In the stanzas on
others' sorrows, far-off in time and in any case gloriously cured,
'Deor' might naturally be detached and gentle, even while hinting at
the agony behind the words. Now, speaking of his own troubles in
the present, the irresistible force of grief ought to cause a change of
style, perhaps to the rawness and confusion of *Wulf and Eadwacer*
and *The Wife's Lament*. But it does not. Instead the style returns to
the curt understatement of the start, perceptibly different from the
more developed sentences of general advice.[44] Treating the present as
if it were already legendary is a practical demonstration of the
controlling power of the mind. And there is a further twist in the
last use of the refrain. In its previous five uses it meant: 'that grief
passed and so can this one'. In the last line, though *þisses* keeps its
meaning—now understood for the first time— *þæs* refers to 'Deor's'
earlier *prosperity,* now passed away as completely as ancient grief.
The speaker recognises change in both directions, and so draws even
a slightly more Stoic moral from his own history than from anyone
else's.

Deor depends on a sophisticated awareness of the gap between raw
experience and poetic formalisation. It acts out the uses of thought
and expression as well as describing them, a process which has led
Professor Morton Bloomfield to compare it to Old English charms.[45]
Though the parallel is not exact—since *Deor* has no immediate
practical purpose, whereas the charms very obviously do—it is
nevertheless very just. *Deor* is a 'performative' poem, a piece of
'action literature', embodying the Old English philosophy of
wisdom with its stress on the strengthening and controlling of the
mind. Yet its structure, for all the subtle alternations of joy and
sorrow, personality and detachment, adds only a slight twist to the
structures of *The Seafarer, The Wanderer* or *The Wife's Lament,*
as these in their turn arise out of the duller advice-poems surrounding
them in the *Exeter Book.* All the 'elegies' depend on some similar
alternation of involvement and detachment, and share as a basic
theme the ability of the mind to control itself and resist its surroundings. The group as a whole exemplifies the great strength of a

traditional literature—the ability to use common thoughts and images as a springboard, so that poets need only small additions to create great effects without baffling their audiences. The group also develops the theme of will-power and its limitations to an extent and with a subtlety matched by no other early European culture.

4

LANGUAGE AND STYLE

Those RULES of old discover'd, not devis'd,
Are Nature still, but Nature methodiz'd;
Nature, like liberty, is but restrain'd
By the same Laws which first herself ordain'd.

POPE, Essay on Criticism

Manuscripts and parallels

Though the two preceding chapters have insisted on the limited
independence of single Old English poems, they have concentrated
ultimately on the small and highly selective groups of 'heroic' and
'elegiac' literature. To understand the true nature of Old English
verse, and the reason for the close inter-relationships already discussed, it is necessary to look at the whole range of surviving material,
and to consider it on the lowest and most inescapable levels of
language and style. The best way to begin is to give some account of
the poems that have been preserved.

There are around ninety manuscripts (and two or three inscriptions) in existence which contain some fragment or other of Old
English verse. Their importance is very uneven, and their distribution
peculiar. Some twenty-nine of the ninety, for instance, are copies of
Bede's Death-Song inserted in the Latin *Epistola Cuthberti,* and
owing their survival only to connection with a scholar of inter-
national standing. Seventeen other manuscripts contain versions of
Cædmon's Hymn, the story of which, again, is part of a Latin work,
Bede's *Ecclesiastical History.* The prestige of one man alone therefore accounts for almost half the manuscripts of Old English poetry
—but for a total of only fourteen lines. Very few of the other poems
are found in anything but a single version, and the majority are quite

short, from two lines (*Winfrid's Proverb*) to a few hundred (*The Battle of Maldon*).[1] Only six manuscripts are of any great length, and two of these are fairly close translations, from Latin (*The Paris Psalter,* over 4000 lines), or from Old English prose (the *Metres* of Boethius, around 1500 lines).[2] Four long and important manuscripts containing Old English poetry are left, each edited separately in volumes 1 to 4 of *The Anglo-Saxon Poetic Records,* and known customarily as the *Junius Manuscript,* the *Vercelli Book,* the *Exeter Book,* and the *Beowulf Manuscript.* These between them contain just over twenty thousand lines of verse, out of the total of just under thirty thousand known. On these collections depends most of the study of Old English literature. But each has marked peculiarities, which must be considered before making any evaluation of the nature of the poems they contain. The nature of the manuscripts gives rise, also, to some disturbing thoughts about the context of poetry in Anglo-Saxon England.

To begin with, the most imposing volume of the four is certainly the *Junius Manuscript.* It contains four poems, *Genesis* (2936 lines), *Exodus* (590), *Daniel* (764), and *Christ and Satan* (729), and nothing else besides. Clearly it was meant all along to be a verse collection, not just a handy miscellany, and there is some evidence of careful planning before the copyist (not the poet) got to work. All the sheets of parchment are the same size, illustrations have been added, and space has been left by the copyist (no doubt acting under orders) for further illustrations which have *not* been added. On page 2 of the manuscript is the profile of a man with the name 'Ælfwine', probably the intended recipient of the book. All these facts suggest that somewhere in early eleventh century England[3] there was at least someone who put a high value on Old English poetry, and who had access to several poems by different authors. Still, the plan was never completed. The illustrations stop less than halfway through the book, the fourth poem is distinctly inferior to the other three, and it was written by a coalition of three scribes, all more careless than the man who wrote out the earlier poems. In any case, obvious mistakes exist, uncorrected, even in the most carefully-done parts of the compilation. Good though it is, the *Junius Manuscript* raises at least a doubt as to whether Old English verse was not already dated and difficult before the Norman Conquest.

This suspicion is not resolved by the *Vercelli Book.* It contains six poems, two 'signed' in runes by a certain Cynewulf (*Elene* and *The Fates of the Apostles*), the saint's legend *Andreas, The Dream of the Rood,* and two shorter didactic pieces. *The Dream of the Rood* is of particular interest since it closely resembles the fragments engraved at a very early date (A.D. 700–750) on the Ruthwell

Cross in Dumfriesshire. These poems total around 3500 lines, but are interspersed through a much greater quantity of Old English prose. It has been suggested that the whole collection was by or for someone with 'old-fashioned tastes', since it contains nothing by the popular contemporary homilists, Ælfric and Wulfstan.[4] And certainly the most striking fact about the book is in any case that it was found seven hundred miles away from England, in Vercelli in Northern Italy, on the pilgrim-route to Rome. It is hard to resist the speculation that it was abandoned there for something thought (at that time) to be more valuable.

The largest purely poetic codex left, the *Exeter Book,* is 'odd man out' in several respects. For one thing, it contains, not two, four, or six poems (as in the *Beowulf, Junius* and *Vercelli* manuscripts respectively), but around 117—the qualification being caused by uncertainty as to where any one poem starts and another leaves off. Furthermore, many of the poems are neither saints' lives nor Biblical paraphrase, but undeniably secular, ranging from obscene riddles to the heroic consolation of *Deor* and the minstrel's catalogue of *Widsith*. The order of the poems is oddly jumbled. The *Riddles* appear in two separate sections; poems thought nowadays to be related are rarely found together; and there is an admixture of poems without any clear form or purpose. Yet in spite of this, the manuscript has been copied by a single scribe, while the language and spelling of the poems is so uniform as to suggest strongly that they had been looked over and corrected even before they were delivered to the copyist. Whoever did this nevertheless resisted the urge to give the poems a rational order—at least one we would think rational. Possibly the compilation dates from an earlier and more tolerant period than the others; certainly its existence since has been much less eventful, for it is almost certainly the *mycel englisc boc be gehwilcum þingum on leoðwisan geworht* [big English book on various subjects made in poetry] which was given to the Chapter Library at Exeter Cathedral by Bishop Leofric between 1050 and 1072, and which has remained there ever since.[5]

The last manuscript, the one containing *Beowulf* and *Judith,* has had the most disrespectful treatment of all from Time. By comparison with the others it might seem a 'poor man's book', containing some illustrations of low quality, and often giving an impression of carelessness on the copyist's part. More than that, as must be acutely painful for any critic to realise, *Beowulf*—so often considered as a literary masterpiece and the culmination of Anglo-Saxon civilisation —survives only in intimate relation with a series of fantastic prose-texts which show all too clearly that the collector's prime interest was not epic dignity or ancient history, but simply stories about monsters! Even more than the other collections, which survived as a result of chance, loss, or the value of their illustrations, the *Beowulf Manuscript* must owe its existence to entirely the wrong reasons. Twentieth-century critics assume that *Beowulf* is a 'classic' fully comparable with the *Iliad* or the *Aeneid* (and they are right). But the opinion was not shared, as far as we can tell, by the Anglo-Saxons responsible for the poem's preservation.

All round, the manuscripts on which we depend for our knowledge of Old English poetry show signs of carelessness, disorder, misreading and downright neglect of anything like literary values. The *Junius Manuscript* is unfinished; the *Exeter Book* confused; the *Beowulf Manuscript* maligned; and the *Vercelli Book* abandoned. It is hard to reconcile these facts with the obvious excellence of much of the poetry they contain. The only way out is to suggest that the circumstances of the poems' transmission were *not* the same as those of composition. In particular, though all four collections as we have them can be dated, from the copyists' handwriting, to around the year 1000 (the *Exeter Book* perhaps fifty years earlier), one poem, *The Dream of the Rood,* is clearly related to the Ruthwell Cross inscription of nearly three hundred years before. Between these dates there was time for a whole poetic tradition to flourish and, we must admit, to wither. Possibly there were once poems which surpassed *Beowulf* as *Paradise Lost* outclasses *Gondibert,* for there is no sign that what remains to us was ever carefully selected. But the speculation has to be resisted; and for other reasons it may be improbable.

The traditional tool for investigating the poem's *original* surroundings, before they happened to be copied out in the collections as they now stand, is historical phonology. There are enough precisely dated Old English prose texts left to show that there were obvious differences between the spelling of early West Saxon, around 900, and that of later West Saxon, around the year 1000, as well as between West Saxon in general and the various dialects of the rest of the country. Attempts to relate these facts to poetry, however, have been only marginally successful. For one thing, a man might well feel that poetry was different enough from prose to be written differently; thus the prose and verse versions of the Boethian *Metres,* though probably by the same man, King Alfred himself, have at times quite distinct vocabulary and inflections, so that if we knew nothing at all about the texts, they might well have been ascribed to different places or times. Failure in this case naturally leads to considerable reservations in others. Moreover, though the Anglo-Saxon dialects were different enough, they were never mutually incomprehensible, and as a result poems coming originally from one area could presumably be 'translated' with little difficulty into the dialect of another—as seems to have happened to some extent with the regularised poems of the *Exeter Book*. *The Dream of the Rood* is once again a case in point, for though itself written in late West Saxon with only 'a few traces of Anglian' left,[6] clearly it goes back to some earlier piece written in the dialect of the Ruthwell Cross, a pure and distinct example of North Northumbrian. There the chain of transmission stretches for 250 years and a thousand miles, while the poem has not been copied so much as rewritten. In such circumstances, distinguishing between the origins of one poem and another is virtually impossible. Professor Campbell voices the general conclusion:[7]

There seems to have been, in fact, a 'general Old English poetic dialect', mixed in vocabulary, phonology, and inflexion . . . an originally dialectally pure poem, which achieved general popularity, would in transmission become approximated to this poetic dialect, while new poems would be written down from the beginning with considerable indifference to dialectal consistency.

No doubt standardisation increased further with the political dominance of Wessex.

Dates for Old English poems cannot, then, be found by phonology, or at least not by any features likely to have attracted the attention of copyists and so been normalised. Nevertheless, the copyists' own ignorance of poetic tradition allowed some peculiarities to escape correction, and so provide a trace back to the times of original composition. A familiar test, for example, is 'the loss of intervocalic *h*'. In some poems, notably *Genesis A* in the *Junius Manuscript,* there are half-lines either abnormally short or badly-stressed. The phrase

$$\acute{/}\quad \acute{/}\;_{x}$$

hea beorgas [high mountains] appears to have only three syllables,

$$_{x}\;_{x}\;\acute{/}\quad \acute{/}$$

whereas the usual minimum is four; with *and on deað slean* [and strike

$$_{x}\;_{x}\;\acute{/}\quad \acute{/}$$

to death] or *on þa hean lyft* [in the high air], both stresses are thrown to the end, in a pattern not regularly found elsewhere, while

$$\acute{/}\;_{x}\quad _{x}\quad \acute{/}$$

metodsceaft seon [to see destiny] splits the stresses equally oddly. However, all these examples (and a score of others), would immediately become normal if one assumed that words like *heah, seon,* and *slean* were intended to be dissyllables, as indeed they were at an early period.[8] The four half-lines given above would then reappear as

$$\acute{/}\;_{x}\;\acute{/}\;_{x}\quad _{x}\;_{x}\;\acute{/}\quad \acute{/}\;_{x}\quad _{x}\;_{x}\;\acute{/}\;_{x}$$

something like **heahe beorgas, *and on deað sleahan, *on þa heahan*

/   / x   x   / x

lyft, *metodsceaft seohan, all recognisable metrical types. Though nothing like these forms ever does appear in the tenth- and eleventh-century collections, the inference seems clear—that the original poet thought of such words as dissyllables, but that later copiers made them conform to their own usage, not recognising that they were spoiling the metres. Arguing further could be dangerous. Poetry can after all be conservative. No one would care to base conclusions on the existence of such pronunciations as 'bewitchèd' or 'utterèd', not part of normal speech for centuries, but still not wholly unfamiliar.

It is interesting to see, however, that with words like *heah Genesis A* consistently uses dissyllabic forms, while *Beowulf* has a number of them mixed with a proportion of forms quite acceptable as mono-

x / x   x   /

syllables, e.g. *in sele þam hean* [in the high hall]. This does not exactly *prove* that *Genesis A* is the older, but with this and similar tests it is possible, in some cases, to reach a tentative order of priority. *Genesis A* and *Daniel,* for example, appear more archaic than *Beowulf, Exodus* or *Guthlac A,* which in their turn precede *Guthlac B* and the Cynewulf poems. Others are too short to offer much evidence, or else contain contradictory indications. The order above was proposed in 1907 by the German scholar Sarrazin, who suggested that it covered a time-span of about 700–780[9]. Since then, opinion has preferred to make all the poems later, as well as discounting even further such abstract methods of working. In her influential book on *The Audience of Beowulf* it is notable that Professor White-lock is prepared to extend *Beowulf's* composition up to almost any date before 835, when the Viking invasions make poems in praise of the Danes increasingly improbable.[10]

There are then some formal distinctions between many of the long epic poems we possess. But such differences are still insignificant compared with the similarities. In *Beowulf* (before 835) the hero says he will resist the dragon, in these words:

> 'Nelle ic beorges weard
> forfleon fotes trem,   ac unc furður sceal
> weorðan æt wealle,   swa unc wyrd geteoð,
> metod manna gehwæs . . .
>   Ic mid elne sceall
> gold gegangan,   oððe guð nimeð,
> feorhbealu frecne,   frean eowerne!'   (2524–37)

['I will not flee the mound's guardian the space of a foot, but at the wall it must go with us as fate grants, the ruler of every man . . . I will gain the gold gloriously, or else battle, the bold and deadly evil, will take your lord!']

In *Maldon* (which must be after 991, when the battle was fought),
Leofsunu declares very similarly that he will resist the Danes:

> 'Ic þæt gehate,   þæt ic heonon nelle
> fleon fotes trym,   ac wille furðor gan,
> wrecan on gewinne   minne winedrihten.
> Ne þurfon me embe Sturmere   stedefæste hælæð
> wordum ætwitan . . .
>   ac me sceal wæpen niman,
> ord and iren'   (246–53)

['I promise this, that I will not flee from here the space of a foot, but will
go forward to avenge my lord in battle. The steadfast warriors of Sturmere
will not need to reproach me with words . . . but the weapon will take me,
point and blade']

The situations are not especially similar. Yet in both there is the
phrase *(for) fleon fotes trym,* the strong opposition *nelle ic . . . ac unc
[furður] sceal / ic nelle . . . ac wille furðor gan,*[11] the final presentation
of two possibilities and acceptance of one, *guð nimeð . . . frean
eowerne / me sceal wæpen niman.* There appears to have been little
change over the best part of two or three centuries.

It may be objected that heroic poetry is bound to be limited in its
structures. But similar parallels are easy to find in the religious
poetry as well. In *Daniel,* apparently an early poem, when the three
Jews are released from the fiery furnace they are described in this
way:

> Wæron þa bende forburnene   þe him on banum lagon,
> ladsearo leoda cyninges,   and hyra lice geborgen.
> Næs *hyra* wlite gewemmed,   ne nænig *wroht on* hrægle,
> ne feax fyre *beswæled,*   ac hie on *friðe drihtnes*
> of ðam grimman gryre   glade treddedon   (434–8)

[The bonds which lay on their bones, hateful contrivance of the king of
peoples, were burnt through, and their bodies protected. Their beauty was
not spotted, nor any mark on their clothes, nor their hair singed by fire,
but they stepped happily from the fierce terror in the peace of the Lord]

In *Andreas* St Andrew is miraculously healed, with rather comparable
phrasing:

> Næs *him* gewemmed wlite,   ne wloh of hrægle
> lungre alysed,   ne loc of heafde,
> ne ban gebrocen,   ne blodig wund
> lice gelenge,   ne lades dæl,
> þurh dolgslege   dreore bestemed,
> ac wæs eft swa ær   þurh þa æðelan miht
> lof lædende   (1471–7)

[His beauty was not spotted, not the hem of his dress quickly destroyed, nor a hair of his head, nor a bone broken, nor bloody wound upon his body, nor anything painful stained with blood from a jagged wound, but again as before he continued his praises, through the noble might]

In Cynewulf's *Juliana,* a comparatively late work, the heroine is saved from the torturers' fires in a passage linked with both the above:

> Ða gen sio halge stod
> **ungewemde wlite. Næs** *hyre* **wloh ne hrægl,**
> **ne feax** ne fel **fyre** *gemæled,*
> **ne lic** ne leoþu. Heo in lige stod
> æghwæs onsund, sægde ealles þonc
> *dryhtna dryhtne* (589–94)

[Still the saint stood with unspotted beauty; neither her hem nor dress, her hair nor skin was marked by fire, not limb or body. She stood in the fire completely unharmed, said thanks for all to the Lord of lords]

The similarities between all three passages have been italicised or emboldened.[12] As significant as their quantity is the fact that they overlap three ways. The *lað . . . lice* alliteration is common to *Daniel* and *Andreas* alone, the word *wloh* to *Andreas* and *Juliana* alone, the *ne feax fyre beswæled / gemæled* construction to *Juliana* and *Daniel* alone. All three poets cannot have known each other's work. Did the *Andreas*-poet copy *Daniel,* and Cynewulf copy both? Might *Andreas* be the last in the chain, or is the *Daniel*-passage a late interpolation, as some have thought? The matter cannot be easily settled, for no passage looks significantly more or less derivative than the others. The three texts are probably from different generations and appear in separate manuscripts, *Junius, Vercelli* and *Exeter* respectively. Yet the poets concerned have all expanded their reasonably diverse Latin sources with a strange mixture of unanimity and independence.

In the early periods of scholarship in Old English such 'parallel-places' (or *Parallelstellen*) were not unnaturally collected eagerly, with a view to establishing chains of borrowing and literary influence. The endeavour soon ran into difficulties. One has already been touched on—the fact that there is no evidence that any of our present collections ever had wide distribution in Anglo-Saxon times. Echoes of *Beowulf* can be found in most long Old English poems. But if it was as popular as that, it is odd that there is *no* direct reference to it anywhere and that (in striking contrast to the Arthurian epics or the Roland story) not even the hero's *name* had any popularity. A second factor was the sheer number of parallels that could be found. An early editor of *Christ and Satan,* for example (totalling only 729 lines), could cite more than seventy passages in it which corresponded more or less closely to pieces from nine or ten other poems.[13] That was not untypical. The extreme case of *Andreas* revealed about 160 'parallel places' with *Beowulf* alone, not to speak of nearly three hundred more with *Christ, Guthlac, Elene* and *Juliana* between them. Of course opinions can vary as to what is and what is not similarity. But if any reasonable proportion of these passages were to be accepted, one would have to go much further than the editor who inferred a 'wide acquaintanceship . . . with the traditions of Anglo-Saxon poetry',[14] and say that the author must have spent much of his time fitting his poem together, like a jig-saw, out of prefabricated pieces.

In the event, arguments over *Parallelstellen* quickly became circular or merely subjective. The controversy of G. Sarrazin and J. Kail in the journal *Anglia* between 1886 and 1892 is a good example. The former wished to show that *Beowulf* and the Cynewulf-group were by the same man (who was therefore a dominant influence on Old English poetry), and amassed similarities of phrase to prove it; Kail could not deny the similarities, but pointed out that poems outside this group also showed so many similarities purely among themselves as well as to the *Beowulf*–Cynewulf group that, by the same reasoning, one could argue for the existence of other, only marginally less dominant authors, or indeed for the single authorship of virtually all Old English verse. To this Sarrazin's answer could only be that some parallels were more important than others. Much the same position is reached even by Claes Schaar's late and very temperate account of the *Parallelstellen*.[15] He too ends with an intricate sketch of influences, and a relatively convincing explanation of them. But the case depends on giving some parallels more weight than others and characterising a few poems, notably *Andreas,* as poor and therefore derivative—a personal critical judgement which might readily be challenged.

In any case, even the few parallels already quoted show one marked difference from the ordinary nature of literary borrowing—here one poet is not trying to copy another *for any particular effect.* The passage from *Maldon* gains no great resonance from Beowulf resisting the dragon; nor do the *Andreas* or *Juliana* pieces actively *use* the memory of the episode in *Daniel.* So the resemblances are not instances of quotation; and if they are mere plagiarisms, it is strange that there is no tendency to copy particularly effective scenes. One might expect that the great aside in *Beowulf* 1202–14, the destruction of Pharaoh in *Exodus,* the Fall of Man in *Genesis B,* to take three leading instances, would make some special impression on poets looking for ideas. But we find no trace of any of them. *Parallelstellen* are scattered evenly, sporadically, uncritically, through the entire corpus of Old English verse. Together with the nature of our four main manuscripts, they raise this problem—that on the one hand we have an excess of evidence to show that all Old English poems are related to most of the rest; on the other, there is no sign that any one poem ever reached popularity or pre-eminence. We do not seem to be dealing with any normal literary situation. In style as in subject-matter, the poems spiral inconclusively round each other.

The oral-formulaic theory

To this whole question, one very positive answer has been put forward in recent years, first by Milman Parry (who was writing about Homer), second by A. B. Lord (who draws his evidence mainly from South Slavic epics), and third by F. P. Magoun, who applied the work of his predecessors to Old English.[16] The theory claims that much classical and modern poetry has been composed by an 'oral-formulaic' process, i.e. by illiterate singers who make up their verse as they go along, retaining no memory of a fixed text, but assisted by an intricately developed grammatical and metrical technique which guides their speech, almost unconsciously, into poetic form. The theory—or rather discovery, for under some conditions there is no doubt that all it claims is true—is in many respects a shattering one, primarily because it forces one to upgrade all previous estimates of human ability. It was also overdue. Reports of epic song in illiterate societies had always been too frequent to be ignored, even if scholars firmly grounded in a written culture found them inexplicable.

However, much of the material on which Lord and Parry based their work was collected with a tape-recorder, actually during per-formance, a situation which can never now be duplicated for Old English poems. As a result, the limits of applicability of their theory remain uncertain. All that can be done is to set out their ideas in a 'pure' form, primarily following Lord, and then see how much it explains of the peculiar phenomena recorded above.

What Lord says—and this applies, for the moment, *only* to twentieth-century Yugoslav epic—can largely be reduced to a series of paradoxes. The first is the paradox of an intensely conservative tradition marked by a 'permanent flux'. The age of the songs recorded in Yugoslavia in the 1930s is in one sense indeterminate—they go back to an age of heroes in a quasi-medieval setting, and versions of them, already old, were taken down from the eighteenth century onwards. Yet in another sense no song is older than the day it is sung; for songs are not repeated. Even if a singer is asked, and agrees, to repeat a song word for word, what he will produce is the same story in the same style, but with hardly a line exactly the same. Lord insists that the concept of a fixed text did not exist among his performers, any more than the idea of an 'original' and 'variants'. All poems are originals, if they have never been performed in exactly that way before; they are also all variants, in that they rely heavily on a style built up by familiarity with other performances. A related paradox deals with the question of authorship. No one can say that the singer is anonymous; he is, after all, bodily present and recognisable. But although he may be famous and influential, with many pupils and imitators, there is no way for him to put his 'signature' on a work and call it his. The story is open to anyone, the style is shared—everything he offers is common property, except his own skill. Since a song performed once and never again *in that form* can hardly be memorised, there is still an inherent guarantee of protection. But everything in the tradition, lines, words, descriptions, stories, is at the same time common and unique.

To any modern man the question is, of course, 'How can this be done?' The answer lies in the word 'formula', defined by Parry as 'a group of words which is regularly employed under the same metrical conditions to express a given essential idea'.[17] Possibly his definition suits the strict metrical patterns of the Greek hexameter better than the relatively loose alliterative line, or half-line; but the essential idea remains the same, even when considering many different languages and types of poetry. The oral poet has at his disposal a vast reservoir of phrases and ideas already partly arranged for him; his job is not so much creation as composition. In composing, though, memory plays little part, and repetition—though it is indeed the outward and visible sign of a formulaic technique—is kept at a remarkably low level, much lower, for instance, than in the 'song and refrain' technique of the traditional ballad. For the poet's reservoir of phrase depends less on single words than on abstract patterns, into which words may be fitted. This is of course implied by the word 'formula'; the essence of even an algebraic formula is to provide a fixed pattern which can be completed by many variables. In the poetic formula, words are only the temporary values for 'x' and 'y', the pattern behind them being at the same time more fixed and more abstract, probably never recognised consciously by the poet himself, who indeed (as Lord says) may be unable to define even the rhythm and metre in which he is composing. It is at this stage of expansion of the formula that the poet's skill enters, allowing him to tell many different stories and to compose almost incredible amounts of verse without wearying even highly critical audiences.

The process may seem mystic and intangible. But it has one analogue with which everyone is familiar—the process by which children learn their native language. Modern investigations have shown that infants learn to form plurals, tenses, and acceptable sentences, all without a

moment of formal grammatical instruction, by setting up special
'classes' in their minds, which approximate more and more closely
as the child grows up to the 'classes' of adult grammar.[18] They make
mistakes—like saying 'digged' for 'dug'—not through imitating
adults but through drawing false, if natural, analogies from other
words. In the end each child can produce effortlessly many sentences
he has never heard before, let alone memorised, through an unconscious knowledge of the acceptable limits of variation within the
structures of their native language. These structures have never been
memorised and cannot be defined by the vast majority of people:
but they *have been learnt*. In the same way the oral poet learns his
formulaic systems without ever consciously knowing them. If he
did try to define and memorise them, we might well expect that an
essentially fluid technique would become rigid, and would collapse.
Since they depend on a 'play of analogy' the systems of oral poetry
are intangible and even—as has been held against them—'crypto-
psychological';[19] in early cultures the poet's gift, denied to other
men, was also no doubt deeply mysterious, seeming to come from
outside. But these are not reasons for blaming or disparaging the
poet. Rather, as Odysseus said of the blind minstrel Demodokos:[20]

> 'All men owe honour to the poets—honour
> and awe, for they are dearest to the Muse
> who puts upon their lips the way of life.'

What has been described above applies most firmly to Lord's
Yugoslav studies, and the Greek epics of Homer. Proving an
'oral-formulaic' style in Old English poetry is naturally more
difficult—since, after all, the poems we have were somehow written
down, and so may have changed their nature. The most common
method of collecting evidence so far has simply been to take passages
of Old English poetry, and to see how many of their lines, half-lines
or phrases are repeated elsewhere in the whole corpus of verse.
The results have shown how extraordinarily schematised this poetry
is. But there are some limitations on evidence gathered in this way.
One is, that it relies on repetitions; and though oral poetry must be
repetitive, it is also part of the poet's job to avoid that as much as
possible by varying elements within a pattern. Furthermore, the
percentages of verse 'demonstrably formulaic' (i.e. repeated elsewhere) contain an obvious qualification in the word 'demonstrably',
which quite undermines their accuracy. At the moment we may well
allow that 72·5 per cent of a certain passage in *Elene* is to be found
in other Old English poems, as R. E. Diamond proves.[21] Nevertheless,
if the *Beowulf Manuscript,* say, had been a little more badly scorched

in the Cotton fire, that percentage would drop; if another collection of poetry had survived, it would almost certainly be higher. There are clear limits to the value of mechanical collection of repeated phrases —as is of course recognised by scholars. What is needed is rather an understanding of the Old English poet's areas of choice and of constraint.

One very brief example may be given. *Beowulf* begins:

> Hwæt! We Gardena   in geardagum,
> þeodcyninga,   þrym gefrunon   (1–2)

[Lo! we have heard of the power of the Spear-Danes, the people's kings, in far-off days]

Andreas echoes it:

> Hwæt! We gefrunan   on fyrndagum
> twelfe under tunglum   tireadige hæleð   (1–2)

[Lo! we have heard of twelve glorious heroes under the stars, in far-off days]

The similarity is so obvious that many people have assumed that the *Andreas*-poet knew and copied *Beowulf.* However, in *Christ I,* we find a similar pair of lines in a different context:

> Ne we soðlice   swylc ne gefrugnan
> in ærdagum   æfre gelimpan   (78–9)

[Truly we have never heard of such a thing happening in former days]

And later on in the same poem there is again:

> Eac we þæt gefrugnon,   þæt gefyrn bi þe
> soðfæst sægde   sum woðbora
> in ealddagum,   Esaias   (301–3)

[We have also heard that a certain prophet, Isaiah, spoke truly of you far-off in ancient days]

In these four examples only one phrase is exactly repeated each time, *we . . . gefrunon.* It is completed with great freedom as regards the verb's grammatical object—a noun, an infinitive, a complete clause— and with rather less freedom by the phrase *in/on . . . -dagum,* where the first element of the compound may be *gear, fyrn, eald* or *ær.* This last choice obviously does not matter in a semantic sense, the words having no individual connotations at all, and therefore being completely interchangeable *except* in so far as alliteration is concerned. Other choices do matter, and lead to greater variety. Still, that the different passages rest on a similar organisation of material is undoubted. A kind of similarity would remain even if the one invariable phrase *we gefrunon* were replaced by *we gehyrdon* (also meaning 'we have heard'), or if the *in x-dagum* half-line became some other adverb-phrase, such as *næfre sið ne ær* [never before or since]. At that extreme there would be no verbal repetition at all, and it might be said that the poetic 'formula' was beginning to merge with the natural features of the language. However, formulaic systems do range all the way from exactly repeated words and phrases to barely discernible abstract patterns. This irritatingly circular and subjective situation may well remind us of the *Parallelstellen*.

Indeed, the great advantage of the 'oral-formulaic theory' is that it clears up without delay the problem of the *Parallelstellen*, a problem recognised long before Parry began his work, and one to which there has never been any other effective solution.[22] To test this assertion—and also to provide more examples of the 'variation-within-similarity' of Old English verse—two passages have been taken which were for long considered to be a clear case of literary borrowing, and which have been maintained as such even *after* the 'oral-formulaic theory' was applied to Old English.[23] They are a dusk-description from *Beowulf* and a dawn scene from *Andreas*, printed here for convenience in half-line columns, with overlapping sections italicised, the closely overlapping in bold:

Beowulf, 1787–92a	*Andreas*, 122–9
Þa wæs eft swa ær	Ða wæs Matheus
ellenrofum	*miclum onbryrded*
fletsittendum	**niwan stefne.**
fægere gereorded	**Nihthelm** *toglad,*
niowan stefne.	lungre leorde.
Nihthelm *geswearc*	Leoht æfter com
deorc ofer dryhtgumum.	dægredwoma.
Duguð *eal aras.*	**Duguð** *samnade,*
Wolde blondenfeax	hæðne hildfrecan,
beddes *neosan,*	heapum þrungon,
gamela Scylding	(guðsearo gullon,
	garas hrysedon),
	bolgenmode, .
	under bordhreoðan.
	Woldon *cunnian*
	hwæðer cwice lifdon . . .
[Then again as before the glorious men sitting in hall were fairly	[Then Matthew was once again much heartened. The cover of

addressed once more. The cover of night blackened, dark over warriors. The company all arose. The old, grey-haired Scylding wished to seek his bed]

night passed away, went quickly; the light followed, coming of dawn. The company gathered, heathen warriors pressed in troops (armour clashing, spears clinking), angry under their shields. They wished to find out whether there remained alive . . .]

The two passages share a good six elements, and put them in the same order. Did the *Andreas*-poet borrow from *Beowulf*? If he did, he borrowed one of the least stressed scenes in that poem, and made some neat changes, such as the introduction of a subject *(Matheus)* into *Beowulf*'s impersonal construction. But the really destructive point for the theory of borrowing is that the *Andreas*-passage overlaps with at least eight other Old English poems to only a lesser degree. If the poet borrowed from them all, then he was a strikingly deft plagiarist; if they are accidents, then the greater resemblance to *Beowulf* might be an accident too.

Taking it line-by-line, the first phrase of the *Andreas*-piece resembles *Elene* 839–41 as much as *Beowulf*:

Þa wæs modgemynd **myclum** geblissod . . .
inbryrded breostsefa

[Then his mind was greatly pleased . . . his spirit heartened]

It is also close to *Elene* 874–5 and *Guthlac* 334–5. The phrase *niwan stefne* occurs as a complete half-line in *Genesis* 1555b and 1886a; *nihthelm toglad* helps to fill out Constantine's dream in *Elene* 78. More interestingly, the *Andreas*-poet himself recombines these elements in a novel and quite un-Beowulfian form later on, in lines 1302–5:

Þa wæs orlege   eft onhrered,
niwan stefne.   Nið upp aras
oþðæt sunne gewat   to sete glidan
under niflan næs.   Niht helmade . . .

[Then the battle was once more stirred up again. Hostility rose, until the sun went gliding to its rest under the steep cliffs. The night became covered (intrans.)]

This piece too contains overlaps with *Judith* 113 and *Elene* 831, and its *Nið upp aras* parallels *Beowulf*'s *Duguð eal aras*. Are we to assume that the poet had been saving up phrases from elsewhere to pad out his second dusk-scene? That would seem to imply an efficient filing-system. It is simpler to think that all the poets mentioned shared some common constructions and useful phrases and that no question of dependence on one another arises.

Further exact parallels can be piled up. *Bolgenmode* is the half-line *Guthlac* 557b; *under bordhreoðan* also forms *Exodus* 236a. As interesting are the near-parallels which bear witness to the flexibility of phrases in patterns. *Exodus* 343–5 compares well with the sixth, seventh and tenth half-lines of the *Andreas*-piece:

> guðcyste on**þrang**
> deawig sceaftum. **Dægwoma** *becwom*
> ofer garsecge

[the warrior-tribe pressed on, dew on spears. Dawn came over the ocean]

Meanwhile, *Elene* provides a line almost exactly similar in form to the seventh and eighth half-lines of the excerpt, though quite different in meaning:

> Him wæs hild boden,
> *wiges* **woma**. *Werod* **samnodan**   (18–19)

[battle was offered him, harbinger of war; the bands gathered]

Later on, the *heapum þrungon* of *Andreas* is varied by *hwearfum þringan* [press in crowds] in *Judith* 249, or *heapum þringað* [press in crowds] in *The Phoenix* 336; *hæðne hildfrecan* resembles *Juliana's hæþen hildfruma* [heathen champion].Though there is no close verbal parallel the phrase *guðsearo gullon* forms part of the alliterative pattern for line 6 of the *Finnsburg Fragment, gylleð græghama, guðwudu hlynneð* [the grey-coat howls, the war-spear clashes]. Through this maze of relationships, one might feel, there is no clear route. In no way can the ten poems involved be arranged to show one 'original' and a number of 'variants'; no one of them has priority.

The point need not be laboured. Any piece of Old English verse is liable to resemble others, those others themselves contain echoes from further away, and so on. Moreover, the resemblances are haunting but inexact, nouns turning into verbs (*nihthelm | niht helmade*), compounds being broken up, words replaced by others of similar length and rhythm but opposite meaning. In one sense the poetic diction is like a Meccano-set; it stays the same but you can do all sorts of things with it. In these circumstances even parallels as close as *Andreas* 122–9 and *Beowulf* 1787–92 cannot prove borrowing (though they do not exactly rule it out). The underlying homogeneity of all Old English poetic diction is also much the best way of explaining the links of *Beowulf* 2524–37 and *Maldon* 246–53, or the *Daniel–Andreas–Juliana* passages quoted earlier. Their differences of date only highlight the expected paradoxes of formulaic composition—stability within change, flexibility within bounds.

One should accept, then, that Old English verse is 'formulaic'. Many studies have proved the point. But is it *'oral*-formulaic'? Be it noted at once that neither Parry nor Lord accepts the distinction that has just been implied. Both assert that oral poetry must be formulaic poetry, and vice versa. Lord, indeed, observing the desire of 'diplomatic' scholars to establish the idea of a 'transitional text', denies it flatly: 'The written technique is not compatible with the oral technique, and the two could not possibly combine to form another, a third, a "transitional" technique . . . The two by their very nature are mutually exclusive.'[24] The root of his objection is that the concept of a fixed text, naturally associated with literacy, is disastrous to an oral tradition. The apprentice poet then strives not to re-create but to remember; his formulas degenerate into fixed tags; the flexibility of pattern becomes rigid form. These conclusions must be accepted—for twentieth-century Yugoslavia. Magoun, in 1953, made a valiant attempt to preserve them for our written Old English texts by pointing out that poets could compose in a traditional, oral way and then either dictate their productions or transcribe them personally. Bede's story of Cædmon certainly implies some such process, since we are told that this man listened to instruction, thought it over 'like a clean beast ruminating', and then turned it into English verse so well 'that his teachers themselves wrote and learned from his mouth'—a process entirely oral for Cædmon, but ending in a written text.[25] The same cannot be said, however, of a good deal of Old English poetry.

For one thing, there is the evidence of the translations mentioned before, the *Paris Psalter* and Boethius *Metres*. Parts of these have been tested and proved to be formulaic;[26] at the same time they are obviously based word-for-word on written texts, the *Psalms* of course demanding particular care as regards accuracy. It is hard to imagine work of this precision being carried out by a committee of Latin reader and explicator, oral poet, and Old English recorder. The conclusion must be that one man combined the abilities of literacy and formulaic composition. The same result emerges from an article by Jackson J. Campbell, showing that in *The Phoenix* (another translation, for the most part) formulas co-exist with an intelligent response to the figures of Latin rhetoric.[27] Such cases are too frequent to be denied. But is there any way of resolving their implications with the firmly and practically based work of Lord and Parry?

One striking difference between twentieth-century Yugoslavia and Anglo-Saxon England is that in the former the oral tradition was quickly overwhelmed by a European culture far superior to the native one economically, scientifically and militarily. Lord gives examples of the singers' respect for the powers of new learning; even the investigator with a tape-recorder must have seemed an oddly superior figure to them. These conditions did not occur in early England. Though the foreign learning of Christianity was accepted whole-heartedly, its teachers seem to have taken over native elements wherever possible, as we can see from our modern retention of words like Easter and Yule, Heaven and Hell, as also from the acceptability, in Christian Old English literature, of words like *halig* [holy] and *drihten* [lord], the cognate forms of which appear to have been cut out of the Gothic Bible for fear of their pagan associations.[28] The deep psychological shock which occurs when a primitive culture meets a more powerful one need never have existed in Anglo-Saxon England. As a result, though literacy and the fixed text may have killed 'oracy' in the long run, the change need not have happened as quickly as in the present century; singer and writer were not opposed in every respect.[29]

Something like this conclusion can also be drawn from the evidence of our surviving manuscripts. In a very few cases we have two versions of a poem, or of part of a poem. For instance the *Exeter Book* contains the prayer of *Azarias,* some 80 lines of which correspond closely to *Daniel* 279–364 in the *Junius Manuscript.* The two passages are very similar, far more so than the *Andreas* and *Beowulf* scenes discussed earlier; there can be no doubt that they go back to something written by one man, the variants being much fewer than would be expected from two different oral 'performances'. Still, there are many variants, and though some are purposeless and facile, others must have required a certain skill. Each poem contains several lines not present in the other (see *Daniel* 343–4 and *Azarias* 57–8), but fitted in neatly in each case, with appropriate rhythmic and grammatical alterations carried out around them. Neither passage is clearly superior to the other. Of these two poems, and other parallel cases, Sisam observed that 'as compared with the variants in classical texts, they show a laxity in reproduction and an aimlessness in variation which are more in keeping with the oral transmission of verse'.[30] This is true, but it is spoken harshly, from the point of view of a literary scholar. The real conclusion is not so much that someone has been lax and aimless, but that whoever it was recovered himself and filled in for his original without difficulty—a situation very different, say, from the evidence of Chaucer manuscripts, where copyists who make mistakes never improve on, or even maintain, a

D

standard appropriate to the author. It looks as if texts were trans-
mitted for some time by people who themselves possessed a fair if
reduced command of formulaic composition; and that this happened
after the introduction of literacy. Again, an overlap of the oral and
the written is to be assumed.

Old English poetry is certainly formulaic though our texts were,
probably not produced orally. On the other hand, their composers
and copiers had not necessarily reached our modern concept of a
fixed text; less original than we at their first writing, they were more
so at subsequent stages. The whole corpus of verse shows, unusually,
a traditional style which reacted well to novel subjects and managed
to exploit them. Nevertheless, this may have taken place only in the
short run, for a century or two. By the year 1000, when our poems
were collected, the tradition was in decline. Concepts of literacy and
memorisation are at least as probable killers as those traditional
villains the Vikings and the Norman Conquest.

The limits of Old English poetry

It is customary by now to end all discussions of the oral-formulaic
theory with a claim that it is still possible to discern originality and
subtle artistry in poems composed in this way. In so far as they are
intended to dispel lurking ideas of the 'unwashed illiterate', such
protestations are worthwhile. It is no good denying, though, that
the patterned and guided nature of the formulaic poet's thinking
presents a great difficulty to modern appreciation. George Steiner,
a critic much concerned with the implications of language, asserts
that:

'A poem is language in the most intensive mode of expressive
integrity, language under such close pressure of singular need, of
particularised energy, that no other statement can be equivalent,
that no other poem even if it differs only in one phrase, perhaps one
word can do the same job. A poem is because nothing exactly like it
has been before.'[31] Regrettably (or so one might think), the cases of
Daniel and *Azarias* just mentioned show instead a cheerful carelessness about particular words or phrases, but it is one which seems to
be followed by no corresponding poetic failure. This is certainly not
because Old English poetry is under-organised; the 'close pressure'
upon it, however, is not one of 'singular need'.

Several well-meaning critics have in the past tried to defend Old
English poems along the lines familiar with later and more literary
verse, finding in them difficulty and particularity. A recent translator
of *Beowulf* argues that its excellence lies in the imagination and
intricacy of its vocabulary, especially its 'compounds (known as
"kennings") that have to be deciphered like riddles or the clues of a

crossword puzzle'.[32] The mechanistic suggestions of this remark are inappropriate. In any case, poetry meant to be read aloud cannot normally allow for much decipherment from its audience, so that the familiar word 'kenning' would probably be better reserved for the genuinely secretive tradition of Norse skaldic poetry. Even the harder Old English compounds, such as *heafodgimmas* [head-gems] for eyes, or *hildeleoma* [battle-light] for sword, have little in common with such contorted Norse phrases as *sára þorns sveita svanr* [swan of the sweat of the thorn of wounds], a 'kenning' which reduces to 'raven' in the end through three mechanical stages. Compounding in Old English verse is not there to tax the audience's ingenuity. Much more, it assists the poet to compose by providing him with a large number of reasonably expressive synonyms which can be introduced into patterns of varying length and, especially, different alliteration. *Beowulf*, for example, contains 107 expressions for the hero himself, 24 for 'boat', 47 for 'sea', these latter ranging from the monosyllabic *brim* or *flod* to the compounds *lagustræt* or *brim-streamas*, the phrases *geofenes begong* or *wado weallende*.[33] Compounds extending such lists are often made up in an obvious way, poetic phrases for 'sea' including not only *ganotes bæð* [gannet's bath], *hronrad* [whale's road] and *swanrad* [swan's road], all cited by the translator of *Beowulf* already mentioned, but also the entire 'system':

⎧ seolhpað =	seal's path
⎩ seolhbæð ⎫	seal's bath
⎧ fisces bæð ⎭	fish's bath
⎩ fisces eðel ⎫	fish's homeland
mæwes eðel ⎬	gull's homeland
⎧ hwæles eðel ⎭	whale's homeland
⎩ hwælweg	whale's way

—and no doubt many others. All ten terms are based on the same observation and inversion—'to this creature the sea is as natural as the land to man'—and could be created and understood quite mechanically. Of course the existence of such phrases in large numbers does have an appreciable effect, creating an overall impression of richness and dignity, reminding the listener at every step that he is not in a prosaic world. Still, they do not call for individual reflection. One wonders whether experienced Anglo-Saxon poets or listeners understood terms like *hronrad* or *hildestræl* as much more than signs for a familiar concept, metaphors as 'dead' as the words *hlaford* for 'lord' (once the periphrasis *hlaf-weard* [loaf-guardian]), or *bord* for 'shield' (once a word with simply its primary meaning,

'board'). Most devices of formulaic poetry remain in this way not
susceptible to individual scrutiny. They are important not singly, but
through their involvement in shared patterns.

Against this defect, as it appears in modern eyes, formulaic
poetry has a corresponding strength. Words commonly used become
imprecise; but that imprecision is the result of tension between
occurrence on a particular occasion and on all other, half-remembered
occasions, a tension which leads to considerable force and resonance.
Words gain a traditional, emotional aura for the poet to exploit.
When Beowulf's retainers wait hopelessly for his non-return from
the dragon, they sit *morgenlongne dæg* [through a morning-long day].
The phrase does not make much sense; it seems a thoughtless
extension of the more obvious *sumorlangne dæg* [summer-long day].
But, as E. G. Stanley pointed out,[34] *morgen* in Old English is a
'loaded' word, carrying with it no associations of dew and freshness,
rather cold, loneliness, the dawn attack, a time implicitly contrasted
with the social union of evening, with its feasts in hall. *Morgenlong*
fits into the series *morgenceald, morgenseoc, morgencolla, uhtcearu,
uhthlem, uhtsceaðu* [morning-cold, -sick, -terror, dawn-care, -blow,
-harm]. It is 'an illogical combination that conveys with great
economy how the lonely fear of early morning is extended into the
day as the band of nobles sat'. Similar 'shorthand' expressions,
relying on traditional associations, can be found everywhere in Old
English verse more or less strongly. In *Beowulf* the dragon is an
uhtfloga [dawn-flier] from more than dragonish habits; there is
unrelieved irony in the Danes finding Grendel's victims gone and
raising *micel morgensweg* [great morning-melody].

Such connections are not easily perceived by the modern reader
familiar with only one or two poems—a fact which makes con-
cordances and fully-itemised glossaries more necessary for Old
English verse than for poems in most foreign languages.[35] But
vocabulary and compounding were not the only levels at which the
Anglo-Saxon poet was under 'close pressure' from forces powerful
but not quite tangible. Another is metre. Perhaps because this is an
expected attribute of poetry, the study of Old English metre began
early and bore fruit quickly, so that it no longer seems mysterious.
Yet in spite of its familiarity, the rhythm of Old English verse
conceals some surprises, the greatest of which is its outward complexity. Neither syllabic (like most later English verse), nor merely
quantitative (like the Latin hexameter), nor based solely on stress
(like a good deal of twentieth-century verse), Old English poems
depend on a restricted range of verbal patterns, fixed overall but
permitting a certain range of variation at each point. The best known
and most immediately useful guide to these is still the '5-Type'

system of Eduard Sievers.[36] The rules governing Old English verse as he interpreted them may be set out briefly as follows.

In each line:

(1) the basic unit consists of two half-lines joined by alliteration, the first generally heavier than the second.

(2) in each half-line there are two stressed points. Two or three of the stresses in each complete line should alliterate with each other, preferably the first and/or second, and the third. The fourth stress does not carry alliteration.

In each half-line:

(3) Stresses must fall on one of these three possibilities:
   (a) a syllable with a long vowel, e.g. *sæ* [sea], or *bat* [boat not bat], or *god* [good not God].
   (b) a syllable ending in a consonant cluster, e.g. *mæst* [mast] or *hors* [horse] or *ecg* [edge].
   (c) *two* syllables conforming to neither of the former types, e.g. *metod* [fate], *faran* [to go, travel], *wine* [friend].

(4) remembering the rule above, each half-line must consist of one of the following five types, as expressed by the symbols / (full stress) \ (minor stress) x (no stress):

A / x / x
B x / x /
C x / / x
D / / \ x   or   / / x \
E / \ x /   or   / x \ /

(5) each x, representing a point of no stress, may include any reasonable number of syllables, usually one to three.

There are a certain number of sub-rules of lesser importance. Types A, D and E may be preceded by one or more unstressed syllables (anacrusis); where two strong stresses follow each other, in the C and D types, the second may be short, in defiance of rule (3) (licence); an extra weak syllable may be inserted after the first stress in the D type. With few exceptions, these rules will fit every half-line of Old English verse in existence. They are so firmly based that variation from them is usually a sign that the copyist has made some obvious mistake—as in the cases cited on p. 84.

Nevertheless, the Sievers 'five types' are in a way unreal. We have no Old English *Ars Poetica* or *Skáldskaparmál*, so the matter is not quite certain, but it seems very unlikely that rules like the above were ever explicitly formulated by any Anglo-Saxon. They are the results of complex statistical analysis, express themselves through relatively modern or learned concepts such as 'stress' and 'vowel length', and are in any case useful only descriptively. From our manuscripts, by contrast, we have no evidence that Anglo-Saxons even knew what a 'line' of their own poetry was, since all the poems without exception are written out without intervals, as if they were prose. A. B. Lord has reminded us recently what a literary concept the 'line of poetry' really is—something only to be seen on paper. Probably if Anglo-Saxons considered the matter at all, they thought the basis of their verse to be rhythm, something apprehended by the ear; and indeed J. C. Pope, realising that lines of poetry *read out aloud* to the Sievers system would sound distinctly odd, has provided an alternative mode of scansion in *The Rhythm of Beowulf*.[37] His approach does not, however, entirely invalidate Sievers. It points rather to the paradox that verse composed on a rhythmic basis, originally to be sung, nevertheless contains within it verbal patterns of an almost abstract order, never perhaps reaching conceptual awareness but still exercising rigorous constraint on generations of poets.

As with the compound-system, knowledge of Old English metre is hard for critics to apply. Since the poets did not control it, there can be no question of 'fitting sound to sense', and the hesitant attempts to declare A-types active, B-types meditative, and so on, have never compelled much agreement. The metrical system was useful primarily to a man composing formulaically. Whether he knew it or not, his ingrained sense of what was acceptable, what sounded right, would keep him from uncertainty and preserve for him the balance of repetition and variation which is the basis of any poetic art. A question *not* to be asked is 'Which came first—the abstract patterns of metre, or the phrases that complete them?' We can only suppose that the two grew up together in an almost evolutionary way, over unguessably long periods—a time-span only hinted at by the similarities between Old English, Old Saxon, and Old Norse poetry, similarities which may go back to a period when the three languages were not as yet fully distinct from each other.

Other systems lie embedded in the habitual usages of Old English verse. One is the hierarchy of parts of speech described by 'Kuhn's Law' which gives a high place in stressing to nouns and adjectives, a lower one to finite verbs, and so on; Lydia Fakundiny has recently shown that some poets gained considerable effects from putting low status words, occasionally and for particular effect, into stressed positions.[38] Less purposeful, at least to our eyes, is the system of 'rank' even between synonyms.[39] For some reason, if the *Beowulf-*

poet wanted to introduce the idea 'lord' towards the end of a line,
or in any non-alliterating position, he decided, or found himself
condemned, to use *cyning* or *dryhten* as a rule, *frea* much more rarely,
but *hlaford* never. The first two are 'low-rank' words which need
not alliterate, the second two 'high-rank', which should or must.
The *Beowulf*-poet is quite normal in observing this distinction, and a
similar one is to be found with many words, *secg* and *guma* being
for instance considerably 'higher' words for 'man' than *leod, mann* or
cempa. The differences are not apparent to us. They are connected
with the growth of formulaic technique and the need for synonyms to
fit different places in the line—so that one might say that the whole
system of 'rank' is highly functional, but meaningless. A third system
—and in this case one leading to effects with which modern criticism
can deal—concerns the 'collocations' of particular words, a force
which in many lines bound together such words as *dom* [glory] and
deað [death], not just because they alliterated conveniently, but
because, we must assume, they were felt to have a real connection.[40]

One example of this system may be given. *Flod* is a 'high-rank' word
for 'sea', alliterating nearly always when it occurs, and compounding
readily. Yet though it might alliterate with any of the (approximately
400) other *f*-words in the poetic vocabulary, it has distinct
preferences for quite a small set.[41] Some are predictable enough, like
famige flodas [foamy seas], *fealone flod* [the grey sea], *on flod faran*
[to travel on the sea]. The opposition with *fyr* [fire], as in *Beowulf*
1764, *oððe fyres feng oððe flodes wylm* [either the grip of fire or the
surge of the sea], may also seem natural. In some cases, though, this
latter link persists *across* grammatical boundaries in a peculiar way,
as in the flood-description of *Andreas*:

> Wægas weoxon,   wadu hlynsodon,
> flugon fyrgnastas,   flod yðum weoll   (1545–6)

[The billows grew, waters clashed, sparks of fire flew, the sea surged with
waves]

What, one might wonder, have 'sparks of fire' got to do with this
scene? Possibly the established alliterative link drew the poet to an
image he would otherwise have neglected.[42] The same might be true,
rather more successfully, of the eerie change in *Beowulf* when the
hero, dragged into a hall on the lake-bottom, sees, perhaps with
regained hope, a fire glowing:

> ne him for hrofsele   hrinan ne mehte
> færgripe flodes; // fyrleoht geseah,
> blacne leoman,   beorhte scinan   (1515–17)

[nor could the dangerous grip of the sea injure him, because of the roofed hall; // he saw firelight, a pale gleam shining brightly]

More than that, even, other words commonly associated with *flod*, as here *fær* [danger], *fæge* [doomed], *feorh aletan* [to give up one's life], and especially *feor*, *feorran* [far, from far off], all help to surround it with an aura of danger, death and mystery, very suitable to the Anglo-Saxon image of the sea and often expressed in memorable lines. The *Beowulf*-poet counts on this to some extent in the passage above. Even better is the line describing the funeral-boat of Scyld at the start of that poem. In a passage dependent, as everyone has realised, on the clashes between respect, riches, display, and a profound feeling of helplessness among the mourners, we find these lines:

> him on bearme læg
> madma mænigo,   þa him mid scoldon
> on flodes æht   feor gewitan   (40–2)

[on his chest lay many treasures, which were to accompany him, travel far into the power of the sea]

The sense of distance and silence come partly from the word's associations, and from the familiar link of *flod* and *feor*. It was the poet's decision, though, which provided the quiet and mysterious *flodes æht* [power of the sea] rather than the commoner *flodes wylm*, *flodes fær*, *flodes fæðm* [surge, danger, embrace of the sea]. Originality was never ruled out for Old English poets; but they also had the opportunity to use powerful and imaginative connections not entirely their own.

Some four types of intangible pressure contributing to the form of Old English verse have so far been identified: compounding, metre, 'rank', the alliterative 'collocations' of particular words. Once again it must be repeated that we are not to imagine the poet *consciously* struggling with all these, muttering to himself lists of permitted collocations and angrily scratching out high-rank words in low-rank places. The constraints are supportive; they prevent the poet from having to grope for inspiration in the unorganised mass of his total vocabulary, and leave him relatively free for the more intricate tasks of overall composition. One last area where the poet was no doubt controlled, but where he was also free to aim deliberately for quite remarkable and varied effects, is that of the patterns of syntax. To illustrate this most important point, a poem has been selected which has never aroused much critical interest, but is nevertheless a sample of how good even average Old English verse can be in that respect: it is the *Exeter Book's Descent into Hell*.[43]

Even a quick analysis of this poem shows how tightly bound the poet was, superficially. The number of syntactic patterns for the half-line is very low indeed; it is said to be about 25 in the whole corpus of verse,[44] and in this poem some types are immediately obvious. Of the first 200 (legible) half-lines, some 27 consist simply of 'Noun + Genitive Noun', e.g.:

æþelinges lic	=	the prince's body
hælendes burg	=	the saviour's town
hæleð Iudea	=	warriors of the Jews
burgwarena ord	=	the best of the town-dwellers, etc.

Another 18 are 'Finite Verb + Subject':

mægenþrym aras	=	the great Power arose
sægde Iohannis	=	John said
wræccan þrungon	=	the wretches pressed, etc.

7 consist of 'Auxiliary Verb + Infinitive', 9 of 'Adjective + Noun' and so on. A score of rough categories like these cover the great majority (perhaps 75 per cent) of all half-lines in the poem. One wonders how anything complex can be said in such a restricted way, and indeed whether there is anything especially suitable about these patterns rather than any others. In fact they do sometimes dovetail oddly with other qualities in the Old English verse style; for instance, the 'Noun + Genitive' types often automatically produce D and E metre-patterns. But as usual it is impossible to say whether the grammar evolved to suit the metre, or vice versa; all one knows is that they suit each other. Meanwhile the limitations give the poet opportunity for subtle and deliberate effects.

The simplest is a repetition of like patterns. Four times in the poem there are appeals from Hell, all in the form, *Eala Gabrihel, Eala Maria, Eala Hierusalem, Eala Iordane* [Oh Gabriel . . . Mary. . . Jerusalem . . . Jordan]. But more commonly, patterns are set up to be broken. Once similarity has been established, very small changes create a disproportionate effect. So, the run of 'Genitive Noun + Noun' types, *æþelinges lic, æþelinges deað, eorles dohtor* [the prince's body, the prince's death, the noble's daughter], is broken by an inversion, *sigebearn godes* [victorious child of God], or an expansion, *ealles folces fruma* [the whole people's leader]; the 'Verb + Subject' pattern (see above) is extended over the half-line, *cwom seo murnende / Maria on dægred* [there came the mourning / Mary in the dawn], or filled out by an adverb, *ongeat þa geomormod* [then the sorrowful man realised]. Nothing repeats itself for long. At times neat effects are created, as when Gabriel is appealed to, *'hu þu eart . . . wis on þinum gewitte ond on þinum worde snottor'* ['how

you are wise in mind and in your word sagacious']. The word-order
is chiastic (i.e. it goes a b b¹ a¹, like Pope's 'To foreign tyrants and to
nymphs at home'), completed by the grammatical parallels *wis* /
snottor and *gewitte* / *worde*, but slightly broken by the fact that
three words alliterate but one does not. A similar pattern becomes
powerful as well as neat in the first hint of Christ's Resurrection.
After the crucifixion and burial, the women go to anoint the body.
The poet comments:

> Ræst wæs acolad,
> heard wæs hinsið; // hæleð wæron modge,
> þe hy æt þam beorge   bliðe fundon   · (6–8)

[The bed was cold, harsh his passing; // the heroes brave whom they found,
rejoicing at the tomb]

The *hæleð* are the angels guarding Christ's empty sepulchre. Their
presence inverts all the grief of the preceding lines, as it does the
whole of human history. The inversion of meaning is the more
marked for the multiple chiasmus and grammatical similarity of the
first three half-lines; for the sudden irruption of *modge* into the
pattern set up by *heard* and *acolad*; for the clash of meaning in words
bound together by alliteration, *beorge* and *bliðe*, happiness at the
tomb. Strong patterns have been set up to be broken more strongly
and surprisingly—a device found continually in this poem, from the
sudden changes of viewpoint like *folde bofode, hlogan helwaran*
[the earth trembled (and so) the hell-fiends laughed], or in the curt,
half-explained summary of John's vision:

> Geseah he helle duru   hædre scinan,
> þa þe longe ær   bilocen wæron,
> beþeahte mid þystre;   se þegn wæs on wynne   (53–5)

[Then he saw hell-gates shining brightly, which had for long before been
locked, covered in darkness; the thane was glad]

Here too, the opposing alliterations of *helle*/*hædre* and *þystre*/*þegn*
seem oddly powerful. They use that favourite device of Old English
poets (on several levels), the concealed antithesis dramatising the
suddenness of change, e.g., *Beowulf* 128, *þa wæs æfter wiste* / *wop up
ahafen* [then after the feast, sorrow was raised], or *Exodus* 5, *æfter
bealusiðe* / *bote lifes* [after the harsh journey, the cure of life]. Such
patterns may have been as ingrained as the common word-pairs
expressing the same idea, *sibbe æfter sorge* [peace after sorrow],
gyrn æfter gomene [sadness after mirth], and all the rest. Both alliteration and syntax impelled poets to write in this manner; but the
result is not less to be appreciated, or admired.

In a recent review, A. J. Bliss hinted a doubt as to the validity of the formulaic theory, suggesting: 'It would appear that the identical recurrence of formulae in Old English poetry is an accidental consequence of the close-knit syntactical and metrical structure of the classical alliterative line.'[45] In doing so, he has perhaps opened up a better way of considering verse of this type. The remarkable thing about it is how 'close-knit' it is, and not only from syntax and metre, but from 'rank', alliteration, and compound-structure as well. None of these systems need have exerted *total* control over the poet at any point—indeed variations are prized—but each of them exerted a kind of pressure, whose effects overall were irresistible, the more so because each system dovetails so well with all the rest. The only word one might object to in Mr Bliss's sentence is 'consequence'; a formulaic style means *the same thing as* 'close-knit structures', and of such structures 'identical recurrence' is an 'accidental' *sign*. Certainly it is more fruitful to study these structures —perhaps in an artificial isolation—than merely to collect recurrences and parallels. By such an approach, one gains awareness also of an oddly 'eighteenth-century' quality in Old English verse—superficial calm, and even monotony, covering a great deal of subtlety and an energetic sense of antithesis. The poetry needs to be read closely and widely to appreciate all its resonances, and translations which ignore parallelisms and destroy word-order (as most of them do) deprive it of all its charm. In an attempt to show how criticism can profitably apply the suggested processes of 'comparison and analysis', a short but well-known passage has been chosen from *The Battle of Maldon*, for discussion on as many levels as possible.

Criticism and translation

The situation of this poem (not quite complete but probably reasonably so) is that a band of Vikings have taken up position on a tidal island in the river Panta (or Blackwater). The East Saxons ride to oppose them, and a confrontation takes place across the river between their leader, Byrhtnoth, and a Viking herald:

> Þa stod on stæðe, stiðlice clypode
> wicinga ar, wordum mælde,
> se on beot abead brimliþendra
> ærænde to þam eorle, þær he on ofre stod:
> 'Me sendon to þe sæmen snelle,
> heton ðe secgan þæt þu most sendan raðe
> beagas wið gebeorge; and eow betere is
> þæt ge þisne garræs mid gafole forgyldon,
> þon we swa hearde hilde dælon.
> Ne þurfe we us spillan, gif ge spedaþ to þam;

we willað wið þam golde   grið fæstnian.

Gyf þu þæt gerædest   þe her ricost eart,
þæt þu þine leoda   lysan wille,
syllan sæmannum   on hyra sylfra dom
feoh wið freode,   and niman frið æt us,
we willaþ mid þam sceattum   us to scype gangan,
on flot feran,   and eow friþes healdan.'
    Byrhtnoð maþelode,   bord hafenode,
wand wacne æsc,   wordum mælde,
yrre and anræd   ageaf him andsware:
'Gehyrst þu, sælida,   hwæt þis folc segeð?
Hi willað eow to gafole   garas syllan,
ættrynne ord   and ealde swurd,
þa heregeatu   þe eow æt hilde ne deah . . .'   (25-48)

[Then there stood on the bank, calling sternly, the vikings' herald, who
spoke his words, announced threateningly the seamen's message to the earl,
where he stood on the bank: 'The bold seamen sent me to you, told me to
say that you must quickly send rings for your defence. And it is better for
you to buy off this spear-charge with tribute, than that we should join battle
so harshly. We do not need to destroy each other, if you are rich enough; we
will fix a truce for the gold. If you who are noblest here so decide, that you
will redeem your people, give the seamen, at their own judgement, property
in return for peace, and take truce from us, we will go to the ships with our
tributes, travel to sea, and hold peace with you.' Byrhtnoth answered,
raised his shield, waved the slender spear, spoke his words, angry and
resolute gave him an answer: 'Do you hear, seaman, what this people says?
They will give you spears as tribute, bitter points and ancient swords, the
tribute that will not help you in battle . . .']

The two most prominent effects here are energy and variety. Both
speeches are introduced in similar terms, at first sight repetitively,
both including the phrase *wordum mælde* (26b, 43b). Yet there are
differences. For the first speech, the Viking herald appears from
nowhere, present suddenly *þa . . . on stæðe*, calling out firmly; for a
second or two the grammatical subject is postponed, as is his purpose,
to create a kind of suspense. This is perhaps increased by a favourite
device, the 'envelope', as the last phrase, *þær he on ofre stod* [where
he (Byrhtnoth) stood on the bank] echoes the first, *þa stod on stæðe*
[then (the herald) stood on the bank];[46] the unresolved opposition of
the two men is mirrored grammatically. More than that, the word
stod can itself have strong associations in Old English verse, primarily
with defiance and opposition—as when Adam resists the devil in
Genesis 522-3, *þær he on eorðan stod, selfsceafte guma* [where he
stood on earth, a man personally created], or the saint his tormentors
in *Guthlac* 323. The word implies 'stood his ground', so that the four
lines of introduction in this passage bring the two sides face to face.

The Viking's speech is then persuasive, and there is a second of doubt before Byrhtnoth's reply. But this is introduced with a blunter energy, destroying the balance momentarily set up. *Wordum mælde* is here only one of five active verbs that mime the answer. They may seem redundant, but frame the one half-line of the six which has no verb, and so stands out—*yrre and anræd* [angry and resolute]. There is a distinct syntactic difference between the two introductions, preparing us for the herald's care and thought, and the English leader's destructive carelessness—of course both characteristics stressed more plainly later.

Inside the 'seaman's' speech other techniques are at work. He begins with a sharp threat in lines 29–33. Rather unusually, verbs are stressed, and they are verbs of command, *sendon . . . heton . . . secgan . . . sendan*. Two slightly more expansive half-lines based on nouns stand out, the self-commendatory *sæmen snelle,* and a phrase which could summarise the relationship he offers, *beagas wið gebeorge*. These two nouns do not commonly alliterate together. The clash is picked up by the contrast of *garræs* and *gafole* in the next line. *Garræs,* a strong word, is not found elsewhere, but clearly formed by analogy with, say, *garniþ* [spear-hostility] and *beaduræs* [battle-rush]. Its honourable associations, here defiled by the Viking, might be summed up by the Exeter *Maxims* list of appropriate qualities, *sinc on cwene, god scop gumum, garniþ werum* [treasure to a queen, a good minstrel to men, for warriors the enmity of spears]. But the threat surrounding this offer is summed up by the alliterative (and assonantal) ring of *hearde* and *hilde* in the next line. Then the tone changes to a more wheedling one, as lines 34–5 grow longer, and a twice-repeated structure is set up. 'We don't need to fight . . . if you (are rich enough) . . . we will (make peace) . . . if you (do all we ask) . . . we will (depart).' The second repetition is expanded almost to a peaceful picture in two 3-part sections. 'If you decide that you will *redeem* your people, *give* us money, and *take* peace, [*lysan, syllan, niman*], then we will *go* away, *travel* to sea, *hold* the peace, [*gangan, feran, healdan*].' Each time, the last infinitive is a little different from the other two, and metrically there is a climax as well on the three isolated C-verses, *us to scype gangan, on flot feran, and eow friþes healdan.* The herald speaks ringingly, positively, conclusively; but embedded in all he says are the dishonourable connections of *beagas wið gebeorge, feoh wið freode,* the alliterative link of *grið* and *golde.*

What Byrhtnoth's speech then does is to take the enemy's assumptions and expose them to violent sarcasm. The alliteration of *gar* and

gafol is picked up and inverted in lines 46–7, and a similar opposition forms the end of his speech, creating finality again by its
'enveloping' technique and also by the double use of *ær* as adverb
and conjunction.

> 'us sceal ord and ecg ær geseman,
> grim guðplega, ær we gofol syllon'   (60–1)

['point and blade must reconcile us before that, grim warplay, before we
pay tribute']

The list of weapons Byrhtnoth is prepared to 'give' is summed up in
line 48, *'þa heregeatu þe eow æt hilde ne deah'* ['the tribute that will not
help you in battle'], and it has been suggested that *heregeatu* is a
word used deliberately in two meanings, its root sense of 'war-
equipment' and also the specialised sense of 'heriot', a type of
tribute.[47] Though unparalleled elsewhere, this is inherently likely;
the poet is original enough to pun, along lines already suggested by the
different senses of *gafol*. Another variation on poetic tradition in
line 48 is the phrase *ne deah*. For the verb *dugan* is another of this
style's 'loaded' words, connected with the *duguð,* the experienced men
at the heart of any noble court, and carrying a range of meanings
centring on success, on being 'good enough'. This quality may be
constantly queried (five out of nine uses in *Beowulf* are qualified by
'when' or 'although'); but it is also something that on occasion is
positively asserted. When Beowulf thanks Hrothgar, all he needs to
says is *'þu us wel dohtest'* ['you did all that was right for us'].
Byrhtnoth's strong *negative* assertion, therefore, though not unprecedented, carries a summary force not adequately represented
by the common 'that will not profit you' (commercial associations),
or 'that will do you no good' (therapeutic ones).

The speech continues powerfully from then on. But enough has
been said to show that any good passage of Old English verse is
likely to contain a good deal of submerged subtlety, grammatical,
alliterative, or semantic. No doubt the poet himself never considered matters this way; no doubt many readers have felt the power
of such speeches without needing to explain them. Nevertheless,
analysis in terms such as these has a justifiable purpose—it is the
only thing that can put us on anything approaching the level of
an Anglo-Saxon audience, whose unconscious familiarity with a
great quantity of verse must have more than compensated for any
modern advantages of printed texts and glossaries. Our cross-
references back and forward are at best only imitations of the
incessant 'play of analogy' characteristic of any traditional style.
Moreover, analysis of this kind is an indispensable prelude to any
thorough attempt at translation.

By now it is established dogma that poems are untranslatable, as one can see from the remarks of George Steiner quoted on p. 98. The dogma has a foundation of fact, in that any language contains in its words and structures its own cultural history, matching that of no other language point for point—a truth especially evident in this century to those engaged in such heavy tasks as translating the Bible into African or American Indian languages.[48] But Old to Modern English is not the same as Hebrew to Hopi; and moreover, an advantage in translating any formulaic poem is that the problems posed tend to recur, without the continuous individual reference characteristic of later poetry, and indeed of much artistic prose. The decisions to be made by any translator of Old English verse can therefore be divided into two groups—those inherent in the nature of the language, and those stemming from the poetry itself. It is the former group which proves most insoluble. Old English, for example, dispenses with articles in many places where Modern English *demands* them. The translator then has to decide, from the context, which one is most suitable; and after he has done that, he finds his structures inevitably swelled by a torrent of little, pattering words that do away with much of the curtness of his original. The same happens as one expands the simple pasts and presents of Old English into the multiple tenses and auxiliaries of modern grammar. These forces are admittedly in the end irresistible, their effects never more that palliated. However, a true understanding of the poetry's nature can cut out completely some common translation faults in other areas.

It is both a temptation and a mistake, for instance, to exchange an energetic syntax for a swollen vocabulary. In a recent translation of *The Battle of Maldon*,[49] the speech of Byrhtnoth discussed above becomes very consciously aggressive in a manner perhaps affected by, and certainly tending to perpetuate, the myth of crude vigour as the sole virtue of Old English literature. The punning and ironic phrase, *'þa heregeatu þe eow æt hilde ne deah'* ['the tribute that will not help you in battle'], turns into 'Weapons to pay you, pierce, slit and slay you in storming battle'; the curt promise *'feallan sceolon hæþene'* ['It is the heathens who will fall'] becomes the bluster of 'We'll sever the heathens' heads from their shoulders'; and later on even the simple *garas beran* [to carry spears] is expanded to 'to clash their spears'. One can sympathise with the wish to stimulate the imagination as powerfully as does the original, but of course what is missed is the pointed understatement, the heroic caution, the fairly subtle variations in and on traditional language. These are not impossible to reach; but one has to respond first to such matters as the power of word-order and of alliterative linkage. A complementary mistake, at the other extreme, is to abandon the attempt to reach poetic power and allow the whole level of style to sink to the unassuming rationality of modern English prose, as is done by David Wright in his version of *Beowulf*.[50] For here the gentle insertions 'really', 'generally', 'not to mention', as well as the in- variant word-order of the modern sentence, all help to iron out the delight of Old English poets in sudden alterations (disguised as repetitions), in inversions that look like explanations, in the harsh contrast of opposed superlatives, all varied by studied understate- ment. There are good translations of Old English in existence, though (perhaps significantly) all make relatively modest claims as to what it is that they have done;[51] all of them seem to be rooted in awareness of the poetry's surprising potential for variety, and the best of them, Professor Tolkien's verse commentary on *Maldon*, shows also a strong sense of the inseparability of style and meaning, with the consequent capacity of Old English verse for fostering a particular type of illusion[52]—that illusion so powerfully felt by the invented character Torhthelm, the Anglo-Saxon counterpart, perhaps, of Ancient Pistol.

The individual voice

The points made during this chapter may be summed up as follows. Old English verse is strangely homogeneous over a long period; this inner consistency is the result of a mode of composition not present in the modern world, nor understood till recently. That mode is formulaic, expressing itself through pattern rather than through single examples, and it needs to be appraised in the same way. Central to all these points is the conviction that Old English poetry has an individual voice distinct from all others, ancient or modern, though, like the voice of any human being, it is capable of great variation while remaining recognisably 'the same'. The best short example to support this belief is that most widely-distributed Old English poem, *Bede's Death Song*. Its Northumbrian version runs as follows:

> Fore thaem neidfaerae   naenig uuirthit
> thoncsnotturra,   than him tharf sie
> to ymbhycggannae   aer his hiniongae
> hwaet his gastae   godaes aeththae yflaes
> aefter deothdaege   doemid uueorthae

[Before that sudden necessity no one is wiser in thought than he needs to be, in considering, before his departure, what will be adjudged to his soul after his death-day, of good or evil][53]

There is little doubt that this poem was linked with Bede's death, and it must therefore be dated 735 (if he composed it), or earlier, if he merely quoted it. The distinction is of little importance. The poem is certainly an early one, but it is as certainly dependent on traditions with which we have become familiar. There is the common alliteration of *dom* and *deað* (to give the words their more recognisable West Saxon forms); the variation of compounds *nydfær, heonongang, deaðdæg* expressing the departure of the soul; the reliance on those 'loaded' words *snotor, þearf, hycgan*; and, overall, the belief in the power of taking thought. More than that, one can see that the whole monitory force of the poem comes from its use of the 'envelope' technique, in the repeated time-phrases of lines 1a, 3b, 5a, with their all-important change from thinking *before* one's departure to being judged *after* it. In this change is the change from freedom to bondage; awareness of it is the true fruit of wisdom. A terrible threat remains implicit, behind the poem's apparently flat and casual understatement that no man is wiser than he needs to be. Many men, we see, are more foolish than they need to be; they take no thought of what the future may bring, and are therefore damned. The stress on decision, understanding, strength of mind may remind us of *Beowulf* or *The Wanderer* or *Deor,* as the style is reminiscent of many poems; in spite of its brevity and early date, we can see that *Bede's Death Song* is in many ways at the centre of a powerful tradition. So, though the plain meaning is indubitably and unexceptionably Christian, it is coloured by a voice heard at all times in the Old English epic style—a voice remote, stony, but impassioned, full of warning that no man can escape decision, a voice neither duplicated nor overwhelmed by any of the urgent messages left to us, in different tongues, from the Dark and Middle Ages. It was available even to England's greatest churchman on his death-bed. His choice of it was neither uncharacteristic nor inappropriate.

5

THE FIGHT FOR TRUTH:

NON-CYNEWULFIAN SAINTS' LIVES

argument
Not less but more heroic than the wrath
Of stern Achilles on his foe pursued
Thrice fugitive about Troy wall; or rage
Of Turnus for Lavinia disespoused,
Or Neptun's ire or Juno's, that so long
Perplexed the Greek and Cytherea's son;
If answerable style I can obtain . . .

Paradise Lost, BOOK IX

'Andreas' and 'Judith'

Old English poetic diction is subtle and full of unexpected resource. But it is also 'retrospective'.[1] Its highly developed military vocabulary and resolutely abrupt syntax prove that it was created originally by and for a warlike society interested in moments of crisis. As many people have suggested, the excellence of *Beowulf* (and perhaps the 'elegies') is based on a strange unity of style and subject; in them the verse is doing the job for which it was created. But what was to happen when Anglo-Saxon poets turned, as they did at a very early date, to Biblical paraphrase and the lives of saints? In these, alien subjects—notably the virtues of humility and passivity—sought expression in a native style. Though it is unlikely that individual poets ever felt any great sense of incongruity in their enthusiastic widening of the poetic field, we can nevertheless see that there was a problem inherent in their situation.

Many would say that the problem was never very successfully solved. With the best will in the world, no critic is ever likely to regain, for poems such as *Guthlac* or *Daniel,* a genuine popularity comparable with that possible for *Beowulf*. Still, the saints' lives and Bible paraphrases deserve more than perfunctory mention. With characteristic resolution, their authors set themselves not just to translate, but to assimilate new forms and new matter, and the way in which the original stories emerge from such treatment gives us a good deal of information, not just about individual poets' decisions, but about the principles of taste and selection which Anglo-Saxons considered necessary. Some of this information can even cast light back on the secular poems already treated.

For several reasons, a good test-case is the poem *Andreas* from the *Vercelli Book*. The story it tells comes ultimately from an apocryphal Greek legend, the 'Deeds of Andrew and Matthew in the city of the cannibals', which recounts how the apostle St Andrew rescued his colleague Matthew from the man-eating Mermedonians, suffered torture himself, but in the end converted his enemies to Christianity by the destructive medium of a miraculous flood. It was a story of some popularity in early England, for there are two Old English prose versions extant besides the poem. Yet, though it was always clear that the Old English works were unlikely to come direct from a Greek source, for some time the expected Latin intermediary could not be found; and even now, only two Latin versions of the story have emerged from the whole of Europe. The scarcity was probably caused by the legend's horrific nature, which could well lead to its censorship or suppression by any reflective Western churchman.[2] Neither of these two Latin texts corresponds exactly with the Old English versions, but one of them (from the *Codex Casanatensis*) is a reliable enough guide to incident and at times to phrasing; taken with the prose stories, it can be used as a basic check on what is original to the *Andreas*-poet, as against what he has taken over fairly directly.

Yet the poem's romantic story is not what has aroused most of the interest in it. Almost from its discovery, it has been seen that, to say the least, *Andreas* resembles *Beowulf* very closely; a majority of scholars would probably go further and say that *Beowulf* is a source only secondary to the Latin *Acta Andreae*, the one providing material, the other style. Verbal parallels between *Andreas* and *Beowulf* run into the hundreds, and though similarities of some kind are to be expected between almost any Old English poems, as has been said, the number in this case is still surprising. What takes the eye even more is the closeness of some of them. When Grendel comes to Heorot,

> Duru sona onarn,
> fyrbendum fæst, syþðan he hire folmum æthran (721–2)

[the door, fastened with forged bands, opened quickly when he touched it with his hands]

When Andreas comes to the Mermedonians' prison to release
Matthew, he too finds that

> Duru sona onarn
> þurh handhrine   haliges gastes   (999–1000)

[the door opened quickly, at the touch of the holy visitor]

Furthermore, Grendel sees the Geats sleeping in the chamber;
though Andreas sees only Matthew, the poet rather inappositely adds
that the guards slept too—in death, killed magically by divine power.
Similar parallels, if not always similar clumsinesses, can readily be
found elsewhere. Like Beowulf's thanes, Andreas's disciples do not
expect to see their homeland again; both poets qualify assurances of
divine assistance to men with *gif his ellen deah* [if his courage holds];
like Wiglaf in the dragon's den, Andreas in his prison sees *be
wealle . . . stapulas standan . . . eald enta geweorc* [pillars standing by
the wall, old work of giants]. More even than these, in two places of
special interest it has been claimed that we can follow the *Andreas*-
poet's mental processes, as he comes to a difficult place, tries to
solve it by copying *Beowulf*, but succeeds only in showing that his
borrowed phrases do not fit what he really meant to say. In one,
Andreas is explaining that he cannot afford to pay his ship-fare:

> 'Næbbe ic fæted gold   ne feohgestreon,
> welan ne wiste   ne wira gespann,
> landes ne locenra beaga'   (301–3)

['I have neither plated gold nor property, wealth nor provision nor brace-
let of wires, of land or of twisted rings']

As it stands, the last half-line is in the wrong case, genitive rather than
accusative. But the same phrase occurs in the genitive, this time
correctly, in *Beowulf* 2994–5, when Hygelac gives the sons of Wonred
hund þusenda landes ond locenra beaga [a hundred thousand (hides?)
of land and twisted rings]. Did the *Andreas*-poet borrow the phrase,
alter the *ond* to *ne,* but foolishly forget to fit it properly into his new
sentence? It could be so.[3] There is another strange instance at the
end, when the devouring flood is called *meoduscerwen . . . biter
beorþegu* [a bitter beer-drinking . . . (too great a) pouring of mead].
The heavy irony is comprehensible, but it reminds one of the (much-
disputed) word *ealuscerwen* which describes the Danes' terror outside
Heorot. As it happens, *Andreas* is in this case rather clearer than
Beowulf,[4] but it is still odd to compare anything 'bitter' to mead,
a sweet drink. The metaphor is muddled, and may have been
borrowed.

From similarities and cruces of this nature the argument of *Andreas'* derivation from *Beowulf* has been created. Against it one has to weigh the very homogeneous nature of all Old English verse. Early scholars had no doubt that the poem was a 'Christian *Beowulf*';[5] but in 1951 (and that was two years *before* Magoun's article on the oral-formulaic theory), L. J. Peters strongly queried the connection, pointing to the great range of parallels between *Andreas* and *Beowulf* and many other poems,[6] so that a certain caution appeared in later statements. Professor Whitelock thought there was a case for literary influence but that it 'stops short of proof'.[7] It is going too far to say, with Rosemary Woolf, that it was 'clearly part of the author's technique to recall *Beowulf* in the same way as it was Milton's to recall the *Aeneid*...in *Paradise Lost*'.[8] That assumes that *Beowulf* was familiar enough to a wide enough circle for such imitation to be worthwhile; and it ignores the sporadic nature of the *Parallelstellen*, which rarely show much literary point.

Regardless of the issue of this argument, one important fact does emerge. Whether he was imitating *Beowulf* or a whole epic tradition which just happens to include *Beowulf*, the author of *Andreas* obviously did his best to subordinate new matter to old form; in any tug-of-war between native and alien traditions he was the man who moved least. Was this conservatism simply stupid, bought at the price of ridiculous discrepancy between style and subject? The first few lines certainly suggest as much, for in them the poet describes the twelve apostles as:

> mære   men ofer eorðan,
> frome folctogan   ond fyrdhwate,
> rofe rincas,   þonne rond ond hand
> on herefelda   helm ealgodon,
> on meotudwange   (7–11)

[famous men on the earth, wise and active war-commanders, fierce warriors, when hand and shield defended the helmet on the battlefield, the plain of destiny]

There is no hint that he means the warfare of the spirit. More likely, the heroic vocabulary has been used simply because it was ready to hand, already developed; and no one could deny the resultant incongruity. But at other places critics have perhaps been too ready to see similar incongruity in passages one might want to defend. Claes Schaar, for instance, in a generally systematic and imaginative study of Old English verse technique, nevertheless complains of the *Andreas*-poet's repeated habit of giving syntactic prominence to characters' emotions, and relegating essential information to

subordinate clauses.[9] He cites the passage where the cannibals arrive
at their now-empty prison, meaning to take Matthew out and eat him:

> Him seo wen gelah,
> syððan mid corðre   carcernes duru
> eorre æscberend   opene fundon,
> onhliden hamera geweorc,   hyrdas deade   (1074–7)

[their hope failed them, once the angry warriors found at the prison the
dungeon's door open, the work of hammers destroyed, the guards dead]

It is true that the worst of this discovery is kept to the end, true also
that Cynewulf (whose technique Schaar prefers) does not often
write in a similar way. But the conclusion should not be that the
Andreas-poet is inferior; rather, he is more susceptible than
Cynewulf to the established methods of heroic narrative. In
fact the passage quoted follows a technique familiar from *Beowulf*
(see pp. 36–8), that of opposing wish and frustration within the one
line, creating for the reader a momentary suspense while he waits for
the explanation. Three of the four passages cited by Schaar as
blunders contain *siþþan*-clauses of this nature; all but one of them
could be said to be effective, giving an excitement not present in the
Latin source.

Indeed, this device is only one of several that *Andreas* shares with
the best heroic verse. Its author likes the strong conjunction of
opposites:

> deor ond domgeorn,   in þæt dimme ræced   (1308)

[bold and eager for fame, in that dim hall];

he changes direction without giving any syntactic indication:

> sorgum geswenced,   sigore gewyrðod   (116)

[torn by sorrows, (but) honoured by victory];

and he ends passages with suggestions of immensity:

> on hronrade   heofoncyninge neh   (821)

[on the sea (but) near to the king of heaven]

None of these lines is incongruous or contemptible. Indeed with a
better knowledge of the conventions of heroic styles and attitudes,
several passages criticised in the past at the very least fall into place
in the general tradition. Considering the value of wisdom to the

Anglo-Saxons, Andreas' praise of his steersman's wit may not have been as 'out of place' as it now seems;[10] again, the decision to change an ironic Latin understatement, *'parvulum negotium habemus ibi agere','* ['we have a little business to do there'], into the taciturn dignity of:

> 'Usic lust hweteð   on þa leodmearce,
> mycel modes hiht,   to þære mæran byrig'   (286–7)

['Our wish, great desire of the mind, urges us to the province, the famous city']

may, in its time and context, have made a good deal of sense. All in all, the epic style, with its insistence on the importance of human action and will-power, casts a wholly acceptable wash of solemnity over the poem, and indeed conceals many of the weaknesses and over-simplicities of its Latin original.

All this does not go to prove *Andreas* a neglected masterpiece, nor is it meant to. The main point is that its local successes and failures often come from the same root, a reluctance or inability to abandon the syntax and vocabulary appropriate for a secular epic. This poem's 'garment of style' is a ready-made one, and it fits where it touches. The theoretical questions which it raises for us derive from the interaction between stylistic units and narrative suitability. Can a style developed for use in one kind of story be made to work for another? How far does it tend to alter the story? Where are the basic overlaps and discrepancies between oriental romance and northern epic? Does style end at the level of selecting phrases?

The last question may be answered first. An interesting series of articles by D. K. Crowne, Alain Renoir and D. K. Fry has recently made it clear that the *Andreas*-poet, like many others, could expand his material in a quite recognisable way, to create not only lines reminiscent of other Old English poetry, but whole scenes.[11] When Andreas goes to the sea-shore to find a boat for Mermedonia, the Latin text reports concisely, *Mane autem facto beatus andreas una cum suis discipulis descendit, et cepit ambulare secus litus maris, uti preceperat ei dominus* [When morning came the blessed Andrew went down alone with his disciples and began to walk with them along the sea-shore, as the Lord had commanded him]. The poem reads:

> Gewat him þa on uhtan   mid ærdæge
> ofer sandhleoðu   to sæs faruðe,
> þriste on geþance,   ond his þegnas mid,
> gangan on greote.   Garsecg hlynede,
> beoton brimstreamas.   Se beorn wæs on hyhte,

syðþan he on waruðe   widfæðme scip
modig gemette.   Þa com morgentorht
beacna beorhtost   ofer breomo sneowan,
halig of heolstre.   Heofoncandel blac
ofer lagoflodas   (235–44)

[Then in the dawn before day he went over the sand-hills to the sea's edge,
sad in mind, and his men with him, walking on earth. The ocean roared,
sea-currents beat. The man was happy, once he boldly met a broad ship on
the shore. Then the brightest of beacons, glorious in the morning, came
hurrying over the sea, the holy creature from darkness. Heaven's candle
shone over the sea-floods]

In its way this is a beautiful passage, moving from glum determination
in the hero's mind to sudden joy, and echoing it by the shift from
'the dawn before day', with all its melancholy associations, to the
bright, powerful sun, hurrying over the ocean, described almost
symbolically as *halig*—all changes not present in the Latin. But before
deciding how much this is due to indivdual talent it is as well to
recall, again, a passage from *Beowulf*, where the hero, returning
from Denmark, lands in his own country:

Gewat him ða se hearda   mid his hondscole
sylf æfter sande   sæwong tredan,
wide waroðas.   Woruldcandel scan,
sigel suðan fus   (1963–6)

[Then the harsh one with his companions went treading the sea-plain
along the sand, the wide shores. The world-candle shone, the sun ready
from the south]

There are only comparatively minor verbal parallels here, and if the
Andreas-poet was borrowing, then for once he improved on his
original. The point is rather that both scenes contain a similar combination of elements—the hero on the beach, with his men, at the
start or end of a journey, linked (remarkably) with the shining light.
A similar combination is to be found several times in *Beowulf*, as also
in *Exodus, Elene, Guthlac, Judith*, and perhaps others. Without taking
the argument as far as Crowne and Fry—who believe this scene was
familiar enough to Anglo-Saxon poets to be used ironically—one can
see that here again an individual talent could receive some help, and
be under some pressure, to compose a scene in a familiar and normally
successful way. The little cluster of ideas lets a poet mark journeys
dramatically. And similar clusters (often called 'themes') can be seen
elsewhere in Old English poetry, filling out battle-descriptions,
scenes of exile, sudden arrivals, travel over the sea.[12] Usually they are
effective, though at times incongruous, as at the end of *Guthlac B*,

where a journey across a Norfolk fen suddenly turns into a full-scale ocean crossing. The poet there has been deflected into the easy and familiar path rather than the right one—as we have noticed also with the incongruous description of the twelve apostles at the start of *Andreas*. Still, it is an exception. Scenes of this nature would not be attractive at all unless felt to be generally successful.

The main conclusion, that habitual patterns are as possible at the level of 'theme' as of 'formula', is an interesting one. Yet these set scenes cannot be said to affect the *shapes* of poems very radically. They are too static. Besides, the true centre of interest in Old English verse lies elsewhere, in the mind rather than its surroundings, depending on insight more than action (as is argued in pp. 29–30 above). Moments of understanding (or lack of it) are most commonly expressed by speech; and in considering the structure and success of *Andreas* it is the stock speeches, rather than the stock scenes, which most repay study.

It is worth remembering at the start that the heroic poems themselves lay stress on the importance of speech in formal surroundings. Both *Beowulf* and *Maldon* refer familiarly to the *gilpcwide* or *beot*, two words often loosely translated as 'boast', but in fact referring more to the future than the past. Sometimes these occasions are quite neatly marked off, as in Beowulf's *gilpcwide* of lines 632–8 or his *gylpword* a little later, in which he promises first to conquer or die, and second to do so without using weapons. Yet although these speeches are taken seriously, it is clear that they are not important for themselves alone. Possibly the promises will not be fulfilled, in which case they become *idelgylp* [vainglory], worse than nothing; and that this likelihood was borne in mind even at the time of the *beot* is proved by the comment in *Maldon*, as many of the English turn in flight:

> Swa him Offa on dæg   ær asæde
> on þam meþelstede,   þa he gemot hæfde,
> þæt þær modiglice   manega spræcon
> þe eft æt þearfe   þolian noldon   (198–201)

[So Offa had told him one day at the meeting-place, when he held council, that many spoke bravely there who later would not endure at need]

Words without subsequent deeds are useless. The importance of the *beot*, then, is that it signals a determination to become involved, and marks the moment when a train of events is set off. Whether the *beot* is fulfilled or not, the situation can never be the same again; the speaker either increases his honour or loses it. The moment of the 'speech of promise' therefore implies within itself a knowledge of later

moments, and these are themselves often signalled in Old English by
formalised speeches of a common type. Unlike the *beot*, these do not
possess agreed names, but a familiar one is the moment of *pearf*
[necessity], when several speakers in *Elene, Judith, Maldon, Juliana*
and *Andreas* itself declare that they have reached the limit of
endurance and ask for help from outside.[13] Another is the opposite
moment, of joy at seeing one's enemy crushed, marked again in
Andreas, and also in *Genesis, Beowulf, Judith* and *Maldon* by some
such phrase as *þa his mod ahloh* [then his mind laughed]—though in
conformity with Old English liking for grim reversals, most of the
examples cited are ironic. They are remarked only to be denied—as
when Grendel sees the sleeping Geats in Heorot and exults, but does
not foresee his own approaching death.[14]

But to return to *Andreas*—although it does contain speeches of the
types suggested, the ones used most dramatically and climactically
are of a slightly different sort. In moments of *beot* and *pearf* one
either predicts the future or recognises the present; the *Andreas*-poet
makes more use of the past. In a fine speech after the coming of the
miraculous flood, one of the Mermedonians, a *feasceaft hæleð*
[desolate warrior] admits defeat and recommends submission, saying
to his fellow-cannibals:

> 'Nu ge magon sylfe   soð gecnawan,
> þæt we mid unrihte   ellþeodigne
> on carcerne   clommum belegdon,
> witebendum.   Us seo wyrd scyðeð,
> heard ond hetegrim.   Þæt is her swa cuð,
> is hit mycle selre,   þæs þe ic soð talige,
> þæt we hine alysan   of leoðobendum,
> ealle anmode,   (ofost is selost),
> ond us þone halgan   helpe biddan,
> geoce ond frofre'   (1558–67)

['Now you yourselves can know the truth, that we unjustly placed the
stranger in prison, in chains, bands of torment. The event injures us, hard
and hateful. So it is known here that it would be much better, as I
consider true, for us to release him from the chains on his limbs, all
unanimously—haste is best—and ask the saint for help, aid and comfort']

There is indeed a source for this passage, and a comparatively long
one, for in the *Acta Andreae* the cannibals too cry out 'woe to us for
all these things which have come upon us; this flood is made because
of that pilgrim we placed in prison, and the universal evils we put
upon him', etc. The difference is that the Old English poet presents
not so much surrender as a retrospective admission; he adds to his
source the idea of clarity and knowledge *(soð, cuð, soð gecnawan)*,

laying stress too on the contrast between what was done in the past and what is apparent here and now *(nu, her)*. If the *beot* is a prediction of the future, a speech of this type is its opposite, showing a revaluation of the past, a new awareness of what happens when human will is crossed by the power of *wyrd* (which is, again, retrospective, 'history' rather than 'fate').

The point would not need to be laboured, except that the author of *Andreas* seems to have considered the whole of his original story as if it were designed to lead to climaxes of this nature. Missionary activity, for him, is a process of presenting the truth, inviting a challenge from heathen visions of reality, and then putting both to the test; the apostles' greatest weapon is recorded history. This idiosyncrasy becomes apparent in the interpolated story of 'the disbelieving Jews'. This is told in peculiar circumstances: Andrew, called by the Lord to Matthew's rescue, has at first been doubtful, and has made his way to the sea-shore only reluctantly. But the boat he finds there is steered by Jesus himself and manned by angels, though they are not to be recognised. As a result, Andrew passes the start of the journey by telling stories of Jesus's miracles to Jesus himself. In the Latin the situation seems to be conceived as basically a *piquant* one, leading to a scene of passionate apology and reconciliation. The Old English poet, however—and perhaps here he did learn something from the structural technique of *Beowulf*—sees the first miracle, the 'stilling of the storm', as a comment on the apostle's presence in the boat, and the second as if it led up to comparison with the Mermedonians. This second miracle is in fact totally unscriptural. It tells how Jesus, entering a Jewish temple, found the elders unbelieving, and so commanded a statue on the wall (in flat contravention of the second commandment!) to speak in his honour. It does so; yet the elders do not believe. The Latin version is content to leave it at that, but the *Andreas*-poet points the moral. At the end of its speech, *his* statue (but not the one in the Latin version) cries out:

> 'Is seo wyrd mid eow
> open, orgete,   magan eagum nu
> geseon sigores god,   swegles agend'   (758–60)

['The event is open, apparent to you. Now you can see, with your eyes, the god of victory and ruler of the sky']

But the elders resist this revelation:

> eft ongunnon
> secgan synfulle,   (soð ne oncneowan),
> þæt hit drycræftum   gedon wære

[They then began to say, the sinful ones—they did not admit the truth—
that it had been done by magic]

For those who refuse to *soð oncnawan,* argument is impossible.
Deeds must replace words. The poet makes it clear that this scene,
this moment of non-recognition, damns the unbelievers to hell and
yfel endeleas [endless evil]. Jesus himself has already said:

> 'Deofles larum
> hæleð hynfuse   hyrdon to georne,
> wraðum wærlogan.   Hie seo wyrd beswac,
> forleolc ond forlærde.   Nu hie lungre sceolon,
> werige mid werigum,   wræce þrowian,
> biterne bryne   on banan fæðme'   (611–16)

['Those heroes eager for death too readily obeyed the devil's teaching, the
evil traitor; the event deceived them, taught false, played false. Now they
shall quickly endure pain, cursed with accursed, a bitter burning in the
killer's embrace']

There is no note of regret in his voice. Yet the poet should not be
considered vindictive. The Jews, after all, have the same chance as the
Mermedonians, and cannot be compelled to take it; in all Old English
verse, decisions are treated seriously, whatever it is they lead to.

It would be too much to go on from these two scenes of conversion or its failure to talk of 'thematic unity' or anything as consciously
contrived as that; like his use of 'themes' and 'formulas', these
speeches may be the result merely of the *Andreas*-poet's preconceived
ideas of what kinds of climax a story could have. They have, however, a general effect at least as important as the 'wash' of epic
dignity already mentioned, and they redeem some of the original
story's basic narrative weaknesses. Why, for example, should Andrew
suffer torture from the Mermedonians for three days? They are converted by the flood, not the saint's endurance; and this could have
come as easily on the first day, at the moment of his capture—as
indeed might have been more dramatic. The *Acta Andreae* offers no
answer to this obvious question, unless it is to show again what one
can only call Andrew's love-relationship with his Lord. *Andreas*
turns our attention more to the saint himself. What has to be tested
is his strength of mind, and of course without torture this would not
convincingly emerge. Before he is seized by the Mermedonians
Jesus says to him:

> 'Scealt ðu, Andreas,   ellen fremman!
> Ne mið ðu for menigo,   ah þinne modsefan
> staðola wið strangum . . .

Cyð þe sylfne,
herd hige þinne,   heortan staðola,
þæt hie min on ðe   mægen oncnawan'   (1208–14)

['You, Andreas, shall perform glory! Do not hide from the multitude, but
fix your mind firm against the powerful ones . . . Make yourself known,
harden your mind, fix your heart firm, so that they recognise my power
through you']

Cyð þe sylfne [Make yourself known] is a typical phrase.[15] Firmness
of mind is not enough unless it *is* made known and admitted,
externalised by events. Once this has happened, though, it has a
value not to be denied by mere physical weakness, as the retainers
demonstrate in *Maldon*. The wish to provide proof (and so compel an
admission) would be enough in itself to motivate the scenes of
torment, but the poet makes further changes to back them up. In
particular, the scenes of temptation and persecution by the devil,
found in the *Acta*, are expanded and turned into a static confrontation reminiscent of the statue's clash with the disbelieving Jews.
The saint and devil do not *argue*, but declare their ideas of truth.
The devil claims that Andreas is in his power, that Christ was killed
by Herod; the apostle shows that they cannot pass the sign of the
Cross and, conclusively, taunts the devil with his Fall. This last fact
cannot be denied, and breaks the devil's power; after another day
and a last speech, Andreas is released, having proved his strength.
Perhaps significantly, it is at *this* point that the poet breaks off
for a short speech in the first person about the *wyrd undyrne* [clear
history] that he has been translating, as if recognising that the
mental climax has now passed and that the physical one (the
miraculous flood) is only a rounding-off.

The structure imposed on his story by the author of *Andreas*
is one of the emergence of light from darkness. Most of the characters
are at one time or another *modblinde menn* [men blind in spirit].
Andreas himself is doubtful at the start, but as a result of his
miraculous sea-crossing 'now knows more readily' the power of
Christ, and shows his conviction by enduring torment. By his actions
the Mermedonians are converted, and admit their new understanding.
In contrast, the Jewish elders, and the devil, their inhuman counterpart, refuse to recognise truth until it is too late. The polarisation,
the subtle attitude to time, and the assertions of power are all
additions to the source, and seem typical of Anglo-Saxon ways of
thought. One might note for instance that although *Beowulf*'s
enemies are all dumb, and so cannot confess their mistakes, that poet
also is very fond of alternations of ignorance and knowledge, signalled by phrases such as *þæt wearþ gesyne . . . widcuð . . . orgete . . .*

undyrne [that became visible . . . well-known . . . obvious . . . clear].
Moreover, he gives Hrothgar, in lines 932–42, a speech contrasting
past and present in a way we might now find characteristic. Elsewhere,
the consistently similar expansion, by several poets, of known
Latin sources, carries even more conviction as evidence of Anglo-
Saxon habits of thought. The devil's plea for mercy in *Juliana*
546–53, and the Jews' confession in *Elene* 1120–4, should both be
looked at as examples of the interest in 'submission and recognition'.
However, the best short parallel to what has been said about *Andreas*
is undoubtedly the poem *Judith*.

In this case the poem's source was early recognised as the Apocryphal *Book of Judith,* which tells how a Hebrew widow, faced by
Assyrian invasion, went to the enemy general Holofernes, insinuated
herself into being alone with him, and then cut off his head and
escaped, to raise her people against a demoralised Assyrian army.[16]
Unlike the *Acta Andreae,* this story is extremely coherent, presenting
quite a realistic tactical situation, laying a sensible plan for the
heroine's escape, and building up well to the invaders' collapse. As it
happens, only some 350 lines (perhaps a quarter) of the Old English
poem are left, but even from this portion it is possible to see what the
poet has done. Several minor characters have been cut out, Judith's
cunning has been much reduced, and Holofernes has been changed
from a certain rationality to a speechless, drunken, Herod-like monster. The whole picture is simplified; everything turns on the one
event of the beheading. However, that event is now surrounded by all
the 'heightening' speeches and contrasts one could hope for. At the
start, Judith's confidence in God is juxtaposed with the equal confidence of the Assyrians at their banquet. But suspense is never present,
for we are told at once:

> hie þæt fæge þegon,
> rofe rondwiggende,   þeah ðæs se rica ne wende,
> egesful eorla dryhten   (19–21)

[They were doomed as they took (the wine), the fierce warriors, even though
the noble one, terrible lord of men, did not expect it]

When Judith and Holofernes are left alone she appeals to God in a
speech of *þearf*; and after she is given the strength to kill him, the
mistakenness of his earlier arrogance is firmly stressed by following
his soul (for some lines) to hell, where it will indeed know truth
butan ende forð [endlessly afterwards]. Even more interesting is the
fact that Judith then goes back to encourage the Israelites, not with
moral reflection but with the assurance that destiny is on their side
and is, moreover, visible:

> 'Fynd syndon eowere
> gedemed to deaðe,   ond ge dom agon,
> tir æt tohtan,   swa eow getacnod hafað
> mihtig dryhten   þurh mine hand'   (195–8)

['Your enemies are judged to death, and you have fame, glory in battle, as the mighty Lord has signalled for you through my hand']

Nor do the Assyrians disagree. Finding his leader dead, a spokesman for them gives a 'speech of admission' very similar to the Mermedonian's, before all turn to flee:

> 'Her ys geswutelod   ure sylfra forwyrd,
> toweard getacnod   þæt þære tide ys
> mid niðum neah geðrungen,   þe we sculon nyde losian,
> somod æt sæcce forweorðan.   Her lið sweorde geheawen,
> beheafdod healdend ure'   (285–9)

['Here our own destruction is made clear, signalled against us, that it has painfully pressed close to the time when we must needs perish, all be destroyed in battle. Here lies, hewn by the sword, our lord beheaded']

This speech is a completely original addition to the source. It expresses perhaps better than any other the belief in the power of events, the delight in sudden and complete changes of opinion, which has been seen to underlie the structure of *Andreas*. There is no reason to suspect any literary influence on either of these poems from the other. Both authors have simply read and recast their stories in the same way, following a mode of thought and narration which is completely explicable in terms of what we know about the Anglo-Saxon heroic ethic. In the process, discrepancies between eastern and northern narrative—notably the deficient sense of human dignity at times evident in the former—have simply been ironed out. No better proof of the strength of a traditional style, with its established concepts, could be found.

Having said so much, it should now be feasible to offer a relatively unbiased valuation of *Andreas*, at least, as a poem. And—as was admitted at the start of this chapter—it is no longer possible to rate it especially high. Justifying such a verdict, though, is not as easy as has sometimes been thought. The poem is not as repetitive as *Maldon* or as confused as the 'elegies'; the credulity which (temporarily) swallows Grendel and the dragon should not balk at magic floods and talking statues; nor can the verse-techniques of *Beowulf* and *Andreas* be consistently seen as beyond comparison. Perhaps a basic flaw is the diminished sense of reality. *Beowulf*'s monsters, after all, retain their physical presence in spite of their intermittent symbolic development; Andreas, on the other hand, too often finds his difficulties whisked away, and so never quite seems to face what we would recognise as essential human limitations. Still, in its place and time, this flaw may not have been so obvious. The great and genuinely heroic efforts of Anglo-Saxon missionaries in pagan Europe are now well known and appreciated; the list of eighth-century martyrs contains a high proportion of English names. It would not be impossible to think of *Andreas* in the same context as Willibrord, 'apostle to the Frisians', or Boniface (Wynfrith), martyred by the heathen at Dokkum.[17] No doubt if these men had had less faith in God's power or an acuter sense of material reality they would have stayed at home and never exerted themselves to convert their distant kinsmen. But they may instead exemplify for us virtues to which *Andreas* can fairly lay claim—a sense of purpose, an unargued confidence in the strength of virtue.

The 'Guthlac' poems

The only other saints' lives in Old English verse, apart from those written by Cynewulf, are the two poems *Guthlac A* and *Guthlac B*, found together in the *Exeter Book*, but clearly separated from each other both by a deliberate break in the manuscript, and by differences of style and treatment.[18] Before considering them in the light of their poetic tradition, it is important to realise that the 'saint's life' genre is not by any means a homogeneous one, and that these poems have quite a different intellectual background from that of *Andreas*. Both depend (loosely and selectively) on the Latin *Vita sancti Guthlaci* of one Felix of Croyland, an English monk. He depends much more closely, and often word-for-word, on several earlier lives, especially the *Vita sancti Antonii* in the Latin version of Evagrius—which, unlike the *Acta Andreae*, was a most widespread and influential work, having many readers and imitators through the Western world, and perhaps especially in Ireland.[19] It may be that St Guthlac himself genuinely modelled his life on that of St Anthony, or it may be that Felix, following the theory of the 'communion of saints',[20] simply decided that what was true of one saint was true in some measure of them all, and so had no compunctions about plagiarism. But whatever the reason, the *Vita sancti Guthlaci* has its hero follow St Anthony in all major respects. Both saints retire from distinguished families to solitude, building their own hermitages; both come under constant attack from diabolic manifestations; and both lives are a scheme of spiritual gradation. As a result of their asceticism they see visions and perform cures, dying cheerfully bereft of all possessions. Both are characterised by a spiritual tranquillity not founded primarily on deeds. Felix introduces the character of a doubting but experienced monk, Wigfrid, who believes that many anchorites are frauds trading on a certain magic power. He is converted less by action than by St Guthlac's strange aura of sanctity. In short, both lives are essentially turned inward, their success measured not by souls saved nor by resistance to tyrants—far different from the goals of missionary-lives like *Andreas* or *Elene*, or martyr-lives like *Juliana*. Behind the *Guthlac*-poems stretches a powerful tradition which has its root in the deserts of Egypt in the fourth century. It is accordingly impossible to find in them anything very close to the scenes of challenge and revelation in *Andreas* and *Judith*.

The effects of Anglo-Saxon ideas of narrative form are nevertheless perceptible, for good or for ill. To take the latter first, both *Guthlac*-poems almost entirely erase one of the best points of the 'Antonian' tradition, its sense of psychology. In the *Vita sancti Antonii* one is never quite sure whether the saint's demonic assailants are external or internal. One devil appears to Anthony *per noctes in pulchrae mulieris vestiebatur ornatum, nulla omittens figmenta lasciviae: hic ultrices gehennae flammas, et dolorem vermium recordans, ingestae sibi libidini opponebat* [during the nights he appeared dressed with the ornaments of a beautiful woman, omitting none of the trappings of wantonness: but (the saint), remembering the avenging flames of hell and the torment of the worms, resisted the lust which was arrayed against him]. Is the adolescent saint fighting himself or the 'powers of air'? Perhaps the two are the same. Similarly, when Felix's Guthlacus hears devils prompting him to fast longer than he should, is this not translatable as that frequent temptation of the desert-dweller, competitive asceticism, with its consequent erosion of humility? These enemies have a certain symbolic and psychological force. But *Guthlac A*, in particular, pays such matters little heed. The saint's conversion from a warrior's life is in Felix a matter of inward conflict, caused by reflection on transience. In *Guthlac A* it seems to be a matter of external direction through divine power. Two spirits fight over the saint, *engel dryhtnes ond se atela gæst* [the Lord's angel and the terrible spirit], urging argument on him:

> Swa hy hine trymedon   on twa healfa
> oþþæt þæs gewinnes   weoroda dryhten
> on þæs engles dom   ende gereahte.
> Feond wæs geflymed . . .   (133–6)

[So they urged him from two sides, until the Lord of hosts made an end to the struggle, for the angel's judgment. The devil was routed . . .]

As so often, the change takes place in a moment, and it is absolute. Thereafter Guthlac makes one move only, to his mound in the fens,

E

his *dygle stowe* [secret place], there to engage, helped by his guardian
spirit, in permanent but successful conflict with the fiends. He never
wavers; nor does he have to go through the prolonged stages of self-
conquest suffered by Anthony. Though visited by what we might
recognise as a sense of earthly duties (192–9), homesickness (353–5),
and despair of earthly virtue (460–6), all these come from outside,
not from the mind but from the devil (sometimes in direct speech),
and so need no explicit answer. Guthlac lacks even the limited
humanity of Evagrius's St Anthony, for he breaks these temptations
(or assaults) without any strain. His virtue is firmness, his arguments,
as in *Solomon and Saturn* or the prison-scene of *Andreas*, simply an
assertion of power:

> 'Wendun ge ond woldun,   wiþerhycgende,
> þæt ge scyppende   sceoldon gelice
> wesan in wuldre. // Eow þær wyrs gelomp,
> ða eow se waldend   wraðe bisencte
> in þæt swearte susl'   (663–7)

['You wished and expected, rebellious in thought, that you should be like
the Creator in glory. // There a worse thing happened to you, when the
Ruler sank you angrily into that black torment']

The reminder is of course unanswerable. But though powerful, the
poem's scheme is barren of any psychological depth or sense of
temptation, and (here unlike *Andreas*) there is little narrative interest
or change in the saint's circumstance. As a result, the energetic style—
very close to that of *Andreas*—is at times a liability. Three times
towards the start we are referred back to the devil's discomfiture
siþþan he for wlence . . . beorgas bræce [once (Guthlac) broke the
mounds in the wilderness, out of daring], *siþþan biorg gestah eadig
oretta* [once the noble warrior ascended the mound], *þa he ana gesæt
dygle stowe* [when he alone settled the secret place]. In these repetitive
structures the poet seems to be projecting effort and triumph when
none is clearly visible. The style is designed for action, and so does not
fit a 'life' of this type; at the same time the poet cannot break entirely
from his own poetic tradition and move to the internalised conflicts
of his source.

To be fair, *Guthlac A* also has a correspondingly independent
virtue, not derived from Felix or any Latin work. It is extremely
purposeful, as can be seen from its long and sinuous prologue. With
a characteristic subtlety in its handling of time, this begins with a
death-scene—the virtuous soul met by its guardian angel and led
to Paradise. But that joy has to be earned. The poet goes back to
insist:

> mæg nu snottor guma   sæle brucan
> godra tida,   ond his gæste forð
> weges willian   (35–7)

These lines could be translated 'the wise man can now enjoy the happiness of fortunate times, and desire his spirit's going forth'.[21] But any suggestion of enjoying the present is ruled out by the firm description that follows of the world's decay. More properly these lines are a compressed statement not dissimilar to *Bede's Death Song*, 'now (is the time when the wise man ensures that) he can enjoy the happiness of fortunate times . . .', that is, when he comes to die. They urge one to a realisation; and this is indeed the poem's whole purpose. The prologue winds on to a description of those who realise the truth and those who do not. The former are broken down into groups including the 'wilderness demon-fighters'; and then Guthlac is introduced as a representative. The poem ends with his death and reward, and the point of the opening is restated: *this* is how righteous souls gain joy in their death-day, *they* have no cause to fear it. So, unlike Felix's story, *Guthlac A* has more than entertainment or historic value. It is meant as proof, a revelation in itself, to open the eyes of sinners (perhaps in this resembling the Mermedonians' flood). The poet argues firmly for the truth of what he records:

> Eall þas geeodon   in ussera
> tida timan.   Forþan þæs tweogan ne þearf
> ænig ofer eorþan   ælda cynnes   (753–5)

[All these things happened in our own times. So no one of the race of men upon earth need doubt it]

His attitude is profoundly different from the derivative and ritualistic claim to reliability of Felix,[22] but shows the characteristic Old English fusion of ideas about time, wisdom, and the importance of proof, equally characteristically subordinating all of them to that one decisive moment of death, *æt þam ytmestan ende . . . nyhstan nydgedale* [at the uttermost end . . . the last compelled parting].

Guthlac B is even more markedly a death-poem, and in it too the poet uses his prologue to set up a temporal perspective, this time looking back to the Fall of Man, the 'bitter drink' that Eve gave to Adam, and death, its inevitable result. In dying Guthlac finds a place in that perspective, not making a last gesture of contempt for the world (as St Anthony did, refusing all burial rites), but showing how men can succeed, transmuting the effects of Adam's sin through rigorous faith. This is the point of the last speech we have, from Guthlac's servant:

'Is hlaford min, . . .
se selesta   bi sæm tweonum . . .
gumena cynnes,   to godes dome
werigra wraþu,   worulddreamum of,
winemæga wyn,   in wuldres þrym,
gewiten, winiga hleo . . .
           ond þe secgan het
þæt git a mosten   in þam ecan gefean
mid þa sibgedryht   somudeard niman'   (1357–72)

['My lord . . . best of the race of men between the seas . . . comfort of the
weary and joy of his friends, has gone to God's judgment from the joys of
this world, to the glory of heaven—that protector of his friends . . . and he
commanded me to say to you that you might always possess a home together
in the eternal joy, with the happy band']

The piled-up variations are troublesome; but they express a sense of
triumph, and an urgent admonition, which do not appear in Felix.
Once again, there are local failures in the poem—the incongruous
ocean-crossing mentioned on p. 121; the rather static nature of the
speeches made by Guthlac; the servant's stress on gloom—rather
curious since he has just seen his lord translated convincingly to
Heaven. They are partly compensated by an insistent attempt to give
the poem unity, and to make it work persuasively on its readers. Miss
Woolf has suggested attractively that the lesson of *Guthlac B* is that
'the Anglo-Saxon melancholy sensitivity to transience and the
Christian confidence in the Resurrection' are not as irreconcilable
as they might have seemed.[23] To this one needs to add only that no
Christian's confidence in his own fate should be total. Both *Guthlac A*
and *Guthlac B* are aware of this qualification, and in their different
ways warn or encourage their readers to follow the right path. The
poems are purposive, show awareness of choice and the strong
attraction of scenes of conflict and decision. In these ways they differ
from the Latin tradition that gives them matter, and resemble the
native one that gives them style.

Conclusion

At the start of this chapter it was suggested that the Old English poet
of, say, the eighth century faced a problem when he came to translate
some types of Latin composition into the formal structures of his own
tradition. It should by now be clear that the problem was not an
ordinary literary one, of the sort that faces any translator. Not only
at the level of phrase, but of scene, speech, and essential situation as
well we find the Old English poet constrained by poetic habits which are
(apparently) those of generations. Some material could be remoulded
easily to fit at least most of these preconceived ideas; but some

resisted. It does not look as if many poets could tell, before they had composed their poems (and some perhaps not even after), whether their efforts led to success or to painful incongruity. There should be no question, though, of going through these saints' lives commending or reproving their local successes and failures. Instead, by seeing what has been done as clearly and wholly as possible, one can come to understand the operative pressures and some even of the ultimate goals of Old English poets, excited by Christian doctrines[24] and loyal to them, but (inevitably) loyal after their own fashion. Circular as this process may seem, it is only by following it that one can come to any understanding of the developments and climaxes actually reached in these uneasy and unstable poems—poems to be taken neither, one feels, as substitutes for nor exactly as rebuttals of that dead heroic literature from which, retrospectively, they must have drawn so much.

6

POETRY AND THE BIBLE:

THE JUNIUS MANUSCRIPT

Whether by this in mystick *Type* we see
The *New-years-Day* of great *Eternitie* . . .
Or that the *Law* be kept in Mem'ry still,
Giv'n with like noise on *Sina*'s shining Hill,
Or that (as some men teach) it did arise
From faithful *Abrams* righteous *Sacrifice* . . .
Obscure the *Cause*; but *God* his will declar'd;
And all nice knowledge then with ease is spar'd.
COWLEY, Davideis, Book II

Sometime in the first decade of the eleventh century, the great Anglo-Saxon teacher and homilist, Ælfric of Eynsham, wrote a summary of the Bible for a layman friend called Sigwerd. He ended this treatise with a curious plea to Sigwerd; 'When I was with you', he wrote, 'you wished to invite me to drink more than is my custom, for joy. But, dear man, know that he who compels another to drink beyond his powers must bear the guilt of both, if any harm come to them from that drink. In his holy Gospel our Saviour Christ forbade drunkenness [*þone oferdrenc*] to all believers: let him keep His command, who will. And after the Saviour the holy apostles put down that vice through their teaching, and taught that one should drink so as not to be harmed, since this drunkenness doubtless destroys man's soul and his health, and misfortune comes of that drink.'[1] These remarks have been taken (especially by Gallic scholars) as no more than confirmation of Englishmen's notorious alcoholic propensities. But if that is all they are, they gain a curiously needless stress from their appearance at the very end of a long and pious compilation; nor is the suppression of drunkenness really a very prominent theme in the New Testament. More likely, Ælfric is here approaching a subject dear to his heart, the 'spiritual drunkenness' of uncontrolled religious knowledge. Both at the start of this treatise and in his *Preface to Genesis* (also written for a layman friend) Ælfric shows the greatest reluctance to provide ignorant men with the raw text of the Bible—not from simple obscurantism, but from a belief that religious doctrine is too dangerous a matter to be handled by any but experts. In the *Preface to Genesis* he mentions some fairly comic examples of Biblical misreading—his old Latin master, for example, much struck by the fact that Jacob was allowed to have four wives, or the priests who argued from St Peter that (monogamous) marriage was lawful even for them.[2] Rites such as Passover or Circumcision were also clearly liable to be interpreted all too literally by well-intentioned enthusiasts, so that, all in all, Ælfric's strongly expressed desire for caution was no doubt justified. In the passage quoted, his implicit parallel between Sigwerd forcing strong drink on him, and himself providing equally pleasant but dangerous knowledge for Sigwerd, appears as a firm, but delicately tactful explanation of his own slowness to comply with his friend's request for English instruction. This attitude would certainly have been supported by almost any major churchman of his day.

Yet Ælfric's treatise is almost exactly contemporary with one of our four major collections of Old English poetry, the *Junius Manuscript*, devoted in great part to translation, or paraphrase, of parts of the Old Testament. We can never know what Ælfric would have thought of this book (though he complains elsewhere of 'the great error in many English books which unlearned men have considered great wisdom, through their simplicity'),[3] but it is unlikely that he would have approved. The poems at times treat sacred texts with considerable freedom, and in an age which could argue that not only the words, but even the *word-order* of the Bible might be significant, any translation at all required a certain justification.[4] The very existence of the *Junius Manuscript* forces us to consider problems of cultural and linguistic adequacy far greater, even, than those surrounding the poems of *Andreas* or *Guthlac*. Were the poets who wrote these Bible-versions less learned and more foolhardy than Ælfric—as they might well have been, since at least some of the poems date back to around 700–50, even though the manuscript itself was copied two or three centuries later? Or were they, like the *Andreas*-poet, perhaps unaware of the effects their traditional methods of style and narrative might have on alien matter? Is it possible to save their face by showing that their poems conceal layers of hidden significance similar to those derived, by scholars like Ælfric, from the raw text of the Bible? It is this last speculation which has proved most acceptable to the poems' modern critics,[5] and there is, to begin with, a certain amount of evidence in its favour; the second poem in the collection, *Exodus*, shows best how much.

Two features of this poem direct readers away from seeing it as a simple re-telling of the Bible story. The first is that the poet has chosen to tell only a small part of the Book of Exodus, roughly chapters xii–xv, dealing with the flight of the Israelites from Pharaoh, their crossing of the Red Sea, the destruction of the Egyptians, and the thanksgiving on the further shore—admittedly a dramatic section in itself, but also, to many minds, an obvious symbolic unit. The nature of the symbolism that may be present is suggested by a second feature of *Exodus*, and one that has *no* good narrative reason behind it—the speed and apparent disconnectedness of its 'flashbacks', of which one in particular demands interpretation. As the tribes of Israel assemble to cross the Red Sea, parted by Moses' power, the poet of *Exodus* breaks off to comment that they all had the same ancestor, and that their genealogy was known to the old and wise. As if to prove himself one of this latter group, he then jumps immediately and without apology to the story of Noah's Ark:

> Niwe flodas   Noe oferlað,
> þrymfæst þeoden,   mid his þrim sunum,
> þone deopestan   drencefloda
> þara ðe gewurde   on woruldrice   (362–5)

[Noah voyaged over new (=unprecedented?) floods, the mighty prince, with his three sons, over the deepest devouring flood that has ever been in the world]

Of course it might be only the association of one 'flood overcome' with another that led the poet to this digression. But he continues blithely from Noah to the story of Abraham and Isaac, again with little narrative connection, and this time with no apparent similarity of scene to excuse him either. The example of *Beowulf* naturally deters one from saying that Anglo-Saxon poets had no reason for their rambling digressions; but the principle here is not easy to find. Biblical commentary provides one possible solution. In his *De Catechizandis Rudibus*, for instance, St Augustine had made an equation out of the very juxtapositions just mentioned, arguing that the Christian Church had been 'prefigured' (to use a technical term) by Noah's family in the Ark, by the people of Abraham, by the Israelites under Moses.[6] In the first and last, he added, one could see the mysteries of Wood and Water, the latter in the Flood and the Red Sea, the former in the Ark and Moses' rod. He associated the one with Christ's Cross, the other with baptism, a process which (as Augustine says) blots out sins like the water covering the Egyptians. References of this nature provide a certain justification for the *Exodus*-poet's sudden and undramatic leaps in time; to his mind they may have been connected thematically, whether or not he expected the connection to be obvious to everybody. Similar arguments can be turned even more convincingly on the organisation of the whole of the *Junius Manuscript* itself, for, as has recently been pointed out, the three major blocks of narrative in it, Genesis i–xxii, Exodus xii–xv, and Daniel i–v, correspond well with the readings appointed by some rituals for the great ceremony of Holy Saturday, the day after Good Friday and one traditionally reserved for baptisms.[7] The Exodus-passage gives a fine symbolic analogue for baptism itself, as the Israelites (or Christian souls) pass out of Egypt (the sinful world), through the waters (of baptism), to the Promised Land (of Heaven); meanwhile Genesis xxii and Daniel iii, with their stories of the 'help of God' granted to Isaac and to the Israelites in the fiery furnace, are well adapted to strengthening the faith of the baptismal candidate about to take his *sacramentum* or (military) oath. All in all, it is hard to deny a certain forethought and symbolic awareness to the *Junius Manuscript* poems, which might have molli- fied Ælfric to some extent. Nevertheless, part of the credit for this may go to the compiler, not the individual poets; and in any case, though general probability is certainly in its favour, particular instances are by no means clear.

One considerable drawback to interpreting all these poems as 'figural narratives', that is, as stories controlled by traditional symbolic association, is the fact that they are in Old English verse, and often show just as obviously as the saints' lives discussed above that their authors were not always capable of resisting the strong biases of their inherited style. A very brief example could be taken from the translation of Genesis, normally closest of all the Junius poems to its source, but still wavering towards narrative climaxes of a type discussed before. In the Book of Genesis xviii, 12–15, the Lord promises Abraham that his wife Sarah will bear him a son, in spite of her age. Overhearing, she laughs; 'And the Lord said unto Abraham, "Wherefore did Sarah laugh, saying, Shall I of a surety bear a child, which am old? Is any thing too hard for the Lord? At the time appointed I will return unto thee, according to the time of life, and Sarah shall have a son".'[8] Without varying from the gist of this, the *Genesis*-poet nevertheless sees in it an opportunity for a speech much less familiar in tone, and closer to that theme of *Andreas,* concealed power becoming apparent even to the wilfully blind:

'Ne wile Sarran   soð gelyfan
wordum minum.   Sceal seo wyrd swa þeah
forð steallian   swa ic þe æt frymðe gehet.
Soð ic þe secge . . .
                        þe beoð wordgehat
min gelæsted.   Þu on magan wlitest,
þin agen bearn,   Abraham leofa!'   (2390–8)

['Sarah will not believe the truth in my words. Nevertheless, the event shall
set out what I promised you at first. I tell you the truth . . . that my promise
will be performed for you. My favoured Abraham, you will look on a son,
your own child!']

Even the idea of 'fulfilling one's vow' [*gehat gelæstan*] appears in the
last few lines, with its military associations. In some such way as this,
the *Genesis*-poet repeatedly adapts the climaxes of his source (see,
for example, Abimelech's covenant with Abraham in lines 2807–16);
and though these have no overall effect on the poem, they show
that there were pressures at work other than those of faithful
translation or dogmatic relevance. The poet could not escape his
background. Some scenes make one think that the poets of *Exodus* or
Daniel did not even make the attempt.

Of these the most obvious example (and perhaps the worst) is the
'parting of the waters' in *Exodus*. In the Bible this is told quite
exceptionally well, with a strong sense of drama, vivid dialogue, and a
series of sharply-focused scenes—the Israelites complaining to
Moses for bringing them to die in the wilderness; God's reassurance;
the command for Moses to stretch his rod out over the sea and part
it; the hot pursuit of the Egyptians hindered by their chariots'
heavy driving; and finally Moses' second clearly-visualised gesture
with its mighty result: 'And Moses stretched forth his hand over the
sea, and the sea returned to his strength when the morning appeared;
and the Egyptians fled against it; and the Lord overthrew the
Egyptians in the midst of the sea.' With his good eye for detail and his
liking for sudden alterations, the *Exodus*-poet might be expected to
amplify, but not radically to change this excellent scene. Yet he did—
and as a result many hard words have been said of him.[9] In particular,
he chose to convey much more of the action through the single
figure of Moses than does the original; and he presented it very
much through formal speech, Moses appearing (rather like Byrhtnoth) as a *hildecalla, bald beohata* [war-herald, maker of bold
promises]. The complaints of the Israelites and God's reassurance are
all but completely cut. Instead, at the moment of crisis in the dawn,
Moses makes a speech which is totally confident but for which we
have not been in any way forewarned. He vows that the Egyptians
will get their reward through his hand:

'Ne willað eow andrædan   deade feðan,
fæge ferhðlocan,   fyrst is æt ende
lænes lifes.   Eow is lar godes
abroden of breostum.   Ic on beteran ræd,
þæt ge gewurðien   wuldres aldor . . .
Þis is se ecea   Abrahames god,
frumsceafta frea,   se ðas fyrd wereð,
modig and mægenrof,   mid þære miclan hand'   (266–75)

['You (the Israelites) will not fear these dead troops, these doomed bodies;
the time of their fleeting lives has come to an end. The knowledge
of God is withdrawn from your hearts. (But) I have a better counsel, that
you should worship the Lord of glory . . . This is the eternal God of
Abraham, Lord of Creation, who defends this army with his mighty hand,
brave and powerful']

There is then an almost imperceptible pause, signalled by the two
lines:

Hof ða for hergum   hlude stefne
lifigendra leod,   þa he to leodum spræc   (276–7)

[The leader of the living lifted up a loud voice before the armies, when he
spoke to the tribes],

and the speech continues. But now it is retrospective, looking *back*
on the 'parting of the waters' that has somehow been achieved
'offstage', in the indeterminate gap between Moses' two speeches:

'Hwæt, ge nu eagum to   on lociað,
folca leofost,   færwundra sum,
hu ic sylfa sloh   and þeos swiðre hand
grene tacne   garsecges deop.
Yð up færeð,   ofstum wyrceð
wæter wealfæsten.   Wegas syndon dryge . . .'   (278–83)

['Lo, now you see with your eyes, dearest of peoples, a sudden wonder, how
I myself struck the ocean's deep, this right hand with a green token! The
wave mounts up, hastily the water builds itself into a wall. The paths are
dry . . .']

In some ways this avoidance of the event deserves all that has been
said about it. Still, there is no need to think that lines have been lost.
Whatever else it may be, the passage is quite typical of Old English
narrative, reminiscent of the *Finnsburg Episode* in its sudden and
virtually unexpressed change from defeat to victory, and of *Andreas*
and *Judith* in its opposition of doubt and belief, resolved by a single,
visible manifestation. Moses' speech may resemble Deuteronomy

xx, 1–4, more than Exodus xiv, 13–14, as a recent editor suggests;[10] but it resembles the statue's speech in *Andreas* 744–60 still more. It is arguable that the poet has not improved on his source, but it is surely undeniable that he knew what he was doing, and that the emphasis on power and unexpectedness may have been more recognisable and stimulating to audiences of his day than any of the subtler stylistic variations of the Latin Bible could be. One may be permitted, therefore, to wonder whether narrative decisions of this type do not deserve at least equal consideration with the vagaries of Biblical commentary and symbolism in analysing the organisation of the poem of *Exodus*.

Looked at in this light, it becomes clear that the *Exodus*-poet, like his colleagues in the *Junius Manuscript* (but with the exception of the author of *Christ and Satan*) was in one way at least quite ill-suited to the symbolic tradition of Augustine and Ælfric, and Biblical commentators as a whole. If there is one thing that characterises the whole 'figural' school, it is a certain indifference to individual facts and motives. Christ heals a blind man on his entry into Jericho: and the commentator (Ælfric) explains that the blind man is mankind shut out from the heavenly light, that Jericho represents mortality, and that Christ's entry into it reminds us of his acceptance of human nature.[11] Or Abram with his 318 servants attacks the kings of the North to rescue his nephew Lot, defeats and pursues them: and the commentator (Bede) points out that 300 is signified by the Greek letter *tau,* which is also a cross, and 18 by the letters for I and H, so that the servants stand for IHesus the Crucified, while the kings of the North are sinners pursued to judgment, damnation, and the drink of death.[12] In each case the incident is directly related to the doctrine of salvation. But, equally, the commentators show no concern for individual blind men or robber-kings; they remain extremely shadowy as to how the Almighty exerted his power in staging these vital and revealing events; and least of all do they offer any political, historical or social explanations whatever. This is not meant, of course, as a criticism of the 'figural' world-view (though Augustine did find it necessary to remind others, and perhaps himself, that events of Scripture had really happened). The point is only that to many medieval minds Scriptural history no longer possessed 'any reality . . . only signification'.[13] But it is just this that one cannot say of the poem *Exodus*, a work marked in several places by interest, not in symbolic or doctrinal commentary, but in other events of Bible story, events related moreover to those being described not as mystic analogues, but as simple, factual motives or results. As the tribes of Israel cross the Red Sea, the poet notes that the tribe of Judah goes first, though by precedence it is only the *feorðe cyn* [fourth race]. He may have taken this order from some unknown commentator, or perhaps directly from the Bible, there being a scene which might carry this implication in Genesis xlix. But his purpose is to show that it is its courage on this occasion that gives Judah practical pre-eminence in the future, a point both moral and historical, but with no wider symbolic meaning. In the same way, as the Israelites first become aware of their pursuers, the poet gives a long (but now much mutilated) 'flashback' to explain—a strikingly original addition!—the motives of the Egyptians, angered not only by the deaths of their first-born but also by jealousy at the Israelites' prosperity. This idea is certainly latent in the Bible itself (see Exodus i, 7–20), and is in itself plausible. But it is a sign of the poet's natural bent towards history that he includes it, while the concern for human motivation on a realistic level is markedly alien to the type of commentary most practised by Augustine and his followers.

This 'flashback' indeed gives something of a clue to the *Exodus*-poet's most dominant interest. At start and end of the digressive passage—practically, indeed, all that is left of it—he takes pains to condemn the Egyptians, not for their attack on the Israelites so much as for their breach of a 'treaty' (again, the poet is perhaps remembering the elder Pharaoh's promise to Joseph in Genesis xlvii, 6). *Wære ne gymdon,* he claims, *wære fræton* [they did not care for the treaty . . . they devoured the treaty]. Within the poem breach or maintenance of one covenant or another seem to be the poet's moral extremes. During the Flood, Noah keeps his agreement, *Hæfde him on hreðre halige treowa* [he had holy faiths in his heart]; while the surprising climax of Abraham and Isaac's gloomy ascent of Mount Zion is that they 'found an agreement there, saw glory, a high and holy faith' [*Wære hie þær fundon, wuldor gesawon, halige heah-treowe*]. God makes the same powerful assertion, as He commends Abraham:

> 'Soð is gecyðed,
> nu þin cunnode cyning alwihta,
> þæt þu wið waldend wære heolde,
> fæste treowe . . .
> Hu þearf mannes sunu maran treowe?'   (420–6)

['Now the King of all creatures has made trial of you, the truth is made known, that you held to your agreement with the Ruler, your firm faith . . . How can a man's son need a greater faith?']

The theme of trial and proof is obviously congenial to Anglo-Saxon minds. But one can perhaps imagine also how the idea of an expressed Law or Covenant might appeal to beliefs about wisdom and 'the sage'. Moses' role as a leader, as we have seen, is essentially to maintain his people's faith, and to remind them of their agreement; the 'Exodus' itself, with the parting of the waters, is the promised (and almost statutory) intervention of God to fulfil his side of a bargain. At start and end of the poem, also, we have concentration on *Moyses domas, wræclico wordriht* [Moses' judgments, a strange law in words], and on the *ece rædas* . . . *halige spræce, deop ærende* [eternal counsels . . . holy speech, a deep message], so that it is perhaps the poet's main intention to direct his audience towards seeing at least this part of the Bible as a 'History of the Covenant'—a covenant between God and His people which is of course extended, in medieval minds, to all Christians by the pledge of Crucifixion and Redemption.

Probably this thought can guide us to an interpretation of a much-disputed—and possibly conclusive—passage towards the end of the poem (in the section edited for the *Anglo-Saxon Poetic Records,* lines 519–48).[14] Here the poet turns from Moses' speech to bring the story up to date:

> Dægword nemnað
> swa gyt werðeode,   on gewritum findað
> doma gehwilcne,   þara ðe him drihten bebead
> on þam siðfate   soðum wordum,
> gif onlucan wile   lifes wealhstod,
> beorht in breostum,   banhuses weard,
> ginfæsten god   gastes cægon   (519–25)

[Races of men still name that day's word, and find in Scripture each of the laws that God commanded them on that journey with true words—if the interpreter of life, the body's guardian, bright in the heart, will reveal the lasting good by the keys of the spirit]

The references to the 'interpreter' and the 'keys of the spirit' have caused many to take this as a plea for symbolic reading of the Augustinian kind, a possibility not to be ruled out.[15] However, one might also see the poet here as turning from his main subject to exhort his readers to apply the story to themselves, using a full apprehension of history to find solid faith (a thought rather similar to the one expressed at the ends of the *Guthlac* poems, see p. 131). Certainly he goes on to praise books and scholars for their guidance towards a personal understanding—as usual, an awareness of earthly transience and the dangers of Judgment—drawing, again, moral conclusions rather than allegorical ones; while the other possible 'final scene' of the poem, the Israelites plundering the drowned Egyptians, offers for all its symbolic possibilities a firmly realistic assurance—success for the Israelites and those who hold to 'holy teaching', death for the treaty-breakers and those who resist. Obviously this scene was not meant to be a mere description with no wider importance. At the same time, the 'reality' of it is very determinedly part of its 'signification'.

Such a reading is of course in no way at variance with religious doctrine; indeed, the Covenant, its breaches and re-establishments, forms the basis for at least half of the eighteen common readings for Holy Week with which the *Junius Manuscript* might be associated,[16] so that it would be quite improper to condemn the *Exodus*-poet for treating his source in a relatively realistic and legalistic way. Nor should there be any suggestion that he knew no better. On the contrary, the poet often shows quite a familiar and minute awareness of the possibilities of allegory, though these are to some extent confused by his very daring (or maybe uncontrolled) compression of traditional language.[17] Nevertheless, a deliberate choice was made as to how to read this part of the Bible, and it was followed through with considerable consistency. The choice may have been shaped by, and might have contributed to, a fairly aggressive and worldly Christianity disliked by some and misinterpreted by others; so that Ælfric's strictures on translation keep a certain force, resting, as they do, on the perception that the cultural values of a society and a language are liable to seep into matters that might be better left unadulterated. Nevertheless, the 'collaboration' of vernacular poet and sacred text could create between them an original kind of strength. This can be seen more clearly, or perhaps more bluntly, in the poem following *Exodus* in our manuscript, the paraphrase of *Daniel*.

In some ways, the Biblical 'Book of Daniel' offers far more of a challenge to a historically-minded poet than most parts of the Old Testament, some problems remaining apparent even to a modern reader. For one thing, there is a distinct gap between chapters i–vi and vii–xii—the first half containing a chronological account of the miracles of Daniel under various kings, Nebuchadnezzar, Belshazzar, and Darius the Persian, the rest describing the poet's (uninterpreted) visions, at various times overlapping with the earlier section. This second half has attracted most attention from commentators, no doubt because of the freedom it offers to anyone wishing to interpret the prophecies for his own ends. The Old English poet, however, ignores it entirely. But even in chapters i–vi one cannot help noticing some oddities. The structure of each chapter is basically the same: Daniel, or his friends Shadrach, Meshach and Abednego, come into some conflict with the Babylonian king or his wise men, being called on to infringe the Jewish law, or else to perform some impossible action. In chapter i, all four Jews refuse to eat the king's

meat; in chapter iii the three friends will not worship Nebuchadnezzar's golden statue; in chapter vi it is Daniel who cannot accept
the king's supreme authority; in the other three chapters Daniel is
asked to interpret some vision of the king's, after the wise men and
soothsayers have failed. In each case divine intervention saves the
believers. But a problem in logic is caused by the lack of continuity
between chapters. At the end of chapter ii, for example, Nebuchadnezzar worships Daniel and admits his God's power, but at the
start of the next he is once more oppressing the Jews. Again, the
start of chapter iv breaks suddenly to a first-person speech from him,
while in view of his generally submissive approach to Daniel it is hard
to see what the 'iniquities' are for which he is eventually punished.
At the same time, the overall similarity of the chapters raises a
narrative problem: how are six closely similar climaxes of divine
rescue to be varied or organised? From the Old English poem, it is
clear that these superficial (but important) questions were as visible
to the poet then as they are now, and that he expended considerable
care (and not impiously) in reshaping his material to explain or
enhance them.

His most efficient, if (in view of the sanctity of his text) his most
daring decision, was simply to omit quite large sections. The miracle
of chapter i, God's miraculous nutrition of the four Jews who have
refused the king's food, not only does not take place but is practically
denied:

> þa se beorn bebead, Babilone weard . . .
> þæt þam gengum þrym   gad ne wære
> wiste ne wæde in woruldlife   (99–103)

[then the warrior, guard of Babylon, commanded . . . that there should be
no lack of food or clothing for the three youths during their lives]

Daniel has been omitted from this scene as well. But the curtailments
are not for reasons of economy—the poet has already expanded the
first couple of verses into some eighty lines—so much as to allow more
dramatic and unexpected entries later. After this 'historical prologue'
there is a fine build-up of the wrath and despair of the 'wolf-hearted'
Nebuchadnezzar as he dreams of his end but can find no one to
interpret the vision for him. It is maintained for some thirty lines,

> oðþæt witga cwom,
> Daniel to dome, se wæs drihtne gecoren,
> snotor and soðfæst, in þæt seld gangan   (149–51)

[until the wise one came, Daniel to judgment, he who was the Lord's
chosen, wise and firm for truth, entering the hall]

Even the syntax of this passage—the 'until' clause connecting despair
and its solution, the postponement of the verb of motion—shows the
traditional skills of Old English narrative; and only afterwards does
the poet explain who this mighty and mysterious figure is. Even then,
he cuts the explanation of the dream right to the bone (15 Biblical
verses to 3 Old English lines), and forfeits all the interpretative
possibilities of the 'idol with the feet of clay'—purely, one feels,
in order to subordinate this minor climax to later and major ones.
The poet's self-control is immense (strikingly different from that
of most medieval vernacular authors); but the benefit of it is felt
much later, in lines 495–592, where Nebuchadnezzar's second dream,
and the prophet's explanation of it, can be given in full without any
sense of repetition. That detailed version in its turn throws a fine and
necessary stress on the moment when Nebuchadnezzar, three times
warned already, boasts of his power and is struck down:

'Ðu eart seo micle   and min seo mære burh
þe ic geworhte   to wurðmyndum,
rume rice.   Ic reste on þe,
eard and eðel,   agan wille.'
    Ða for ðam gylpe   gumena drihten
forfangen wearð   and on fleam gewat,
ana on oferhyd   ofer ealle men.
Swa wod wera   on gewindagum
geocrostne sið   in godes wite,
ðara þe eft lifigende   leode begete,
Nabochodonossor,   siððan him nið godes,
hreð of heofonum   hete gesceode   (608–19)

['You are the great, the famous city of mine, which I built for my honour, a
broad kingdom. In you I will have rest, earth and home.' Then for his
boast the lord of men was struck down, and fled away, alone in his pride
beyond all men. Like a madman Nebuchadnezzar, under God's anger,
trod the weariest path in days of strife that ever might come to living men,
once God's stroke, power from the heavens, hurt him with hate]

The suddenness is not hindered even by the voice of God (as it is in
the Bible), while the poet alone is responsible for the dramatic irony
of lines three and four. But the process of reaching this climax—
Aufgipfelung, or 'steepling-up', as the Germans call it—extends
deliberately over some hundreds of preceding lines; while that one
'moment of truth' is carefully matched by a second one, when, after
his years of bestiality in the *wildeora westen* [wild beasts' desert], the
winburge cyning [king of the wine-hall] looks up at the sky, and, like
the Ancient Mariner, sees truth and sheds his burden.
    Noticeably, the Old English poet then finds it necessary for the

king, replaced in his kingdom, to admit his fault and tell his experiences to all, rounding it off with the authorial remark:

> Wyrd wæs geworden,   wundor gecyðed,
> swefn geseðed,   susl awunnen,
> dom gedemed,   swa ær Daniel cwæð,
> þæt se folctoga   findan sceolde
> earfoðsiðas   for his ofermedlan   (652–6)

[The event had taken place, the miracle been made known, the dream confirmed, punishment endured, the judgment given, as Daniel had said before, that the ruler would come upon times of trouble because of his pride]

Yet in adding this the poet is only tying off a thread of comment continuous almost from the start—a cycle of prosperity, arrogance, and downfall seen first in the Jews destroyed by Babylon, then in Nebuchadnezzar's first unparticularised dream and his behaviour after the 'fiery furnace', and finally in the bragging of Belshazzar. On each occasion the poet is careful to point out that they prospered *oðþæt hie wlenco anwod* (line 17) . . . *oferhygd gesceod* (489) . . . *oðþæt him wlenco gesceod* (677) [until confidence struck them . . . pride injured him . . . until confidence injured him], but that all the time there was waiting *yfel endelean* (187) . . . *he þæs hearde ongeald* (597) [an evil repayment in the end . . . he paid hard for it]. Proleptic hints of this nature make the poem almost a grave comedy of over-confidence against unheeded knowledge; and it has not escaped notice that there are remarkable parallels with the speech of Hrothgar in *Beowulf*, who foresees much the same cycle for all men as Daniel does for his Babylonian masters.[18] But the consistency of the references in *Daniel*, and the evident suitability of Hrothgar's speech to its context in *Beowulf*, make it unlikely that either poet was borrowing clumsily from the other. Rather, they share a view of life. And (as we have come to see from modern analyses of novelistic technique) views of life may be communicated through simple decisions, individually almost imperceptible, about no more than the selection and presentation of a writer's raw material.

All in all, *Daniel* enjoys a certain shapeliness, more than most Old English poems. At the end Daniel's appearance before Belshazzar is verbally almost identical with his appearance before Nebuchadnezzar (compare lines 735–6 with 149–51 quoted above), while he rebukes Belshazzar for using the holy vessels of Israel in words very like those describing the Jews' first downfall (compare lines 749–52 with 17–20). The similarities were probably recognised by the poet, even if he did not expect listeners or readers to pick them up. Yet they would be enough to gain the poem a certain modern repute, if it were not—in our eyes—marred by the disproportionately long central section devoted to the adventure of the three 'children' in the fiery furnace, with their canticle of praise, the 'Song of Azarias'. The text of the Bible is itself in some confusion here, our Authorised Version having a palpable gap between verses iii, 23 and iii, 24, while the 67 verses found in that gap in older versions (including undoubtedly the one known to the *Daniel*-poet) make the story clumsy and repetitive, and still embody slight failures in narrative logic. In these circumstances one could hardly expect the Old English poet to succeed.[19] Still, it is strange that the crux was not dealt with in the same free and sensible way as several of the others mentioned already; and suspicion is increased by the poem *Azarias* in the *Exeter Book*, which gives a text parallel to *Daniel* 279–364 but with the similarities oddly fading out several lines *after* the start of the canticle of praise, not at any obvious point of junction.[20] Several scholars have argued that a section has been interpolated into *Daniel* as we now have it, a theory one would like to believe. But there is no denying that the original poet would have had to put *something* in this place. Just possibly the supposed interpolation is his own work, though he may have been inhibited from his usual freedom by the liturgical importance (especially on Holy Saturday) of precisely this lyrical section. Whatever the reason, a large part of *Daniel* displays a gracelessness oddly at variance with its otherwise tight construction. The contrast at least serves to point out the skill with which the poet at times draws philosophy and morality from what must have been a difficult, and even recalcitrant, text.

Nevertheless, the real clash of doctrinal and narrative interests was reserved for parts of the poem of *Genesis*. There is no doubt at all, here, that we are dealing with an original poem and an (unsignalled) interpolation from quite a different period and even a different country. In 1875 Eduard Sievers prophetically argued that lines 235–851 of *Genesis* (normally known now as *Genesis B*) must have been a translation into Old English from Old Saxon, a backwash from the eighth-century missionary activity mentioned on p. 128. His guess was confirmed nineteen years later when a fragment of an Old Saxon poem was found, and proved to be undoubtedly the original of lines 791–817 in the poem we have.[21] The two 'layers' of *Genesis* are an odd contrast. The earlier, longer, Old English sections stick fairly close to the Bible text, omitting a few passages (such as Abraham's 'horror of great darkness' in chapter 15), and adding others (mostly learned but merely explanatory details such as the names of the wives of Noah and his sons, or the identification of the 'sons of God' in Genesis vi with Seth's children),[22] but by and large

following the original almost verse by verse. In contrast, the translation from Old Saxon deals with the Fall of the Angels and the Fall of
Man, stories in great part *created* by commentators enlarging on a
part of the Bible notoriously difficult to reconcile with a Christian
scheme. As a result this poet is both guided by orthodoxy and
menaced by heresy at almost all points; a simple retelling of Bible
story was never a choice open to him. Where *Genesis B* succeeds,
then, it does so dangerously. And in some areas one ought to admit
that it fails.

Indeed, probably the first and most obvious impression that this
section makes on a reader is one of technical inferiority. In place of
the neatness and control of *Genesis A*, the later *Genesis* continuously
produces extended lines in great number and in close conjunction
with normal ones, leading to general diffuseness and occasional
startling rhythmic clashes:

> Worhte man hit him to wite, (hyra woruld wæs gehwyrfed),
> forman siðe,   fylde helle
> mid þam andsacum.   Heoldon englas forð
> heofonrices hehðe,   þe ær godes hyldo gelæston . . .   (318–21)

[It (Hell) was made for their torment, (their world was overturned), for the
first time He filled Hell with enemies. From then on the angels who had
performed God's service kept the height of Heaven . . .]

The syllable-length of each half-line—admittedly not always a
significant measure, but one not to be completely discounted—varies
from 8,8, to 4,4,5,5,6,9, Stresses are as weak in *mid þam andsacum*
or as far apart as in *Worhte man hit him to wite*; and there is a
superfluity of words with merely grammatical importance. All of this
results in a verse lacking the powerful virtues of most Old English
handlings. Still, it is probably unwise to blame the Old English
translator for this, since the few lines surviving both in his version
and in the original Old Saxon prove that he did his best to alter
his source back to something like normality, cutting it whenever he
could and also breaking some single, unwieldy, Old Saxon phrases into
two shorter Old English equivalents.[23] His intentions were good, but
(as might be expected) they proved incomparably weak against the
deeply embedded linguistic features inherent in Saxon poetry as in
Anglo-Saxon.[24] This failure—for it must be counted as one—should
act as a basic check on any exalted claims for the poet-translator's
artistic control.

Yet to modern readers, technical inferiority is totally outweighed by a literary (and intellectual) force quite unprecedented in Old English, and of a kind we are for once well equipped to appreciate. Consider Satan's first speech from Hell after his overthrow:

'Is þes ænga styde   ungelic swiðe
þam oðrum ham   þe we ær cuðon,
hean on heofonrice,   þe me min hearra onlag,
þeah we hine for þam alwaldan   agan ne moston,
romigan ures rices.   Næfð he þeah riht gedon
þæt he us hæfð befælled   fyre to botme,
helle þære hatan,   heofonrice benumen;
hafað hit gemearcod   mid moncynne
to gesettanne.   Þæt me is sorga mæst,
þæt Adam sceal,   þe wæs of eorðan geworht,
minne stronglican   stol behealdan,
wesan him on wynne,   and we þis wite þolien,
hearm on þisse helle.   Wa la, ahte ic minra handa geweald
and moste ane tid   ute weorðan,
wesan ane winterstunde,   þonne ic mid þys werode—
Ac licgað me ymbe   irenbenda,
rideð racentan sal.   Ic eom rices leas'   (356–72)

['This narrow place is most unlike the other home we knew, high in heaven, which my Lord gave me—though because of the All-ruler we could not possess it or aim at our kingdom. Still, he has not done right in casting us down to the fire-bottom, to hot Hell, taking Heaven away. He has designed to settle that with mankind. That is the greatest of my sorrows, that Adam, made from earth, should possess my strong throne and be in joy, and we endure this torment, pain in this Hell. Alas! If I had use of my hands and could be out one hour, one short winter-hour, then with this company!—But iron bands lie around me, the weight of chains pulls me. I have no kingdom']

A fully-developed Satanic character appears through the repeated turns and variations of this speech. Concern for lost rule is its main theme, emerging from the first contrast between Heaven and Hell, the past and the present, and developed as Satan recollects that Adam will possess what was once his land; this makes his final acceptance of loss, *'Ic eom rices leas'*, the more heavily laden with bitterness against the race of man. At the same time, his sense of constraint and frustration is built up from the word *ænga* [narrow] in the first line to the wish for revenge and then the sudden anti-climactic realisation, in line 15, that though his mind is free his body is held fast. But these two revelations of defeat and subordination contrast with the mighty and positive energy of Satan's speech. The first phrase, with its inversion, cannot be reproduced in modern English with quite the same force; yet it conceals a deliberate and self-assured understatement. The same mixture of energy and restraint reappears in the definiteness of '*þæt me is sorga mæst*', in the truthful, arrogant, '*Adam . . . þe wæs of eorðan geworht*'. Over the whole speech hangs an awareness of power, which we do not have to analyse, and which creates the right response without needing any special preparation. Though there are few verbal correspondences, it is not simply the situation that has made critics speculate on a connection with *Paradise Lost*: the energy, the sense of contrast, the well-focused but inordinate imagination are all there as well. In fact there is little likelihood that Milton knew the Old English poem (though he had the opportunity);[25] but the comparison does raise a valid question. Were the Fall of Man and the figure of Satan ideas sufficiently well-developed in traditional commentary to guide these two poets (and others) along roughly similar tracks? Putting this another way, what is it that is original in the Old English poem; can one see bias or re-arrangement of the kinds used in *Exodus* or *Daniel*? The multiple branches of this question are not to be answered simply, though the basic problem is clear.

The first point is, that though a bare-bones version of the Fall of Man is probably known even now by many members of western civilisation, it has no firm basis in any part of the Book of Genesis. The whole story of Satan's pride and revenge is a later creation,[26] there being no reference to the Fall of the Angels or indeed to Satan (in his familiar guise) anywhere in the Old Testament. Even the expulsion from Eden, which *is* told in Genesis iii, contains there some discrepancies which in a simple reading suggest weakness or doubt on the part of the Almighty—for He drives Adam and Eve out of the Garden seemingly as precaution, not punishment (Genesis iii, 22), and His promise of instant death (ii, 17) is never carried out. Nor is the reason for His temptation (?) of Adam and Eve through the tree of knowledge at all clear, in the original, basic account. Of course solutions to all these problems were rapidly and necessarily forth-coming after St Paul's connection of the Fall with the Redemption on the Cross, solutions which culminated in the powerful Augustinian synthesis of theories involving 'original sin', the corruption of nature, and the trials of free will.[27] Nevertheless, round this dangerous text there soon clustered more 'distinct damnations' than with almost any other. Even orthodox views of it might not be pleasant, as we see with Bishop Avitus of Vienne, who in composing *his* Latin version of the story found time to see in it the damnation of all unbaptised infants, and to offer his sister the consolation that by avoiding marriage she was at least spared that risk.[28] There is no doubt that both poet and translator of *Genesis B* must have been in some sense aware of such theories, since it was the theories which controlled the development of the story. But even Milton's alleged heresies and dangerous independence begin to seem almost anaemic in comparison with some of the implications of the Saxon story.

For one thing, the fall of Adam and Eve is in *Genesis B* not caused by temptation directed to their baser instincts—gluttony, avarice, lust, pride, or the other sins so often seen by medieval commentators in the act of eating the fruit—but by a deception addressed to their sense of duty. Though *on wyrmes lic* [in a snake's body] Satan's emissary presents himself as an angelic messenger with a command from God (Himself unconcerned to take the journey, lines 513–16!) to eat the fruit of the tree of knowledge. Adam rejects the command, but Eve accepts it, partly under threat of punishment. The poet stresses her good intentions as she urges the fruit on Adam:

> Heo dyde hit þeah þurh holdne hyge,   nyste þæt þær
>   hearma swa fela,
> fyrenearfeða,   fylgean sceolde . . .
> ac wende þæt heo hyldo   heofoncyninges
> worhte mid þam wordum   (708–13)

[But she did it because of her obedient spirit, she did not know that so many harms and hardships should follow there . . . but she thought that by these words she was doing the heavenly King's service]

In accordance with this view, Eve's continued deception after she has eaten is explained as a diabolic illusion; while once the trick is exposed—by the devil's gloating—there is none of the drunkenness or copulation presented by Milton, but instead expressions of sorrow and apology.

The corollary of such an approving view of Adam and Eve is of course that the guilt must lie elsewhere—largely, on the devil. Still, without exactly blaming God, the poet does express a certain surprise at His inactivity:

> Ne wearð wyrse dæd
> monnum gemearcod!   Þæt is micel wundor
> þæt hit ece god   æfre wolde
> þeoden þolian,   þæt wurde þegn swa monig
> forlædd be þam lygenum   þe for þam larum com   (594–8)

[A worse deed was never assigned to men! It is a great wonder that the eternal Lord God would ever endure it, that so many a man should be misled by lies, which came as teaching]

As if to compound his dangerous fluctuations, the Saxon poet also denies the evidence of Genesis iii, 6—'that the tree was good for food, and that it was pleasant to the eyes'—and with it the Augustinian thesis that God created nothing intrinsically evil, by making from the start a strong contrast between the tree of life and the tree of knowledge of good and evil—the latter indeed presented as *eallenga sweart, dim and þystre; þæt wæs deaðes beam* [entirely black, dim and dark; that was the tree of death]. It is this change, though, that perhaps points most clearly to the cause of these momentous and barely paralleled rewritings of Christian doctrine. We have earlier seen pp. 29, 113, 131) that if there was one theme no Old English poet could resist, it was that of choice and decision—a feeling that energises the heroic dilemmas of Hengest or Ingeld as well as the warnings of *Bede's Death Song* and the 'elegies', and the conversion-scenes of religious epic. The results of choice, even when made in ignorance, preoccupied many poets as part of the overall sense of the 'ironies of time' and the awareness of transience; we can see this in Hygelac (pp. 34–5) or in Nebuchadnezzar (p. 146). To this impulse the Saxon writer of *Genesis B* seems to have offered little resistance. He makes the Fall of Man into a familiar situation, a feud begun with every excuse and even warning, but one whose consequences are, just the same, inescapable. God is not to be blamed; for, as the poet observes ruefully:

> Bið þam men full wa
> þe hine ne warnað   þonne he his geweald hafað!   (634–5)

[Sorry is the man who does not warn himself while he has the power!]

Yet criticism of Adam and Eve is minimised, even if their responsibility is not. Furthermore, their choice between the trees is presented (again with a certain independence) as only a part of the eternal choice of all men. The two trees stand in the Garden:

> þæt þær yldo bearn   moste on ceosan
> godes and yfeles,   gumena æghwilc,
> welan and wawan.   Næs se wæstm gelic!   (464–6)

[so that the children of men, and every man, could choose, of good and evil, of prosperity and sorrow. Their fruit was not the same!]

The thought is similar to that of the *Death Song*, of Cynewulf's *Elene* 605–8 and 621–6, of *Christ* 889–98, and of more diffuse scenes in many places. A powerful sense of the irrecoverability of fact and decision informs them all, and keeps this poet in particular from changing surprise into complaint. Indeed, though it may ignore such problems as the loss of innocence and birth of sin, it does add a feeling for the long perspectives of time to the single and pivotal moment of the Fall:

> He æt þam wife onfeng
> helle and hinnsið, þeah hit nære haten swa (717–18)

[He received Hell and death from the woman, though it was not called that]

In most of these respects, no source or analogue for *Genesis B* has ever been found, though the otherwise stiffly orthodox Alcuin of York surprisingly repeats the idea of the opposing nature of the two trees—an aberration carefully excised by Ælfric, when he translated Alcuin's work into Old English.[29] It is certainly possible that a learned source did exist, and a 'minimising' account of the Fall may even have been topical at some time in ninth-century Saxony.[30] Still, there should be no doubt that the nature of vernacular narrative was an even greater shaping force, on this poem as on much of *Exodus* and *Daniel*, and even parts of *Genesis A*—a force not necessarily palpable or even irresistible, but powerfully insidious, causing Anglo-Saxons and Continental Saxons not only to write their poems, but also, we may feel, to read their Bibles, within the framework of their own, familiar cultural references.

As has happened before, overall valuation of this group of poems does not come easily. In recent years their differences from each other have been more obvious than their similarities. Yet there is one feature common to all of them, something that is most readily apparent from any comparison with the last poem in the manuscript, *Christ and Satan*.[31] Though in many ways even a slavishly conventional poem, this does two things that the others do not: first, it asserts a thematic connection between widely separated events—the Fall of the Angels, the Harrowing of Hell, the Temptation of Christ in the Wilderness; second, it shows the poet very ready to address his readers directly, and to draw 'applications' from the events he is telling. Of course there *are* themes in the other poems—the Covenant in *Exodus,* the cycles of pride and downfall in *Daniel*—but that similarity only points the difference more acutely. The four poets of the earlier part of this manuscript seem more willing to allow their stories to speak for themselves, drawing only such conclusions from them as are most obvious from the events recorded. They are all 'devoted to the story as story',[32] concerned less with the 'Why?' of events than with the 'How?' It is this quality which has made the poems resistant to allegorical or figural readings. It is not that the poets were ignorant, heretical, or proto-Protestant, but that they were imbued with a passion well described by William James: 'the passion

for distinguishing . . . the impulse to be *acquainted* with the parts
rather than to comprehend the whole'. The poets prefer 'any amount
of incoherence, abruptness and fragmentariness (so long as the
literal details of the separate facts are saved) to an abstract way of
conceiving things that, while it simplifies them, dissolves away at the
same time their concrete fulness'.[33] A grip on facts, however rambling,
has been put before that skeletal coherence so often produced by
(modern) figurative interpretations; and this deserves to be recognised
as an acceptable variety of religious experience. It is something like
this, moreover, which has led several sensitive critics to detect an
'instinctive historical sense' in early English poetry,[34] seeing it in
such original and remarkable moments as the sudden vivid flash of
description, in *Exodus*, of the unplumbed sea-bottom revealed by
the parting of the waters but never seen by men before or since. Even
at this moment of crisis the poet is fascinated by the instant of discovery set against an almost completely hidden past. Such a frame of
mind did not perhaps altogether disappear with the Conquest.
Beryl Smalley, discussing a later period, noted how often English
medieval churchmen swerved towards a linguistic, informative,
historical interpretation of the Bible, often pedantic but also prag-
matic in ways alien to the dominant traditions of Paris or Rome; she,
too, thought of *Exodus* as an early example.[35] Arguments from
'national character' are of course unpopular, but national cultures do
exist, and show a considerable power of resistance to change. It might
not be too far-fetched to suggest that the Junius poems are in the end
less inaccessible to modern English readers than are, say, the works of
St Augustine.

POETRY AND THE INDIVIDUAL:

CYNEWULF

Some in this task
Take off the Cypress vail, but leave a mask,
Changing the Latine, but do more obscure
That sense in English which was bright and pure.
So of Translators they are Authors grown.

MARVELL, To his worthy Friend Doctor Witty

The anonymity of most Old English poetry does not seem to be merely historic accident. It is as if the poets had felt a certain delicacy about adding their names to poems so extensively public and traditional, their composition drawing also on forces for which no single individual could take full credit. That this anonymity was breached, probably sometime in the ninth century,[1] by the name of Cynwulf or Cynewulf, might therefore be a fact of some importance. W. P. Lehmann saw in it 'the shift to a reading audience', and compared it to the similar identification of the German monk Otfrid of Weissenburg,[2] whose Old High German poem on the life of Christ was a genuine turning-point in its introduction of rhyme and regularised Latin metre. Others, arguing from the same premise, have felt that Cynewulf's 'signing' of his poems symbolises not only a point of change but also a point of decline—that his work, in part at least, 'comes at the end of a period', bringing Old English poetry 'into a blind alley'.[3] There is no doubt that the Old English tradition reached a point of decline somewhere. But one might find reason to deny that it is Cynewulf alone who 'marks the spot', both in considering the fact of his work and the symbol of his 'signatures'.

To begin with, Cynewulf's method of giving his name at the end of his poems is clearly not entirely that of a man who thinks of his work in a literary context. Otfrid of Weissenburg, the German rhymer, gave his name acrostically, beginning the first line of one of his prefaces with S . . . the second with A . . ., and so on till he had spelt out (among much else) the legend SALOMONI EPISCOPO OTFRIDUS [Otfrid, to Bishop Salomon]. This device is of course much more comprehensible on paper than read aloud. Cynewulf, however, embedded his name in poetry through the use of runes, and in three cases out of four used the runes syllabically rather than alphabetically.[4] Thus the 'signature' of his section of the poem *Christ* runs as follows:

> Þonne ·ᚻ· cwacað, gehyreð cyning mæðlan,
> rodera ryhtend, sprecan reþe word
> þam þe him ær in worulde wace hyrdon,
> þendan ·ᚱ· ond ᛏ· yþast meahtan
> frofre findan. Þær sceal forht monig
> on þam wongstede werig bidan
> hwæt him æfter dædum deman wille
> wraþra wita. Biþ se ·ᚹ· scæcen
> eorþan frætwa. ·ᚢ· wæs longe
> ·ᛚ· flodum bilocen, lifwynna dæl,
> ·ᚠ· on foldan. Þonne frætwe sculon
> byrnan on bæle . . .   (797–808)

Here the name is certainly spelt out— ᚻᚱᛏᚹᚢᛚᚠ , or CYNWULF. But the poetry also makes a kind of sense. To understand it, one needs to know that Germanic runemasters employed a system (rather like our modern radio-alphabets) by which each runic letter not only had a name, but could also stand as an abbreviation for that name; and as it happens, the letter-names survive, carefully-defined, in the *Rune Poem* of the Otho B. x manuscript.[5] To take a clear example of one of the runes used in the 'signature' above, this *Rune Poem* informs us that

> ᛏ byþ nearu on breostan, weorþeþ hi ðeah oft niþa bearnum
> to helpe ond to hæle gehwæþre, gif hi his hlystaþ æror (27–8)

[ᛏ is constricting in the heart, yet it often becomes a help and luck to the children of men, if they are aware of it in time]

The alliteration of this (incidentally rather characteristic) proverb shows that the ᛏ-rune stands for N; and the word that fits best, here and elsewhere, is NYD, 'Distress' or 'Necessity', as Cynewulf clearly intended his readers, or listeners, to recognise. With other runic definitions, unfortunately, he was bound to have more trouble, for the context of Judgment Day, which he is describing at the end of his part of the *Christ*, could hardly accommodate some of the objects familiar to the pagan world of early runic inscriptions. The ᚢ-rune, for example, appears to stand for UR, 'a bison or aurochs', a word never found in Old English, and guessed at here only through Continental analogues and the *Rune Poem*'s description,

> ᚢ byþ anmod and oferhyrned,
> felafrecne deor, feohteþ mid hornum,
> mære morstapa; þæt is modig wuht (4–6)

['The bison' is brave and horned, a daring animal that fights with its horns, a notable moor-strider; that is a bold beast]

Obviously bisons and Doomsday hardly fit together; and the same is true for the ᚳ-rune, *cen,* 'a torch', and the ᚣ-rune, *yr*, 'a bow'. Probably Cynewulf did not leave these to be taken as inappropriate or nonsense-syllables, but assumed they could be replaced by other and more common words—for instance *cene* 'a brave man' for *cen* 'a torch', *yfel* or *yrmþu* 'evil' or 'poverty' for *yr* 'a bow', and the possessive pronoun *ure* 'our' for *ur* 'the aurochs'.[6] By accepting these compromises one can reach a sensible version of the 'signature' quoted above, something to this effect: 'Then (the brave man) trembles, hears the King, the heavens' Ruler, judge and speak harsh words to those who had obeyed him feebly in the world, when (poverty) and (distress) could most easily find comfort. There many a man shall be afraid, waiting sadly on that plain for what bitter torments shall be judged him for his deeds. (The joy) of earthly treasures has gone; for a long time (our) share of joys in this life was enclosed by (sea) floods, all the (wealth) of the world.[7] Then the treasures shall burn in the fire . . .'* And Cynewulf goes on to describe the destruction of the earth, to urge his audience to take warning while there is time, and to compare life to a dangerous sea-voyage that may end in a heavenly harbour—ideas, of course, that are all quite familiar from other Old English poems.

The evidence of the 'signatures' could, then, be turned several ways. In Anglo-Saxon times they would not have to be seen on paper to be understood. A man who knew what words Cynewulf had accepted for his rune-symbols could easily read the pieces out as poetry, to be

* To sum up, the runes used in the 'signature', with their sounds, names, and probable meanings, are respectively:

ᚳ, C, *cene*, a brave man (?)
ᚣ, Y, *yrmþu*, poverty (?)
ᚾ, N, *nyd.* distress or necessity
ᚹ, W, *wynn*, joy
ᚢ, U, *ure*, our (?)
ᛚ, L, *lagu*, sea
ᚠ, F. *feoh*, wealth or property

Four of these are obvious and unchallenged, the other three more doubtful. In two 'signatures' the ᛖ-rune, E, *eoh*, a horse, is added.

understood by all; while those literate people who were 'in the know' (or alerted by a warning from the poet, as happens in *The Fates of the Apostles*, lines 96–8), would also be able to interpret the runes alphabetically and spell out the poet's name. It is possible that Cynewulf intended his poetry for an audience of mixed literacy, and very probable that he did not intend it for private and silent reading alone. Meanwhile, he certainly relied on ancient and native runic techniques (except in the poem *Juliana*), and he also shows at times a turn of thought characteristic of the rest of the Old English poetic tradition. All in all, though the idea of 'signing' poems was certainly novel, it need not be treated as a sign of imminent modernity, a death-portent for the traditional style, or a mark of the conscious and deliberate artist. Cynewulf's motive in inserting his name, after all, was not pride in his work but a desire to be remembered in prayers; and in spite of his undeniable authorship of four poems, it is fair to say that they give no clue to his personality. Just as much as the anonymous poets of *Beowulf* or *Daniel* or *The Wanderer*, Cynewulf allowed himself to be guided by the potentialities, and the defects, of an established style and narrative mode.

Nevertheless, to have four poems *(Elene, Juliana, Christ II*, and *The Fates of the Apostles)*, known beyond doubt to be by the same man, is of the utmost importance to any study of Old English verse or of traditional epics in general. It gives a unique opportunity to see where, in an orally-based and highly schematised technique, the line between fixed tradition and the individual skill is to be drawn— the more so as the three longer poems, *Elene, Juliana* and *Christ II*, all have well-known but fairly diverse Latin sources. Are there any poetic qualities that deserve to be called 'Cynewulfian'? If they exist, how far are these genuinely original and individual? To answer these questions one need no longer consider the once-popular speculations as to whether Cynewulf wrote any other of our surviving poems without actually 'signing' them, since these have been all but totally disproved.[8] Instead, the composite poem *Christ* can be used with some confidence for a comparative analysis.

This poem, the first, the longest, and in some ways the most impressive poem of the *Exeter Book,* falls into three distinct sections, marked in the manuscript by punctuation, double spacing, and large capitals, so that they 'may be interpreted either as separate poems or as parts of a single poem'.[9] They deal with Christ's *Advent*, His *Ascension*, and His second coming at *Doomsday*, and relate to each other very much as do the separate panels of a triptych (for which these three occurrences were a common artistic motif). The section 'signed' by Cynewulf is the second, the *Ascension*. But it is noticeable that the poem, like its source, a part of Gregory the Great's 29th homily on the Gospels,[10] begins with a reference to the Nativity and ends with a reminder of Doomsday. One cannot tell how the three Old English poems were fitted together; but if any of the three poets concerned wrote in awareness of the others' work, it is likely to have been Cynewulf, possibly selecting his source deliberately to bridge the gap between the other two sections. His free handling of the source, however, is revealing, for Gregory's homily is a very fine example of that 'figural' conception of reality discussed earlier (see pp. 136–7), in which all events of the Bible are seen as intimately connected, and which assumes also that the events and their cross-references have meanings not apparent immediately, but directed to the faith of believers hundreds of years in the future. The rather hesitant reactions of the 'Cædmonian' poets to such possibilities have already been discussed, and seen as justified. But it is important (though for many modern readers difficult) to realise that this bent towards allegory and interpretation is not merely aberrant and pedantic, but often oddly attractive, even in purely literary terms. The dominant quality of Gregory's homily, perhaps unexpectedly, is a serious, deliberate, passionate *wit*, occasionally reminiscent of English seventeenth-century poetry. His method is actively to seek out discrepancies and difficulties in Gospel texts (here Mark xvi, 14–20), in order to resolve them on a higher level through allegory and metaphor. So, in this text, Christ orders the apostles to preach *omni creaturae* [to every creature]. Does that mean what it says, asks Gregory, i.e. to rocks and plants and animals? No, he argues, it means only 'to all men', but is important as a reminder that mankind resembles but consummates all other aspects of creation. Again, Christ promises that those who act in His name shall cast out devils, and speak with tongues, and take up serpents, and heal the sick. Instead of accepting this promise literally—as do some extremist sects in our own day—Gregory admits that believers in his day can do no such things, but holds this to be further proof that Christ spoke allegorically. To take up serpents, he suggests, is to drive malice out of others' hearts through friendly counsel; those who help others through their own good example are healing the (spiritually) sick; those who leave their old lives to preach of God's power are genuinely speaking with new tongues; and so on. Furthermore, quoting Matthew vii, 22–3, he even turns the tables by saying that those who ask fruitlessly on Judgment Day 'have we not prophesied in thy name? and in thy name have cast out devils?' will indeed be those who have done these miraculous things physically, but not spiritually; they will be doctors and psychologists, we may say, rather than priests. The whole account urges one to read the Bible not as narrative but as plan, its basic and preliminary paradox being the laudable doubt of

Thomas: *Ille etenim dubitando vulnerum cicatrices tetigit, et de nostro pectore dubietatis vulnus amputavit* [For he touched the scars of wounds doubtingly, and (by so doing) he cut from our heart the wound of doubt itself]. Thomas was *meant* to doubt, for in his doubt was summed up and dispersed that of future ages; no event is without its parallels and its signification, even Christ's Ascension being the culmination of a series of 'prefigurings' from the Old Testament begun by Enoch and Elias. Persuasive, flexible, intelligent, the whole homily is a masterpiece of metaphoric logic.

In many ways one could hardly expect any Old English poet to reproduce this source at all fully. Gregory was writing for an audience not just intelligent, but also knowledgeable and sophisticated. He could assume that his quotations would be recognised even with an unfamiliar twist to them; he could present a distinction between the *coelum aereum* and the *coelum æthereum* [the aerial and ethereal heavens] and expect it to be understood; most of all, he could rely on his readers to grasp the major point of his wit—that is, the simultaneous perception of (spiritual) similarity and (physical) dissimilarity. None of this is really imaginable for an Anglo-Saxon poet or audience. Yet Cynewulf did not turn his back entirely on the multiple meanings of the 'figural' view. He used them, though, not instructively, to resolve contradictions, but emotionally, to express the sense of universal rescue and triumph caused by the single fact of Christ's Resurrection and Ascension. His adjuration to the reader is therefore not the relatively cool one of Gregory, 'Hence, dearest brothers, it is necessary for us to follow Him there in our hearts where we believe Him to have ascended in the body'. Instead, Cynewulf makes the demand *modcræfte sec þurh sefan snyttro, þæt þu soð wite hu þæt geeode* [seek shrewdly through wisdom of the mind, so that you may know truly how it happened]—advice focusing as usual on the power of facts, but also requiring insight into their hidden meanings.

To take only one example, Cynewulf goes on from that insistent beginning to take up a single (rather quibbling) point from Gregory and expatiate on its eternal meaning. Gregory had observed that angels appeared at the Ascension dressed in white garments, according to Acts i, 10, but that this is not said of the angels who appeared at the Nativity. The reason, he says, is that the white clothing of the Ascension expresses joy at seeing the Resurrection of a fleshly body, i.e. *humanitas exaltata* [humanity exalted], while this joy would be out of place at the entry of the Son of God into mortality, i.e. *divinitas humiliata* [divinity humiliated]. Cynewulf notes this discrepancy twice, but never actually troubles to explain it. What he does is to pick up the idea of angelic jubilation and to

express it in a series of aggressive and triumphant speeches, not
directly introduced but seemingly spoken by the angels themselves.
These speeches turn, not on description or explanation, but on a
sense of the contrasts of time, passing not simply from Nativity to
Ascension (as with Gregory) but through all epochs, from remote
past to immediate present. The second speech turns obviously on a
series of time-words, as the angel comments on what has happened
in the moment of Christ's Ascension:

> 'Hafað *nu* se halga   helle bireafod
> ealles þæs gafoles   þe hi geardagum
> in þæt orlege   unryhte swealg.
> *Nu* sind forcumene   ond in cwicsusle
> gehynde ond gehæfte,   in helle grund
> duguþum bidæled,   deofla cempan.
> Ne meahtan wiþerbrogan   wige spowan,
> wæpna wyrpum,   *siþþan* wuldres cyning,
> heofonrices helm,   hilde gefremede
> wiþ his ealdfeondum   anes meahtum,
> þær he of hæfte ahlod   huþa mæste
> of feonda byrig,   folces unrim,
> þisne ilcan þreat   þe ge her on stariað.
> Wile *nu* gesecan   sawla nergend
> gæsta giefstol,   godes agen bearn,
> æfter guðplegan.   *Nu* ge geare cunnon
> hwæt se hlaford is   se þisne here lædeð,
> *nu* ge fromlice   freondum togeanes
> gongað glædmode'   (558–76)

['Now the holy one has harrowed Hell of all the tribute it swallowed
unrighteously in that contest in far-off days. Now are the devils' champions
overcome, bound and fixed in living torment, bereft of their hosts, in the
depths of Hell. Nor could the adversaries succeed in war by cast of
weapons, once the glorious King, Protector of Heaven, made war against
his ancient enemies through the power of One, when He led from captivity,
the stronghold of their enemies, the greatest of bands, uncounted people,
this same troop that you look at here. Now God's own child, Saviour of
souls, will seek the throne of spirits after battle. Now you know well what
the Lord is who leads this army, now go cheerfully and gladly to your
friends']

This speech is based directly on nothing in the Bible or in Gregory,
and as with Moses' speech in *Exodus* one is left to infer what is
happening from what is said.[11] The angel appears to be explaining a
vision of the Harrowing of Hell to the assembled disciples, looking
back on a climactic battle and seeing it as a final proof of divine
power ('*nu ge geare cunnon*') in the manner especially congenial to

F

Old English poets. What is, however, remarkable is the way in which each of the five 'now's' refers to a slightly different time or place and develops a different aspect of the same action. The speech begins with the idea of vengeance, the Harrowing as counter-stroke for the Fall of Man, far off in the depths of time but never forgotten by God or the devils. The next 'now' shows the *effect* of that stroke—the devils fettered from the moment of Christ's incursion; still fettered as the angel speaks; and indeed fettered 'now', as Cynewulf writes. The long third sentence, with its subordinate clauses introduced by *siþþan* and *þær*, jumps back to a fractionally earlier time, when the devils still tried to resist. But it also relates three reflections of the same event—Christ's attack (in the *siþþan*-clause), mankind's relief (in the *þær*-clause), the devils' frustration (in the main clause); while at the end the word *her* reminds us of the apostles watching the vision in amazement. Many emotions are pulled together in the sentence—surprise, relief, defeat—but all contribute essentially to the sense of power and the angel's own implacable delight. The speech turns next to the future, with Christ's intended return to Heaven, and then to the result which this speech and its proclamation of victory should bring to those who are listening, both the angel's audience and Cynewulf's. Now they know who their Lord is, let them abandon former despair. All along, we receive a profound impression, not merely a description, of that *humanitas exaltata* which Gregory saw in the Ascension. Or, if one preferred to find a native and heroic word for the same thing, to match Cynewulf's own heroic vocabulary and syntax, one might say that the disciples' misery and the angel's joy, the apparent victory of death and its real defeat, are contrasted here to express the suddenness of change in a moment of universal *edhwyrft* [reversal]. Certainly the 'perspectivism' and sensitivity to time of heroic poetry have penetrated this speech in a manner quite alien to Gregory. Yet this has been used for the same ends as Gregory's rather tamer temporal comparisons.

Further perspectives are introduced as that speech draws to its end, relating the events of A.D. 33 to Cynewulf's own ninth-century present. The angel ends with a timeless assertion in the present tense:

'Wær is ætsomne
godes ond monna,   gæsthalig treow'   (583–4)

['There is a pledge together between God and men, a sacred agreement']

And this is picked up by a sudden return to the first person, the author himself drawing the conclusion that as a result of what has happened every man now alive has the freedom to choose—

swa helle hienþu   swa heofones mærþu,
swa þæt leohte leoht   swa þa laþan niht,
swa þrymmes þræce   swa þystra wræce . . .
swa lif swa deað,   swa him leofre bið   (591–6)

[either the disgrace of Hell or the glory of Heaven, either the radiant
light or the hateful night, either the throng of glory or the misery of
darkness . . . either life or death, whichever is dearer to him]

But these conclusions are so familiar from other Old English poems—
say, the enthusiasm for a covenant in *Exodus* or *Daniel*, or the
delight in decision from *Genesis B* or *Andreas*—that they raise the
question how far, in these passages with their display of control over
time, Cynewulf was writing independently. Is his response to and
amplification of Gregory's homily not in some ways a characteristic
one, differing certainly from the 'Cædmonian' poems in its unconcern
for human history, but resembling them in its dedication to the
explanation of unseen chains of cause and effect? Probably this is
true. And one might add that if the qualities displayed so far in
Christ II are to be called 'Cynewulfian', then there are indeed several
'Cynewulfian' poems in existence other than those actually written by
him. Both *Christ I* and *The Dream of the Rood*, for example, show a
distinctly similar ability to turn theology into drama through
complex series of repeated contrasts.

Of these two poems, the 'Advent lyrics' of *Christ I* deserve a prior
mention as being less well known (though they have recently been
receiving some deservedly close attention).[12] This first section of
the *Christ*-poem is divided into twelve parts, most of them based on
liturgical Antiphons, that is, phrases sung during church services
before the celebration of Christmas and consisting essentially of
a description of Christ and an appeal to Him to descend to mankind.
The one underlying the start of the Old English poem, for instance,
runs: *'O rex gentium et desideratus earum, lapisque angularis qui facis
utraque unum: veni, et salva hominem quem de limo formasti'* ['O
King of nations and their desire, cornerstone who make both one,
come and save man whom you formed from slime']. Phrases of this
kind the Old English poet expands to some 20–70 lines, using, as we
now know, a highly developed knowledge of the network of prophecy
and metaphor from which the Latin Antiphons themselves originated,
and using it to great purpose. The poem works very largely through
its sudden shifts of style and setting, unexplained and violent, which
nevertheless gradually reveal themselves to be centred on one and
the same thing. In the sixth and seventh appeals, for example (lines
149ff.), we move from the tormented cry of the patriarchs in Hell
before Christ's coming, *'Bring us hælolif, werigum witeþeowum'*

['Bring us salvation, weary slaves of pain'], to a realistic and earthly scene between Joseph and Mary, as he too wonders what is to be done, faced by the shame of Mary's seeming faithlessness. The two scenes, one of timeless frustrated knowledge, the other of almost homely bafflement, seem to have nothing in common. Yet both the patriarchs and Joseph are saved from their different predicaments by Christ; and Mary, as she explains to Joseph, says also *'ic his tempel eam'* ['I am his temple'], and so takes the reader back to the start, where Christ is the 'cornerstone', the *weallstan þe ða wyrhtan iu wiðwurpon to weorce* [wallstone that the makers once rejected from the work]. Now He completes the temple, seen simultaneously as Mary; as the *healle mærre* [great hall] of the Church; as the *leomo læmena* [earthy limbs] of the human body—all three now changed, perfected, and saved. As the poem continues, divided and impulsive as it seems, the reader becomes more and more aware of such hidden symbolic unities, and is possessed by the vast importance of the single event that relates them—Christ's fleshly Advent, with its paradoxes of damnation become salvation, Divinity become Humanity, birth from a Virgin, the separation and the unity of Son and Father. It is not too much to say that this is one of the most moving and most intellectually appealing of all Christmas poems in any variety of English.

Nevertheless, there is no need to think of the poem as created entirely cerebrally (as Robert B. Burlin generally does in his valuable 'typological commentary' on it).[13] The poet's learning is obvious. But he may not have needed a set and predetermined plan. The traditional symbolism surrounding the Advent is so dense that one feels that the poet could—like some modern novelists—have arranged his parts in almost any order, and that they would *still* have been mutually illuminating. Moreover, the 'simultaneous perspectives' and 'penetration of consciousness' that Burlin rightly sees in the *Advent* bear such a close similarity to the techniques of the *Ascension* and indeed to much other non-figural Old English verse that one might see them partly as a product of verse-technique as well as of religious learning. It is, again, probably no accident that *The Dream of the Rood,* also a learned and dramatic poem, is marked above all else by the stylistic device of the *communicatio idiomatum,*[14] that is, a very close connection of apparent opposites: as, *Geseah ic weruda God þearle þenian* [I saw the Lord of Hosts *severely stretched*], or, *Aledon hie þær limwerigne . . . beheoldon hie þær heofones Dryhten* [there they laid down the limb-weary man . . . there they saw Heaven's Lord]. From start to finish, and on several stylistic levels, the *Dream* is characterised by its sudden changes of scale and its readiness to present events in several aspects—the Cross as resplendent throne and instrument of torture; Christ as king and victim; the Dreamer as sinner and saved.[15] No doubt it was shaped by the doctrines of its time; but one might think also that these were expressed so well because they corresponded to a technique of wide-ranging but understated contrast already inherent in the nature of Old English poetry.

To sum up, Cynewulf's second part of the *Christ* shows a remarkably powerful response to the religious parallels, at times recondite, of his source, the homily by Gregory. Nevertheless, the poet's ability to see many things in one event, and to pull together disparate times and situations with sudden and effective force, is not quite unique, and may have been partly instinctive; in both *The Dream of the Rood* and *Christ I* we can see something of the same *wræclic wrixl* [miraculous interchange].[16] Cynewulf's true originality lies in an area perhaps less immediately exciting, but in the long run not less effective—his control over extended patterns of syntax.

For instance, in spite of all the merits of the *Advent* poem, one is aware of a difference immediately one reads the first few lines of Cynewulf's *Ascension*:

> Nu ðu geornlice   gæstgerynum,
> mon se mæra,   modcræfte sec
> þurh sefan snyttro,   *þæt* þu soð wite
> *hu* þæt geeode, *þa* se ælmihtiga
> acenned wearð   þurh clænne had,
> *siþþan* he Marian,   mægða weolman,
> mærre meowlan,   mundheals geceas,
> *þæt* þær in hwitum   hræglum gewerede
> englas ne oðeowdun,   *þa* se æþeling cwom,
> beorn in Betlem   (440–9)

[Now, famous man, seek eagerly and shrewdly through wisdom of the mind, in spiritual mysteries, so that you may know truly how it happened that, when the Almighty was born in a pure manner, after he had chosen the protection of Mary, the famous maiden, flower of women, the angels did not appear there enclosed in white garments, when the Prince came, the Warrior to Bethlehem]

In this sentence a string of six subordinate clauses, of five different types, is set out with unnoticed skill, the poet never losing his way or allowing the variations appropriate to poetry to interrupt his progress. The conjunctions have been italicised; and with this as a guide, one can see also the device of contrast between the two *þa*-clauses, one stressing the birth of a child, the other the entry of a potentate. The achievement perhaps does not seem striking—though it is harder to write a complex connected sentence than it perhaps looks. But control of this kind does give Cynewulf's poetry

a consistent neatness and variety denied as a rule to the *Advent*
poem and at times painfully absent in the last section of *Christ*, the
poem on *Doomsday*.[17] Its effect is pervasive, more obvious in the
breach than in the observance. Still, the feature has been recognised,
if not analysed, by almost everyone, leading to a general agreement
that Cynewulf's style is 'classic', and that it is also 'the style of a
man trained to read and write Latin, to admire the orderly progress
of a Latin sentence, and to prefer its clarity to the tangled profusion
of the native style'.[18] There is more than a touch of 'faint praise'
about these (and similar) remarks, an assumption that even in this,
the one area where Cynewulf's poetry can easily be distinguished
from the rest of Old English verse, the poet must still be in some way
derivative. No doubt a knowledge of Latin did make a considerable
impact on Cynewulf as on other writers. But it is worth noting that
his syntactic control is generally much *greater* than that, at least, of
his immediate sources, themselves at times not free from the banal
and the unsophisticated. Even when Cynewulf is following a Latin
model very closely, he habitually tidies it up without any false
modesty—as for instance in his translation of *Elene*. Here the hero,
Judas Quiriacus, is praying that God may reveal the whereabouts of
the Cross, hidden for many years. In the Latin saint's life, he is
betrayed into a rather unfortunate argumentative delay. *'Et nunc,
Domine',* he says, *'si tua voluntas est regnare filium Mariae, qui
missus est a te (nisi autem fuisset ex te, non tantas virtutes fecisset:
nisi vero tuus puer esset, non suscitares eum a mortuis) fac nobis,
Domine, prodigium hoc.'* ['And now, Lord, if it is Your will that the
son of Mary should reign, who was sent by You (if he had not been
from You, he would not have done so many brave deeds: if he had
not been your son, You would not have raised him from the dead)
perform, Lord, this miracle for us.'] Obviously a quite trivial re-
arrangement would avoid the long delay in the middle. But Cynewulf
keeps it, while trying to rearrange it artistically. The parenthesis
above runs as follows:

> '(gif he þin nære
> sunu synna leas,   næfre he soðra swa feala
> in woruldrice   wundra gefremede
> dogorgerimum;   no ðu of deaðe hine
> swa þrymlice,   þeoda wealdend,
> aweahte for weorodum,   gif he in wuldre þin
> þurh ða beorhtan   bearn ne wære)'   (776–82)

['if he was not Your son without sins, he would never have performed so
many true wonders in the world during his lifetime, nor, Ruler of peoples,
would You have raised him so mightily from death before the companies
if he had not been Your child in glory through the bright Virgin']

One notes that the order is now chiastic, i.e. that the two *gif*-clauses are at beginning and end, with the two main clauses in the centre, while furthermore a quite new distinction has been introduced, the contrast of *woruld* and *wuldor*, earth and Heaven, both supplying arguments for Christ's status as the Son of God. The result is a rather striking double argument and reassertion of the main point. But this has been constructed by Cynewulf, quite deliberately, on the basis of what may have been the Latin author's mistake or at best infelicity! Similar rearrangements are not uncommon. They do not catch the eye. It is all too easy, for example, to read straight through this fine concealed parallel in *The Fates of the Apostles* and never notice its force:

> Æðele sceoldon
> ðurh wæpenhete　weorc þrowigan,
> sigelean secan,　ond þone soðan gefean　　　　　(79–81)

[Through armed hatred the noble ones had to suffer torment (but by so doing) to seek the victor's reward and true joy];

or, equally, to miss the summary force of the last chiasmus in the empress Elene's speech to the Jews:

> 'Ne magon ge ða word geseðan　þe ge hwile nu on unriht
> wrigon under womma sceatum,　ne magon ge þa wyrd
> 　　　　　　　　　　　　　　　　bemiðan,
> bedyrnan þa deopan mihte'　　　　　　　　　　(582–4)

['You cannot prove the words which you have for a long time now concealed wrongly beneath the surface of your sins, you cannot conceal those events, darken that profound strength']

Yet such devices are neither sparse nor accidental. Cynewulf's deliberating intelligence is apparent, and however great the background influence of Latin literature upon him, it is clear that he put its lessons to work *within* a native tradition of rhetoric, relying hardly at all on the style of his originals.[19]

Once again, it is this deep and multi-levelled influence of style which enables Cynewulf to vary his material. Like the *Andreas*-poet, he makes something of what might easily have been depressingly poor stories, the saints' lives of *Elene* and *Juliana*, his longest works. Both these poems are translations, their (proximate) sources now among the gigantic collection of the *Acta Sanctorum*, the 'deeds of saints'.[20] Even to look at the thousands of closely printed Latin pages in this collection makes one realise what a prolific form hagiography once was. Yet the popularity of such stories can seem inexplicable. Too many of them show a totally uncritical attitude to the miraculous, and are debased by a respect for spiritual success alone which transforms central characters into superhuman heroes, whose indifference to pain deprives them of visible courage and whose contempt for their opponents leaves them without any sign of charity. The legend of Juliana turns particularly in this direction, while that of Helena and the *Inventio Crucis* has in addition a potentially unpleasant alliance of ferocious piety and imperial power. Yet though Cynewulf translates these stories (as has been seen) at times with remarkable fidelity, he also bends them away from their dangerous naïveté through methods with which we are by now familiar. His technique, essentially, is to build up the forces of evil from the inadequacy of the Latin originals to a state in which, though finally overcome by miracles, they have a reasonable being and a certain strength. The poems turn into choices, conflicts of will, in which the side of right is exalted only through its demonstrations of power, after challenge.

These changes have been noticed before with regard to *Juliana*. Claes Schaar observed that in the Latin life (as we have it) the virgin martyr first attempted to evade marriage with the pagan governor by making false stipulations—that he would have to be promoted before she would marry him.[21] Cynewulf (if he had exactly this version before him) cut out the procrastination and made the pagan Heliseus, as well as Juliana's father Africanus, into figures of rigid and powerful ferocity, who have to be defied publicly, and whose aim from start to finish is to break Juliana's will, *mod oncyrran, fæmnan forepanc . . . gewitt onwendan* [to change her spirit, the girl's intention . . . alter her understanding]. In *Elene*, though, a similar clash is reached more elaborately and with rather greater difficulty—for in the basic story there is almost no contest to be found. The Roman emperor Constantine is converted to Christianity; he despatches his mother Helena to Jerusalem to find the True Cross; she interrogates the Jews and especially their main representative Judas Quiriacus, until he breaks down, confesses that he knows of Christ, and is miraculously aided to recover the Cross. Since neither the Jews nor Judas actually knows where the Cross is, the interrogation seems oddly irrelevant, and the true point of the story may have been only to rehearse the arguments for Christ's reality, and to demonstrate the path of conversion, first with the pagan Constantine and then with the Jew Judas Quiriacus. In all these respects Cynewulf and his Latin source are in agreement; but though it has been argued that there is little originality in *Elene*, Cynewulf has in fact made a series of changes of emphasis in his poem.[22]

The most obvious of these are the 'Anglo-Saxonisms' connected, not with battle and sea-voyages, but with the theme of darkness and mystery opposed to the searching power of wisdom. This crops up in the most unexpected places. In the Latin, after his victory Constantine enquires what the cross-sign stands for, and as one might expect in the year A.D. 233[23] finds many ready to tell him. In the Old English poem, however, this knowledge is reserved to *þa wisestan* [the wisest men], who explain themselves moreover through *gæstgerynum* [spiritual mysteries]. In the same way, the empress's narrowing-down of the Jews from three thousand to one thousand to five hundred to one becomes a peeling-off of layers of darkness down to the man who can *'onwreon wyrda geryno . . . æriht from orde oð ende forð'* ['reveal the mystery of events . . . the Law from its beginning through to the end']. A basis for this is always present in the Latin. But the references to wisdom and folly are in the Old English all-devouring; even the Crucifixion becomes not a matter of destiny but a willed rejection of the truth, for the Jews *'nahton foreþances, wisdomes gewitt'* ['had no forethought, no understanding of wisdom']. What hangs in the balance, then, is not so much the finding of the Cross as the acceptance or refusal, in single minds, of what is known to be true—in Judas's case an internal struggle against racial and filial piety, a bludgeoning of his *own* will. This gives great power to some of his speeches, where Cynewulf could operate most freely—in particular the start of Judas's long, foreboding address to the other Jews in lines 419–35 (where he first confesses that he knows what the empress wants), and also his speech of refusal to her, when, seeing both earthly and heavenly life threatened for him, he nevertheless perseveres with sullen heroism in a bad cause:

> 'Hu mæg ic þæt findan   þæt swa fyrn gewearð
> wintra gangum?   Is nu worn sceacen,
> tu hund oððe ma   geteled rime.
> Ic ne mæg areccan,   nu ic þæt rim ne can . . .'   (632–5)

['How *can* I find that which happened so far off in the course of years? A great many have now passed, two hundred or more, counted by number. I cannot declare it when I do not know the number . . .']

In such speeches a powerful sense of obscurity through the passage of time is generated. It joins with the repeated images of burial and darkness to express the determination of the empress's penetration, and the strength of her enemies' resistance.

Perhaps typically, the poem's main turning-point, Judas's break-down and confession, is then treated quite curtly in eighteen lines (691–708). After a week's starvation Judas gives in to the empress's demand that he should abandon his lies and make known the truth,

F*

and delivers a speech acknowledging not only that he can bear no
more but also that he

> 'ær mid dysige   þurhdrifen wære
> ond ðæt soð to late   seolf gecneowe'   (707–8)

['was before permeated with folly, and myself acknowledged the truth too
late']

Once again physical defeat is identified retrospectively with seeing the
truth. The miracle of the Cross's discovery, Judas's successful
encounter with the devil, the further discovery of the nails, all
exemplify cumulatively the rightness of Judas's compelled choice.
In a final speech, even the other Jews are brought to this realisation,
accepting the evidence of their eyes in a thoroughly typical 'speech of
submission' after the pattern of the Mermedonian in *Andreas*:

> 'Nu we seolfe geseoð   sigores tacen,
> soðwundor godes,   þeah we wiðsocun ær
> mid leasingum.   Nu is in leoht cymen,
> onwrigen, wyrda bigang.   Wuldor þæs age
> on heannesse   heofonrices god!'   (1120–4)

['Now we ourselves see the sign of victory, God's true miracle, though we
earlier rejected it with lies. Now the course of events is revealed, has come
into the light. May the God of heaven in the heights have the glory of it!']

The *nu* . . . *nu* structure, the visibility of truth and *wyrd*, the retrospective admission of falsity, and the stress on a *tacen*—all are
characteristic of similar speeches in other poems, and no less forcefully create an anticipated climax in their own right. At the same time.
the neatness of the two two-and-a-half line units, the repetition in
lines 3b and 4a, the chiasmus in lines 1b and 2a, all display Cynewulf's own sense of order. It is the coexistence of these two attributes
which gives *Elene* its marked narrative structure and considerable
verbal excitement. On the one hand the poet has worked within a
tradition to add a sense of power and mystery to his relatively
predictable source; on the other, he has deployed his own poetic
skill so as to make some of the formal speeches at the poem's
turning-points into works of considerable subtlety.

   One could (and should) say the same of the poem *Juliana*, in
which a rather similar structure is visible, based on the opposed
wishes to 'alter the mind' or 'know the truth' [*mod onwendan, soð
gecnawan*]. Yet it is perhaps fairer to point out in that poem some of
the drawbacks which inevitably accompany the rigidly powerful
style of Old English epic. Kenneth Sisam once wittily observed how a

sense of conscious merit struggled with humility in many an Anglo-
Saxon heart, citing the Northumbrian Aldred who began his text
with the conventional formula 'I, Aldred, *presbyter indignus et
miserrimus*' ['unworthy and most wretched priest'], but nevertheless
felt constrained to add in the margin 'the excellent son of Tilwyn, a
good woman'.[24] Not that the heroine Juliana shows any great sign of
humility herself. But her story is told very much in the style of the
sermo humilis[25]—racily, even sensationally—with more than a
touch of comedy. As she waits for execution she is tempted to recant
by a devil, whom she subdues by simple physical force (though without going to the lengths of St Dunstan, who caught *his* devil by the
nose with red-hot tongs). After a conversation, she throws him into a
mudheap and strides off to martyrdom; but he reappears behind the
executioners and exhorts them to their duty with an urchin's rhetoric,
well translated for once by the Early Middle English *Seinte Iuliene*,
some four centuries later than Cynewulf. There the devil cries out:
*'A! Stalewurðe men, ne spearie ȝe hire nawiht! Ha haueð us alle
scheome idon. Schendeð hire nuðe! ȝeldeð hire ȝarow borh efter þet ha
wurðe is. A! Stalewurðe men, ne studgi ȝe neauer, doð hire biliue
to-deað buten abade!'* ['Hey! You strong men, don't spare her at all!
She has done us all shame. Now destroy her! Pay her back what she
deserves! Hey! You strong men, don't stop, do her to death quickly
without delay!']. And then, as the maiden glances warningly at him,
he cowers back 'as if from a shot arrow', and rushes off with the
cry *'Ah ilecche ha me eft, ne finde ich na leche. Igripe ha me eanes,
ne ga i neauer mare þrefter o grene'* ['If she catches me again, I'll
never find a doctor. If she gets me once, I'll never walk on the green
again'].[26] Admittedly this Middle English text expands on its original;
but it does so in the right spirit, picking up a colloquial sensational-
ism genuinely present. It hardly needs to be said that any such effects
are right outside the range of Cynewulf or any Old English poet.
The two speeches corresponding to the above in Cynewulf's *Juliana*
sound more like the complaints of *Deor*, serious and painful,
while the whole 'little boy and schoolmistress' approach vanishes
entirely. It makes one wonder whether Cynewulf was capable of
realising the full stylistic force of his original, or whether he merely
realised that he could never reproduce it. Probably the former is
true, reminding us once again of the almost sovereign power of
cultural patterns and ideas of acceptable narrative. But what then *did*
Cynewulf see in the legend of Juliana that led him to want to translate
it? Quite likely, the answer is 'a devil'.

In fact, though *Juliana* is a heavily mutilated poem with something
like 130 lines missing, mostly from the section in which the saint
interrogates the devil, that interview still takes up some 317 of its

731 lines (242–558), or about 43 per cent, as opposed to just over a quarter of the Middle English *Iuliene*. Clearly the devil's confessions had an interest of their own, and in many ways one which called out the best in an Old English poet. The devil is made to describe his assaults on the soul in military terms (382–409), listing his many temporal victories over the martyrs, John the Baptist, Peter and Paul, St Andrew, and Christ Himself (289–315)—a succession, as he says, of *'sweartra synna . . . heardra heteþonca'* ['black sins . . . harsh thoughts of hate']. The result is that he becomes himself almost a heroic figure, brooding without compunction over his past life of 'endless evil', and praising by contrast the power and wisdom of St Juliana, with a touch of surprise at his own reversal:

> 'Næs ænig þara
> þæt mec þus bealdlice   bennum bilegde,
> þream forþrycte,   ær þu nu þa
> þa miclan meaht   mine oferswiðdest,
> fæste forfenge,   þe me fæder sealde,
> feond moncynnes,   þa he mec feran het,
> þeoden of þystrum,   þæt ic þe sceolde
> synne swetan.   Þær mec sorg bicwom,
> hefig hondgewinn.   Ic bihlyhhan ne þearf
> æfter sarwræce   siðfæt þisne
> magum in gemonge,   þonne ic mine sceal
> agiefan gnorncearig   gafulrædenne
> in þam reongan ham'   (518–30)

'There was none of them who laid me in bonds so boldly, overwhelmed me with pains, until you now seized me firmly and overcame my great power, which my father, the enemy of mankind, gave me when he told me to travel out of darkness and make sin pleasant to you. There sorrow came on me, a heavy struggle. After this suffering I have no need to boast of my exploit among my friends, when, sadly, I must render my account in our gloomy home']

After the multiple subordinate clauses of the first sentence the two half-lines of defeat are especially sudden; and in his speech the devil ranges over past, present and unhappy future in much the same spirit as the messenger of *Beowulf* 2900–3027, reaching a moment of despairing greatness. Again, the Old English style *adds* this to the speech's Latin source. And it is worth noting that the overtones of heroic power are produced by the style alone, for within the speech itself there is an overt condemnation of the old heroic situations. As if remembering the stories of Finn or Ingeld, Cynewulf has the devil admit that he has deceived men in many ways, some by direct assault, poison, or drowning, but some also

'þæt hy færinga
ealde æfþoncan   edniwedan,
beore druncne.   Ic him byrlade
wroht of wege,   þæt hi in winsele
þurh sweordgripe   sawle forletan'   (484–8)

['so that they suddenly renewed old enmities, drunk with beer. I poured them out sin from their cups, so that in the winehall they gave up their souls through the bite of swords']

The old motives of honour are here diabolic promptings, wholly sinful. And yet the sense of resolution and triumph associated with them still permeates the poem to the exclusion of all else, preserved in its distinctive vocabulary, poetic technique, and habit of mind.

In many ways Cynewulf was a deeply conventional poet, his desire to identify himself carrying with it no connotations of rebellious individuality. This might have been guessed from the fact that at an early stage in the history of Old English studies it was realised that several other poems possessed 'Cynewulfian' qualities (though now that we know that none of them is likely to have been by him the adjective becomes useful rather than precise). The old distinction between 'Cynewulfian' and 'Cædmonian' is also beginning to show signs of wear, for though there *is* a difference between, say, the *Christ*-poems, and those of the *Junius Manuscript*, that difference can now be seen to arise from the slightly variant reactions to similar material of poets operating basically within a single technique; there is nothing revolutionary in either body of verse. Moreover, some of the charges levelled against Cynewulf in the past—formlessness, dependence on Latin sources, concentration on single scenes rather than entire stories—are those made against Old English poetry in general. It should now be clear that they are not especially truer of his poetry than they are of *Beowulf* and *The Wanderer*. As with other poems, any reading of Cynewulf's work depends on a developed awareness of the types of interest and narrative climax which we have a right to expect from Old English poetry, and we may recognise it as something subtler but more consistent than is generally allowed.

More reasonable, perhaps, is the feeling of several critics that though Cynewulf's verse has the merits of being plain, pleasant, 'classic', it is also monotonous and lacking in vigour. Certainly Cynewulf (unlike, say, the authors of *Andreas* or *Guthlac A*) had begun to discard some of the more obvious devices of heroic poetry, and so lost a certain energy, though of course at the same time avoiding the occasional startling incongruities of those less well-considered poems. Still, once more it is worth remembering that Old English verse, and especially Old English formal speech, does not quite consist of the solid blocks of homogeneous difficulty that many people imagine. Control of syntax and word-association often gives dramatic speeches a kind of flexibility that responds well to modern analysis, and that may well have aroused considerable and justifiable poetic excitement in properly experienced audiences. In this field Cynewulf is distinguished, if not supreme. Perhaps more than any other Old English poems, his deserve to be revalued in the light of our recent increased awareness of the potentialities of Old English technique, and the probability of deliberate control exercised within certain areas of it—a control that issued from cooperation with traditional practice, not from any attempt to break out of it.

8

THE DECLINE:

KING ALFRED AND AFTER

It may be safely affirmed, that there neither is, nor can be, any
essential difference between the language of prose and metrical
composition.

WORDSWORTH, *Preface to the Lyrical Ballads*

The quotation from Wordsworth is intended as an epitaph for the
Old English poetic tradition. It may be a mistaken one, but one is
decidedly necessary—not simply because of the obvious truth that the
tradition is dead, but because it seems to have expired unchallenged.
During the three centuries of its existence (700–1000), there is no
sign of revolution, no Milton or Wordsworth to declare himself
dissatisfied with his predecessors and strike out on his own. Nevertheless, as we have seen, our late manuscripts show some signs of
incomprehension on the part of copyists, and *all* the long narrative
poems which form the backbone of the tradition belong to the first
half of this three-hundred-year period.[1] What caused this decline?
The easiest and most favoured explanations are the external, social
ones. Some suggest the Norman Conquest, others the Viking invasions
two hundred years before; the complaint of King Alfred about the
low standard of culture in England around the year 890 is well
known. These are undeniable as historical facts. Still, in poetic terms
at least the Norman Conquest is too late to be anything more than a
coup de grâce, while the limitation in using the Danes as scapegoats is
that the long period of peace and Anglo-Saxon success, all through
the middle of the tenth century, seems to have produced virtually
nothing of any importance in poetry—a marked contrast to contemporary Anglo-Saxon achievement in many other directions.
Even *Maldon* is the record of a defeat; and though the battle of

Hastings, one might think, provided just as much opportunity for heroic treatment as Byrhtnoth's 'last stand', no English poem on that subject has survived, and it is unlikely that one was ever composed. The tradition did not die prematurely or by violence, but it died of unknown causes, so that some investigation is necessary.

For some preliminary clues it may help to look at what is possibly the last Old English poem to survive, the twenty-one-line piece in praise of Durham, usually dated on internal evidence to between 1104 and 1109.[2] This is a neat but thoroughly derivative example of that schoolboy exercise, the *encomium urbis*. It mentions the fame of the city, its rivers and forests, and then goes on to list the great relics of the cathedral, the bodies of St Cuthbert and the Venerable Bede and the head of St Oswald among them. Unexciting in itself, the poem nevertheless contains some remarkable and unexpected features. Though all its connections are with Northumbria, it is written (unlike, for instance, *Bede's Death Song*) in a reasonable variant of West Saxon, apparently established even in the far North as the native literary language.[3] Moreover, many of the poem's half-lines correspond to recognisable formulas, phrases such as *on floda gemonge* [in the midst of waters], *in deope dalum* [in the deep dales], *bearnum gecyðed* [made known to men], *ðes ðe writ seggeð* [as writings say]. The inference is that the poet was reasonably well-acquainted with other Old English poems, and that even at this late date he was trying deliberately to echo them. But he did not succeed all the time. The river, for example, is described in one half-line as *ea yðum stronge* [river strong in waves],[4] a phrase that almost perfectly fits the pattern of *Beowulf* 1364, *wudu wyrtum fæst* [wood firm in roots] or *Maldon* 210, *wiga wintrum geong* [warrior young in winters]. But not quite. The final -*e* in the *Durham*-poem's half-line is intrusive, and prevents the verse from being the normal D type (see p. 101) half-line it should be. Of course the point is in itself very minor, but it serves to indicate the great drawback of traditional styles being imitated in a period of decline. With the best will in the world, the poets *have no secure knowledge of what they are doing*. Obviously no Old English poet at any period knew what a 'D type half-line' was. He followed the patterns of his verse—which do genuinely exist—out of a combination of instinct and experience, a guiding force with many advantages. But if anything happened to upset that perfect balance of imitation and re-creation, there could in the nature of things be no external check, no appeal to rules and reasons. Like a boy riding a bicycle, once the traditional poet or singer began to think about what he was doing, he was liable to fall off.

In some ways it is clear that the poet of *Durham* has already fallen off. Consider the short section of the poem scanned and printed below:

(A?)	Is in ðere byri eac bearnum gecyðed	(A)
(C)	ðe arfesta eadig Cudberch	(A)
(?)	and ðes clene cyninges heafud,	(A)
(?)	Osuualdes, Engle leo, and Aidan biscop,	(A)
(A)	Eadberch and Eadfrið, æðele geferes.	(A)
(B?)	Is ðer inne midd heom Æðelwold biscop	(A)
(?)	and breoma bocera Beda and Boisil abbot,	(A)
(D?)	ðe clene Cudberte on gecheðe	(?)
(A)	lerde lustum, and he his lara wel genom	(B)
		(9–17)

[Also in the city, known to men, is the noble and faithful Cuthbert, and the head of that pure king, Oswald, protector of the English, and bishop Aidan, Eadbert and Eadfrith, noble companions. Inside with them is bishop Æthelwold, Bede the famous scholar, and abbot Boisil, who gladly taught the pure Cuthbert in his youth, and he received his teaching well]

The material is not inspiring, but simple enough. Still, though the poet is trying to write conventionally, many of his half-lines fit Sievers' 'Five Types' only through our goodwill. Some have three main stresses; some only one; some call for a stress on very weak syllables. Of course it does no immediate harm to abandon the Sievers system—one cannot just rap the poet over the knuckles for being 'incorrect'. The point is, rather, that once poets of this type begin to diverge from the traditions that help them compose in *one* particular, they are very likely—considering the strong interactions of formal patterns in Old English verse—to diverge from them in most, and so to lose the powerful turns of syntax, methods of word-compounding, and alliterative associations which constitute much of the traditional verse's excellence. In short, though the *Durham*-poet's ambitions are meagre and his intentions conservative, he does show accidentally something of an inability to respond dynamically to change, a failing which may account for the very complete disappearance of Old English poetry, once external conditions started it on the path of decline. The absence of a formal prosody or any critical art of poetry means that poets in a period of decisive change are at the mercy of forces which they cannot recognise or analyse.

The *Durham*-poem is too late to give any information about the start of what must have been a gradual and strongly-resisted process. A figure who ought, at least, to be more useful in this direction is King Alfred (849–99). He was born not long after the approximate period of Cynewulf's work; but after he died, few long poems seem to have been written in Old English. Besides spanning this crucial period, his life also represents a remarkable fusion of learned and native interests, evident in his well-known scheme of widespread education in the vernacular. Moreover, he is the only person to whom we can confidently ascribe a quantity of Old English verse, as well as a much larger quantity of Old English prose. In several ways, culturally and politically, he seems a man moving freely between two worlds. His work therefore has more than an immediate or personal interest. One might reflect on the story told about him by his *familiaris*, the Welshman Asser, Bishop of Sherborne, in *De Rebus Gestis Alfredi*.[5] One day, Asser reports (when Alfred must have been less than eight years old), his mother showed him and his brothers 'a certain Saxon book of the poetic art' (*quendam Saxonicum poematicae artis librum*) and told them that whoever could 'learn' the book first—the word used is *discere*—could have it. As if to check on the terms of the competition, Alfred asked if it would be given to whoever could most quickly 'understand and recite' the book (*intelligere et recitare*). Once this was agreed, he found his master to read him the book, and then returned to his mother and recited it. As partial explanation of the feat, we have been told a little earlier that he 'listened intelligently to Saxon poetry, night and day, and hearing poems spoken many times by others, being an apt pupil, he kept them in his memory' (*Saxonicum poemata die noctuque solers auditor, relata aliorum saepissime audiens, docibilis memoriter retinebat*). Does this make Alfred an 'oral-formulaic' singer? Asser after all was a foreigner and might not have been able to distinguish feats of memory from those of composition. One cannot tell, and the story itself is not wholly reliable.[6] But one might at least suggest that, as Asser stresses, Alfred remained illiterate to a late age, and during this period was in the habit of hearing Old English verse recited aloud, so that he would be familiar with its distinctive patterns. On the other hand, we know quite certainly that in middle age he learnt Latin and produced at least three long works in Old English prose—his translations or paraphrases of Gregory's *Pastoral Care*; Boethius's *Consolation of Philosophy*; and Augustine's *Soliloquies*. Alfred thus straddles the worlds of oral and literary culture, of the Latin and Old English languages, and of prose and verse—for the *Pastoral Care* has a verse preface and epilogue that may be by Alfred, while a considerable quantity of the prose of Boethius has been turned back into verse with this fairly credible ascription:

> Ðus Ælfred us   ealdspell reahte,
> cyning Westsexna,   cræft meldode,
> leoðwyrhta list.   Him wæs lust micel
> ðæt he ðiossum leodum   leoð spellode,
> monnum myrgen,   mislice cwidas,
> þy læs ælinge   ut adrife
> selflicne secg,   þonne he swelces lyt
> gymð for his gilpe   (Proem, 1–8)

[So Alfred, king of the West Saxons, told us an ancient story, showed his art, the skill of making songs. He had a great desire to tell songs to his people, many sayings, a warning for men, lest burning desire should drive out the man wrapped up in himself, when in his pride he thinks little of such a thing][7]

The motive—a wish to warn the careless and complacent—is typical of Old English thought; it also fits Alfred's own earnest nature. But this, and the obvious skill of the poet in the ascription, should not disguise the fact that in the Boethius *Metres* we have, uniquely, a case not of translation directly from the Latin (as with Cynewulf and many other authors), but of Old English verse based from the start on Old English prose.

This may not seem a very damaging situation. As Wordsworth would have it, there is 'no *essential* difference' between the two. Certainly King Alfred for much of the time appears to agree with him, following his own prose version closely, not quite word for word, but making only such changes as are necessary to preserve the metre. One might look, for example, at his two versions of the great Boethian question, whether it is possible to reconcile true happiness with the world's instability. (The earlier prose version is given on the left,[8] the verse, in half-lines, on the right. Words added to the verse have been set in bold, substitutions in italic.)

Me ablendan þas ungetreowan woruldsælþa, and me þa forletan swa blindne on þis dimme hol, and me þa bereafodon ælcere lustbærnesse þa ða ic hi æfre betst truwode; þa wendon hi me heora bæc to, and me mid ealle from gewitan. To hwon sceoldon la mine friend seggan þæt ic gesælig mon wære? Hu mæg	Me þas woruldsælða **welhwæs** blindne on ðis dimme hol **dysine** *forlæddon,* and me pa *berypton* **rædes and frofre** for heora untreowum, þe ic him æfre betst truwian sceolde. Hi me to wendon

se beon gesælig se þe on þæm
gesælþum þurhwunian ne mot?

heora bacu **bitere,**
and heora blisse from.
Forhwam wolde ge,
weoruldfrynd mine,
secgan **odde singan**
þæt ic gesællic mon
wære **on weorulde?**
Ne synt þa word sod,
nu þa gesælða ne magon
simle gewunigan.   (2: 10-19)

[These untrue worldly joys blinded
me, and left me blind in this dim
hole, and took away from me each
pleasure which I had always trusted
best. Then they turned their back
on me and went away completely.
Why indeed should my friends
say I was a happy man? How can
he be happy who cannot continue
in happiness?]

[These worldly joys led me, a fool,
wholly blind into this dim hole,
and then deprived me of advice or
comfort, because of their untruth-
fulness, those which I always
trusted best. They turned their
backs bitterly to me, and their joy
away. My worldly friends, why
would you say or sing that I was a
happy man in the world? The
words are not true, now that the
joys cannot always continue.]

[The changes made in the verse passage are visibly minimal, amounting
to re-ordering of sentences, plus a few descriptive or emphatic words
to maintain alliteration. Far greater changes had been made in
translating Boethius's sharp and sophisticated Latin verse into the
blunt assertiveness of Old English prose. Yet it has been shown that
when analysed in a formulaic way these Boethius *Metres* are as
traditional in their phrasing as most Old English poetry;[9] if we did
not know the prose source, it could be assumed that they had been
composed normally. Does this mean that Wordsworth was right,
that the transition from prose to verse can be made without disturbance? It may be true up to a point. But another conclusion is possible:
that verse produced in this way can be superficially regular, but may
be weak.

The quality of the Boethius *Metres* is admittedly (and interestingly)
variable, but a short section can be given without especial unfairness
from one of the solidly argumentative, rather than narrative, parts
which form the bulk of the verse. Alfred is explaining that all
human virtues derive from God:

Is ðæt micel gecynd
þines goodes,   þencð ymb se ðe wile,
forðon hit is eall an   ælces þincges,
þu and þæt þin good.   Hit is þin agen,

forðæm hit his utan   ne com auht to ðe,
ac ic georne wat   þæt ðin goodnes is,
ælmihtig good,   eall mid ðe selfum.
Hit is ungelic   urum gecynde;
us is utan cymen   eall þa we habbað
gooda on grundum   from gode selfum   (20: 26–35)

[That is the great quality of Your goodness, consider it who will, because
it is a unity in every way, You and Your goodness. It is Your own, for none
of it came to You from outside, but I know well, almighty God (or good?),
that Your goodness is entirely in Your self. It is not so with our kind. All
the good we have in this world has come to us from outside, from God
Himself]

This passage expands slightly on a fairly economical piece of prose,
though only the sixth and seventh lines diverge very far from the
original. But unlike the passage quoted previously, it has several
failings, the most obvious (if superficial) ones being, again, those of
metre. How is one to scan the half-line *þu and þæt þin good*? Since
the alliteration is on -*þ*, and since the argument is to distinguish
human from divine good, one might assume a main stress on the
possessive *þin*. Then there are two other alliterative words, *þu* and
þæt, jostling for the second stress; whereas in fact, from the sense, one
might prefer to stress the noun *good*; which would, however, produce
the unscannable pattern $_{xxx}//$. Possibly a native speaker of Old English
would decide quickly and produce something reasonable. But he
would be faced with similar problems in several places, e.g. in lines
3a or 5b; the alliterations are also poor, tending to fall on weak
words or on unexpected ones. The reason is not hard to see. Neither
the original Latin nor the Old English prose has offered any way of
giving rise to the noun compounds, variations, and expanded
phrases so useful in maintaining the alliterative rhythm; nor does the
straightforward argument suit a style founded on 'hurry and delay'.
In keeping up his progress Alfred has been forced into a pattern
of pronouns and possessives and connectives of low 'gram-
metric' value. His verse here is prosaic in more senses than one—in
rhythm, in vocabulary, ultimately even in the structure of his
sentences.

It may be said that all this proves is that the Boethius *Metres* are
not very good poetry—something no one troubles to deny, and which
may have many possible explanations (lack of individual talent, for
one). But that would not be entirely fair to King Alfred. The Old
English *Boethius*, in both its versions, is a thoroughly remarkable
work, far more than just paraphrase, and introduces many changes
not to be accounted for merely by the existence of some traditional
Christian commentary (though no doubt Alfred had one). A recent

study by F. Anne Payne has admirably pointed out what an original
and individual book it is, in a way which can hardly be summarised.[10]
But briefly, one might say that Boethius presents us with the spectre of
a planless and chaotic universe in which evil is random and unjustified, only to solve it by arguing for an ultimate coherence—in which
one might see, however, the seeds of predestination and determinism.
Alfred's view, on the other hand, is of a universe in which good and
evil are well-enough defined, but where good seems basically weak.
He solves it, not with a vision of coherence, but with one of divine
power; and in his universe the importance of free decisions and
human will quite overpowers Boethius's late-antique sense of hidden,
controlling forces. Again and again in Miss Payne's work one comes
across conclusions that should now be familiar. Alfred sees human
reward as 'the pleasure of good work accomplished *or willed so
strongly that the projection becomes a kind of reality*' [my italics].[11]
Can one avoid remembering the mind-reinforcing spirals of *Deor* or
The Wanderer? Again, Alfred's ultimate goal is 'an insistent effort to
prepare men for these extreme moments which will come with
increasing frequency as their human involvements take them into
increasingly complex battles to prove their worth'.[12] Can one not
think of Hrothgar's words to Beowulf? All in all, we should have no
doubt of the effect on Alfred—testified to by Asser—of the concepts
and preoccupations of Old English poetry. With this achievement in
mind, to dismiss Alfred as just a poor poet would be daring. In
fact, when he frees himself from the grip of his own prose, as he does
in telling the story of the Gothic invasion of Italy (section 1) or of
Ulysses and Circe (section 26), Alfred's poetic talent increases
enormously, the verse regaining its due rhythm, its large scale, and
so its sense of compressed power. Parts of the *Metres* are just as good
as *Judith* or *Maldon*; they are parts where Alfred is pursuing a
narrative without interference from the profoundly alien but already
established structures of his own prose.

The general weakness of the *Metres* is, then, not individual, but
inevitable in the circumstances of composition, founded on King
Alfred's reluctance to make a more obvious separation of verse from
prose. In such a case Wordsworth's assertion is not safe at all. Is it
possible that the decline of Old English poetry from the tenth century
on was linked in any way to the development of prose? Naturally few
poets are likely to have begun work by writing out a non-metrical
version to be subsequently versified, as King Alfred did. Nevertheless
the influence of prose-rhythms can be detected; the *Metres*, for
instance, sound not unlike the poem on *Durham* quoted at the start.
Possibly what happened historically was a blurring of categories,
never in any event very consciously defined. At an early period one

knew that there was one form of language employed in speech, and
another, quite distinct, marked by all kinds of special features and
probably sung as well, to be used by some people in special social
circumstances. With the coming of literacy this latter form, poetry,
was no doubt detached from its special circumstances by the very
fact of being written down. As rather later a stylised form of the
spoken language also began to be written down as prose, the two
types may have started to look the same (especially as there was no
convention of writing verse out in lines or half-lines). To some minds,
the specialised linguistic features of poetry might then seem as
inessential as the specialised social and physical ones. And indeed
they would have been right, to a certain extent, there being no
doubt that in its origins Old English poetry is 'really conditioned
prose . . . a tidied form of the spoken language'.[13] But great weight
should be laid on the words 'conditioned' and 'tidied'. There is
nearly always a *reason* (sometimes a very abstract and long-term one)
for even seemingly inessential parts of the 'conditioning' of Old
English verse; to ignore any one of them is to discard something
potentially valuable. But, as has been said, Anglo-Saxons were not
equipped to make such analyses. They therefore found themselves
without the means to detect or restrain, a crumbling away of very
deep-rooted linguistic and literary features. Even if the suggestions
above as to how that process took place are false, the evidence for
this crumbling, this 'blurring of categories' is in the post-Alfredian
period quite overwhelming.

In an important essay, Angus McIntosh has pointed out that in the
tenth century it is not possible to make a single, clear distinction
between prose and verse, there being instead 'at least five clearly
separable stylistic genres between which there are important and
significant rhythmical distinctions'.[14] He warns that his 'at least' is
meant seriously; further distinctions are possible, if less obvious.
But, to take the five styles, they are: those of 'classical' verse and
'ordinary' prose; a third type described as 'debased' verse, of which
there are few extant examples (though a good deal of Middle English
seems influenced by it); and then the two highly characteristic styles
of Ælfric and Archbishop Wulfstan. These two latter, both working
in the period 990–1020, knew each other and clearly understood each
other's stylistic principles; nevertheless they persevered in their
separate answers to the problem of associating verse and prose. It is
Wulfstan that Professor McIntosh is primarily concerned with, and
he shows how the Archbishop would, for hundreds of 'lines' at a time,
maintain a regular rhythm of short, two-stress phrases rather similar
to those of 'classical' poetry and even capable of supporting a
rudimentary scansion:

Leofan men, / gecnawað þæt soð is: / ðeos worold is on ofste, / and hit
nealæcð þam ende, / and þy hit is on worolde / aa swa leng swa
wyrse, / and swa hit sceal nyde / for folces synnan / fram dæge to
dæge / ær Antecristes tocyme / yfelian swyþe / . . .

[Dear men, know what is true, that this world is in haste, and grows near to
the end, and so in the world the longer it goes the worse it is, and so
necessarily for the people's sins it must grow worse from day to day before
the coming of Antichrist . . .][15]

By comparison, Ælfric writes rather similarly on a two-stress pattern,
but his lines are longer and further removed from the rhythm of
normal verse; however, unlike Wulfstan, he maintains a regular if
loose alliteration obviously taken from poetic models. The start of
his *Life of St Oswald* runs as follows:

Æfter ðan ðe Augustinus / to Engla lande becom, // wæs sum æðele
cyning, / Oswold gehaten, // on Norðhymbra lande, / gelyfed swyþe on
God; // se ferde on his iugoðe / fram freondum and magum // to
Scotlande on sæ, / and þær sona wearð gefullod // . . .

[After Augustine came to the land of the English, there was a certain noble
king called Oswald in Northumbria, who believed greatly in God. In his
youth he went from friends and kinsmen by sea to Scotland, and was
quickly baptised there . . .][16]'

There is no doubt that these patterns are deliberate, for both writers
produce many lengthy sermons which can be broken up in this way in
totality, with no words left out and no real doubt as to where the
phrases begin and end. Clearly they were oratorically functional in
their time; yet it is sterile to argue whether they 'are' prose or verse.
(Both writers have been printed both ways in modern times.) The
patterns are like verse in that they superimpose a rhythmic structure
on a syntactic one, the two-stress phrase on the sentence. On the
other hand, they have none of the peculiar grammar and vocabulary
of earlier Old English verse, and neither writer seems to want those
effects. The existence of such hybrid forms proves that what was once
a stable distinction had now broken up; and McIntosh suggests that
the variety of forms points to a break-up not very far in the past, at

some time in the tenth century, between Alfred at one end and Ælfric at the other.

Bearing all this in mind, one might feel some sympathy for the condition of an aspiring poet during the tenth century. The primitive circumstances in which poetry was almost a daily social act were in the past, or much in decline.[17] Latin learning could not compensate by providing rules or handbooks on how to write in the vernacular. Unable to learn easily by study or by imitation, the 'poet' may not even have been too sure as to what he was aspiring to, there being no clear definition of verse and several blurred categories overlapping it. And yet the intense conservatism of Anglo-Saxon culture could not let the matter drop. At least some heightening of style was felt to be necessary in some places, while there was still at least some memory of how to produce it. Reading through a conflated text of the *Anglo-Saxon Chronicle* for the tenth and eleventh centuries is, as a result, an interesting experience, for every so often great formal events (or, later on, just dramatic ones) are marked by occasional poetry of one kind or another.

First in the series, of course, is the great panegyric on King Athelstan's destruction of the Norse and Scots in *The Battle of Brunanburh* (937), with five years later a shorter but comparably skilful piece on King Edmund's *Capture of the Five Boroughs* from the Norwegian kingdom in York.[18] The first of these in particular shows much of the complication of tone which is so attractive and unexpected a part of some of the Old English war-poems discussed earlier. The power and glory of the West Saxon kings are naturally celebrated in the active lines of the start, and perhaps mirrored by the sun-references of lines 13–17. But to this is added a touch of reflection at the wretched plight of the enemy—Anlaf the Norseman fleeing dishonourably back to Dublin, *on fealene flod, feorh generede* [over the grey sea, he saved his life], and the old Scottish king Constantine escaping, though he

> his sunu forlet
> on wælstowe   wundun forgrunden,
> giungne æt guðe.   Gelpan ne þorfte
> beorn blandenfeax   bilgeslehtes   (42–5)

[left his son beaten down by wounds on the battlefield, a young man in war. That grey-haired warrior had no need to boast of the clash of swords]

Not that the poet feels any sympathy for them. He is attracted rather by the suddenness of their downfall, and he observes it with a touch of grim humour and a run of variations to express the totality of their disillusionment:

mid heora herelafum   hlehhan ne þorftun
þæt heo beaduweorca   beteran wurdun
on campstede   cumbolgehnastes,
garmittinge,   gumena gemotes,
wæpengewrixles,   þæs hi on wælfelda
wiþ Eadweardes   afaran plegodan.   (47–52)

[with the relics of their army they had no need to exult that they were better
in warlike deeds on the battlefield, in the clash of banners, in the meeting of
spears, in the encounter of heroes, in the exchange of weapons, in all this
that they played out on the field of the dead with the children of Edward]

Clumsy as it sounds in modern English,[19] the 'framing' of the words
for battle by *on campstede . . . on wælfelda* is in the Old English
thoroughly successful in reaching a sense of climax. After that, the
poet lets his piece die away by commenting on the different departures
of the two armies, mentioning the dead left behind for the carrion-
birds, and slipping into historical perspective by comparing this
battle with all those fought since the coming of the English to Britain.
As in the *Five Boroughs* poem, the author shows a considerable
mastery over techniques of 'envelopment' and 'framing'.[20]

Yet the precedent may have been a dangerous one. Clearly
someone at the West Saxon court thought this composition of
panegyric verse a good idea; but thirty years later, the equally
glorious reign of Edgar found only embarrassing commemoration.
The two poems on *The Coronation of Edgar* (973) and *The Death of
Edgar* (975)—he was not crowned till well on in his reign—are
superficially correct in a painfully laboured way,[21] but are also totally
lifeless. As long as the poet sticks to chronology, as in the first poem,
he escapes certain detection; but in his attempt to add a little history
to the second he reveals quite extraordinary limitations. He comments
on the dispersal of the monasteries, and then adds:

And þa wearð eac adræfed   deormod hæleð,
Oslac, of earde   ofer yða gewealc,
ofer ganotes bæð,   gamolfeax hæleð,
wis and wordsnotor,   ofer wætera geðring,
ofer hwæles eðel,   hama bereafod   (24–8)

[And then the brave man Oslac, the grey-haired man, was also exiled from
his land, over the rolling of the waves, over the gannet's bath, over the
tumult of waters, over the whale's homeland; wise and skilled in words, he
was robbed of home]

Every half-line here, except perhaps the first, is quite respectable and
might be found in a better poem (from which, indeed, such lines
presumably came). But though the repetitions in lines two and three

or four and five look superficially like the variations for 'battle' in
Brunanburh, they clearly have no artistic purpose at all. Like the
meaningless variations *deormod hæleð . . . gamolfeax hæleð,* they are
there merely to pad out the alliteration and keep the lines going.
Or perhaps the author thought this was what 'poetry' was! One
could not ask for a better example of what happens when a creative
and flexible formulaic tradition degenerates into a system of tags and
fillers.[22]

Under that same year the Worcester *Chronicle* also added a piece of
rhythmic prose (as we would call it) to its encomium of Edgar.
Archbishop Wulfstan was probably responsible, and he may have
inserted a similar piece under the year 959. But for good measure
there is another poem under that year, also on Edgar's death, which
begins accurately enough for four lines, but then breaks into a
rhymed jog-trot. Surrounding one event, then, are three different
pieces, two regular and one confused, but all in their way suggestive of
poetic decadence. After that, the *Chronicle* seems to have lapsed into
no more than rhymed proverbs or bits of rhythmic prose, the nadir
of Old English verse being reached by a lumpish piece on *The Death
of Alfred* under 1036. It comments on the capture and betrayal of
King Ethelred's son Alfred by earl Godwin, King Harold's father:

> Se æþeling lyfode þa gyt;   ælc yfel man him gehet,
> oðþæt man gerædde   þæt man hine lædde
> to Eligbyrig   swa gebundenne.
> Sona swa he lende,   on scype man hine blende,
> and hine swa blindne   brohte to ðam munecon,
> and he þar wunode   ða hwile þe he lyfode   (16–21)

[The prince was still alive; they promised him every torment, until they
advised that he should be led like that, bound, to Ely. As soon as he landed,
they blinded him on the ship, and brought him like that, blind, to the
monks, and he stayed there while he lived]

The material itself is barbarous in a way found nowhere else in
Old English verse; it is matched by the uncertain jumps from rhyme
to alliteration, the shaky rhythms, the feeble connections. After
such a piece one might think ignorance all-embracing. And yet under
1065 we find in two manuscripts some thirty lines, on the death of
Edward the Confessor, not especially distinguished but as good as
any of these occasional poems except perhaps for *Brunanburh.*
The existence of these lines reminds one again of the total uncertainty
of poetic conditions in a period at one and the same time highly
unstable and deeply conservative. In these *Chronicle* poems antiquarian
endeavour is seen at grips with chaotic fluidity over about a hundred

and forty years.[23] But the wild variations in quality are not the result
of individual talent or lack of it. They mirror a deep uncertainty
over goals and methods.

The poem of *Maldon* perhaps deserves the final word. Obviously
written after 991, it is the only unquestioned success of this late
period, and is clearly the work of a man determined to write after the
manner of his ancestors. Words, situations, sentence-patterns, all
conform willingly to the modes of heroic epic. But often something
gets in the way. At the start of the poem, for instance, we have the
little vignette of the young warrior, 'Offa's kinsman', realising the
imminence of battle as the horses are sent away:

> Þa þæt Offan mæg   ærest onfunde,
> þæt se eorl nolde   yrhðo geþolian,
> he let him þa of handon   leofne fleogan
> hafoc wið þæs holtes,   and to þære hilde stop;
> be þam man mihte oncnawan   þæt se cniht nolde
> wacian æt þam wige,   þa he to wæpnum feng   (5–10)

[When Offa's kinsman first realised that the earl would not endure irreso-
lution, he let his dear hawk fly from his hands to the wood, and advanced
to battle. By that one could understand that the young man would not
give way in battle, once he took up arms]

The economy of the gesture is in the best tradition of heroic
narrative. Extravagant but understated, it displays purely from the
outside the boy's 'moment of understanding', as he sees that, win or
lose, he will not worry about his hawk again. Yet the rhythm of the
piece is quite distinct from that of earlier warlike preparations in
verse. For one thing, those relatively weak words, auxiliary verbs
taking an infinitive, gain a certain prominence, occurring four times
in six lines (*nolde, let, mihte, nolde*); in the fifth line indeed, *let* is the
strongest word, taking the first alliterative stress. Such uses could be
found in *Beowulf*, but not in such concentration. Relative lack of
force is increased by the large number of small, unimportant,
'grammatical' words. *Gewac æt wige*, for instance, is a phrase found
in *Beowulf*; but in *Maldon* it is *wacian æt þam wige*, as it is *to þære
hilde* and *wið þæs holtes*, all phrases that might earlier have been
shortened. Individually the extensions are not noticeable. But overall,
they make the lines more diffuse and relaxed, unlike the dense,
crowded texture of the best of *Beowulf* or *Exodus* or *Elene*. Three half-
lines out of the twelve here have four unresolved weak syllables, one

$$\overset{\text{x x   x}\quad /\; \text{x x}\quad /\;\text{x}}{(\textit{be þam man mihte oncnawan})}$$ has six, the average is nearly four.
Of course such a short passage is not typical, and indeed the poet at

times writes with great verve and regularity for some length—so much so that it has even been suggested that he was aiming deliberately at a kind of stylistic variation.[24] But that is improbably sophisticated in late tenth-century conditions. More likely this author, as traditionally minded but nearly as uncertain stylistically as the *Durham*-poet, keeps within the bounds of 'classical' verse structure while composing derivative or familiar scenes and speeches, only to fall back (without realising it) to more prosaic uses as he loses the support of his unknown models. The poet's native talent indeed bursts out in many places, especially at start and end. But like many of the poets previously discussed, that talent is subordinated to, or disguised by, the more accidental circumstances of date, method of composition, and suitability of material to the demands of an inherited style. Only with this reservation can one make sense of the apparently contradictory (and equally justified) opinions about *Maldon*, that it is a 'popular' poem of slightly coarse sincerity and that it is the 'high water mark of Old English narrative verse'.[25]

Many readers may feel that in this last chapter more space might have been given to the virtues of some of the later poems, for the very fact of our tenth-century manuscripts suggests that the age was not wholly decadent, while some of the poems mentioned at least succeed in telling lively stories. To them I would reply with the words of Roger Ascham:

Ye know not what hurt ye do to learning that care not for words but for matter, and so make a divorce betwixt the tongue and the heart. For mark all ages, look upon the whole course of both the Greek and Latin tongue, and ye shall surely find that when apt and good words began to be neglected and properties of those two tongues to be confounded, then also began ill deeds to spring . . .

Not that I would connect literary with political decline quite so firmly as Ascham (though some of the best qualities in Anglo-Saxon civilisation—its stubbornness in the face of violence, its eager receptivity to learning—do seem to be mirrored from time to time in its poetry). The point is rather that in this late period one can see, if only by hindsight, the beginnings of a 'divorce' between subject-matter and its expression ultimately more powerful and important than individual efforts to preserve the older unity. If nothing else, the evidences of change and decline should remind us what an extraordinary and glorious period that must have been when the great religious and secular epics were being composed—so many of them, with so little apparent strain! In the break-up of Old English verse one is lamenting not merely a loss of individual potential (like

the early death of Keats), but the disappearance of a whole state of
mind; in its achievement, one is praising qualities in some senses
deeper and more pervasive than might be produced by unassisted
men in single lifetimes.

BIBLIOGRAPHICAL ABBREVIATIONS

ASPR	Anglo-Saxon Poetic Records
BAP	Bibliothek der angelsächsischen Prosa
CL	Comparative Literature
CCSL	Corpus Christianorum Series Latina
EETS OS	Early English Text Society (Original Series)
E&GS	English and Germanic Studies
ELH	English Literary History
ES	English Studies
HSCP	Harvard Studies in Classical Philology
JEGP	Journal of English and Germanic Philology
Med. Stud.	Medieval Studies
MLN	Modern Language Notes
MLR	Modern Language Review
MP	Modern Philology
Neophil.	Neophilologus
NM	Neuphilologische Mitteilungen
NQ	Notes and Queries
PQ	Philological Quarterly
PBA	Proceedings of the British Academy
PMLA	Publications of the Modern Language Association
RES	Review of English Studies
RES NS	Review of English Studies (New Series)
SP	Studies in Philology
TPS	Transactions of the Philological Society

NOTES

Chapter 1
An apology for verse: Introduction

1. Pioneer work in this area was done by Milman Parry, whose collected papers have now been edited by his son Adam Parry under the title *The Making of Homeric Verse*, Oxford 1971. More useful for students of Old English is the work of his collaborator A. B. Lord, *The Singer of Tales*, Cambridge, Mass. 1960.

2. N. K. Chadwick and V. M. Zhirmunski, *Oral Epics of Central Asia*, London 1969. Mrs Chadwick's section is a reprint of a chapter in her and H. M. Chadwick's *The Growth of Literature*, 3 vols, Cambridge, 1932–40.

3. There is no convenient edition of Priscus. For an account of the incidents with translation of relevant parts, see E. A. Thompson, *A History of Attila and the Huns*, Oxford 1948, pp. 102–20 and Appendix A.

4. Sidonius Apollinaris, *Carmina XII*, Loeb ed. with translation by W. B. Anderson in two vols, London and Cambridge, Mass. 1936.

5. *Widsith: a study in Old English Heroic Legend*, Ed. R. W. Chambers, Cambridge 1912, pp. 1–2.

6. See Tennyson's *Battle of Brunanburgh*; Pound's *The Seafarer* in *Ripostes*; Graves' remarks in *Goodbye to All That*, ch. 27.

7. The remark comes from T. S. Eliot's 'The Metaphysical Poets' (1921), reprinted in *Selected Essays*, 3rd ed. London 1951, pp. 281–91.

8. W. K. Wimsatt, *The Verbal Icon*, Lexington 1954, p. 83.

9. Northrop Frye, *An Anatomy of Criticism*, Princeton 1957, p. 277.

10. Gavin Bone, *Beowulf in Modern Verse*, Oxford 1945, p. 12.

11. Wimsatt, op. cit., pp. 190–1.

12. See J. E. Cross, 'On the Genre of *The Wanderer*', *Neophil.* 45 (1961), 63–75; and Murray F. Markland, 'Boethius, Alfred and *Deor*', *MP* 66 (1968), 1–4.

13. For basic information, see J. D. A. Ogilvy, *Books known to Anglo-Latin Writers from Aldhelm to Alcuin*, Cambridge, Mass. 1936. This is applied, in different ways, by B. F. Huppé, *Doctrine and Poetry*, New York 1959, and Margaret E. Goldsmith, *The Mode and Meaning of Beowulf*, London 1970, among many others.

14. D. W. Robertson jr, 'Historical Criticism', *English Institute Essays* (1950), 3–31. See also the same author's 'The Doctrine of Charity in Medieval Literary

G

Gardens', *Speculum* 26 (1951), 24–49, for some interpretations based on Christian Latin writings.

15. See W. Ullmann, *Principles of Government and Politics in the Middle Ages*, London 1961, p. 118 and the chapter following on 'Theocratic Kingship'; and also William A. Chaney, *The Cult of Kingship in Anglo-Saxon England*, Manchester 1970.

16. One might add that this 'ring of archaic truth', difficult but not impossible to define, is often markedly present in *Beowulf*. The confidence and consistency of the poet's references to ancient history have impressed all readers. Though his information is often unsupported—as is shown by Jane A. Leake in her book *The Geats of Beowulf*, Madison 1967—it is still quite different in tone from the garbled and learned mythologising of medieval 'historians' in Latin.

17. It is only fair to say that the school of thought which turned its back on Christian learning and hunted greedily after pagan and 'Germanic' vestiges gave this whole subject a deservedly bad name for some time. See E. G. Stanley, 'The Search for Anglo-Saxon Paganism', *Notes and Queries* 209 (1964), 204–9, 242–50, 282–7, 324–31, 455–63, and 210 (1965), 9–16, 203–7, 285–93 and 322–7.

Chapter 2

The argument of courage: Beowulf *and other heroic poetry*

1. A. J. Toynbee, *A Study of History*, 12 vols, London 1934–61, vol. II, p. 200.

2. For the best expositions of these (and other) facts, see R. W. Chambers, *Beowulf: An Introduction,* 3rd ed. with supplement by C. L. Wrenn, Cambridge 1959, esp. pp. 2–13, 13–20, 25–31.

3. The phrase comes from J. R. R. Tolkien's 'Beowulf: the Monsters and the Critics', *PBA* 22 (1936), 245–95.

4. K. Sisam, *The Structure of Beowulf*, Oxford 1965, p. 9. See also Sisam's comments in 'Anglo-Saxon Royal Genealogies', *PBA* 39 (1953), 287–348, esp. the conclusions on pp. 345–6.

5. The point is made by Sigurthur Nordal, 'The Historical Element in the Icelandic Family Sagas', 15th W. P. Ker Memorial Lecture, 1954, published by Glasgow University. See also that author's detailed analysis of one family saga, *Hranfnkels Saga Freysgotha: a Study,* trans. R. G. Thomas, Cardiff 1958.

6. Like most decisions about this piece, such an interpretation depends to a large extent on debated readings, here of lines 1080–85. Klaeber suggests that their meaning is basically that Finn 'could be successful neither in the offensive nor in the defensive', i.e. that Hengest is in control; see *Beowulf,* Ed. Fr. Klaeber, 3rd ed., Boston 1950, pp. 171–2. But if Hengest were in control, would he not kill Finn immediately? For a more credible reading, see Carleton F. Brown, *MLN* 34 (1919), 181–3.

7. The best statement of this is still H. M. Ayres, 'The Tragedy of Hengest', *JEGP* 16 (1917), 282–95.

8. Again, interpretation and even translation is in doubt. For a clear summary and a good rendering, see A. G. Brodeur, 'The Climax of the Finn Episode', *Univ. of California Publications in English* III, 8 (1943), 285–361. A very different reading is given by R. Girvan, 'Finnsburuh', *PBA* 26 (1940), 327–60.

9. One might note, for example, Gilbert Murray's remarks in *The Rise of the Greek Epic,* 4th ed. Oxford 1934, pp. 90–2; or Peter Hallberg's in *The Icelandic Saga,* trans. P. Schach, Lincoln, Nebraska 1962, pp. 107–8.

10. R. W. Chambers, *Introduction*, pp. 245–89, 543–6. This explanation is

largely accepted by the modern editions of Klaeber (1950), C. L. Wrenn (rev. ed., London 1958), and A. J. Wyatt (revised by Chambers, Cambridge 1948).

11. The story is told, at an early date, by Geoffrey of Monmouth in his *History of the Kings of Britain*, pp. 164–5 in the Penguin ed. of 1966, trans. L. Thorpe. A. S. C. Ross's article, 'Hengist's Watchword', *E&GS* 2 (1948–9), 81–101, implies that there may be a basis of fact for the famous cry 'take out your knives!'. Chambers' own edition of *Widsith*, Cambridge 1912, suggests that there were stories of Hengest and Horsa in existence, see Appendix K, p. 254.

12. The *Finnsburg Fragment, Waldere*, and the *Hildebrandslied* are all given in Klaeber's edition of *Beowulf*, pp. 245–9, 283–5, 290–2. *Waldere* is also edited by F. Norman, 2nd ed. London 1949. One should consult *The Battle of Maldon*, rev. ed. by E. V. Gordon, London 1957, while the 'Cynewulf and Cyneheard' episode is best known from *Sweet's Anglo-Saxon Reader*, 15th ed. by D. Whitelock, Oxford 1967, pp. 1–3. Other attempts to define common elements in these (and many other) stories, and to describe the characters of heroes, are provided by B. S. Phillpotts, 'Wyrd and Providence in Anglo-Saxon Thought', *Essays and Studies* 13 (1928), 7–27; by G. N. Garmonsway, 'Anglo-Saxon Heroic Attitudes', in *Franciplegius: Medieval and Linguistic Studies in Honour of F. P. Magoun*, Ed. J. B. Bessinger jr, and R. P. Creed, New York and London 1965, pp. 139–46; by J. de Vries, *Heroic Song and Heroic Legend*, trans. B. J. Timmer, London 1963, pp. 180–226.

13. Several articles have appeared recently in attempts to elucidate this (not particularly difficult) text, of which the most measured is Ruth Waterhouse, 'The Theme and Structure of "755 Anglo-Saxon Chronicle"', *NM* 70 (1969), 630–40.

14. Again, many articles have come out recently to argue that *Maldon* is or is not reliable historically or effective poetically. The most valuable are J. B. Bessinger jr, '*Maldon* and the *Óláfsdrápa*: an Historical Caveat', *CL* 14 (1962), 23–35; W. F. Bolton, 'Byrhtnoth in the Wilderness', *MLR* 64 (1969), 481–90 (an article which points to the influence on the poem of another literary form, the saint's life); and O. D. Macrae-Gibson, 'How Historical is *The Battle of Maldon*?' *Medium Aevum* 39 (1970), 89–108.

15. This duality is also pointed out by N. F. Blake, 'The Battle of Maldon,' *Neophil.* 49 (1965), 332–45. Failure to appreciate it has probably been at the root of much of the wrangling over Byrhtnoth's 'mistake', started by J. R. R. Tolkien's critical but still sensitive *prosimetra* 'The Homecoming of Beorhtnoth Beorhthelm's Son', *Essays and Studies* 38 (1953), 1–18.

16. This feeling is extremely prominent in Old Icelandic literature, especially in the very common 'egging' scenes, where someone, usually a woman, urges sometimes *strangely* reluctant heroes to their revenge. Even though their actions may be justified, it is very rare for the people who urge on the hero to escape criticism or even punishment for their insensitivity. A well-nigh perfect example is the story translated as 'Thorstein Staff-Struck' in the Worlds Classics volume *Eirik the Red and other Icelandic Sagas,* trans. Gwyn Jones, London 1961. In this the two protagonists, Thorstein and Bjarni, do their best not to fight each other, and are reconciled in the end, the real conflict being between each of them and a succession of men and women who urge them to fight. Bjarni in particular deals ruthlessly with these foolish people; but such reluctance (not cowardice) is common, if not always so extreme. It has become common practice to discount Icelandic evidence, on the ground that it is so much later than the Heroic Age or Old English poetry. Still, the similarity of tone and situation is often quite undeniable—see Theodore M. Andersson, *The Icelandic Family Saga,* Cambridge, Mass. 1967, pp. 65–93.

17. *Harðar saga ok Hólmverja,* Ed. Guthni Jónsson, Reykjavik 1934, ch. 11.

18. See references to Saxo in *Beowulf and its Analogues*, trans. G. N. Garmonsway and Jacqueline Simpson, London and New York 1968; or Saxo Grammaticus, Books I–IX, trans. O. Elton with commentary by F. Y. Powell, London 1894.

19. See Sisam, *Structure*, pp. 33–9, 80–2.

20. A. G. Brodeur gives a good account of this passage in *The Art of Beowulf*, Berkeley and Los Angeles 1959, pp. 78–87.

21. Fr. Klaeber made an early attempt to relate *Beowulf* to the *Aeneid* in his 'Aeneis und Beowulf', *Archiv* 126 (1911), 40–8, 338–59. The idea was given powerful but indirect support by E. R. Curtius, *European Literature and the Latin Middle Ages*, trans. Willard Trask, London 1953, pp. 167–76. But for all his deserved influence, Curtius does not seem to have read *Beowulf* for himself; and if the Anglo-Saxon poet did know the Latin epic, it is curious that he followed its letter only occasionally, and its spirit not at all.

22. Laurence Lerner makes the point about Old English ideas of colour in 'Colour Words in Anglo-Saxon', *MLR* 46 (1951), 246–9, an article which could be compared with Stephen Ullmann's description of an aphasic patient in *Language and Style*, Oxford 1964, pp. 207–12. With his usual understated brilliance J. R. R. Tolkien uses the point in his description of the cloaks of Lorien in *The Fellowship of the Ring*, London 1954, p. 386.

23. Bruno Snell, *The Discovery of the Mind*, trans. R. G. Rosenmayer, Cambridge, Mass, 1953, p. 37. Snell's qualification means that he does not consider 'Homer' to have been one individual; 'Homer' means the shared style of Greek epic in general.

24. See Klaeber's edition of *Beowulf*, Glossary, p. 399, and also Introduction, p. lvii.

25. The figure is necessarily based on Klaeber's edition, the only one to provide a completely itemised glossary. Comparison with other usages is not easy, since the word is not commonly used as a conjunction in prose, its functions being taken over by *þa* and *þonne*. Thus in the first 10 of Ælfric's *Catholic Homilies*, 1st series, Ed. B. Thorpe, London 1844, it occurs twice (in over 80 pages), and both times the order is the reverse of the Beowulfian one, i.e. the subordinate clause precedes the main one. If one considers the more frequent *gif*-clauses, the figures are, for *Beowulf*, 26 examples of main+subordinate and 3 of sub+main, for the first 10 *Catholic Homilies*, 33 of main+sub and 50 of sub+main—quite a convincing reversal. See, however, R. Quirk and C. L. Wrenn, *An Old English Grammar*, London 1967, p. 95.

26. Coleridge, *Biographia Literaria*, ch. 18.

27. This has been discussed by Edward B. Irving jr, *A Reading of Beowulf*, New Haven 1968, pp. 31–42. Here, as elsewhere, I owe a great deal to this exceptionally stimulating author.

28. See the comments of E. van K. Dobbie in the Introduction to vol. IV of *The Anglo-Saxon Poetic Records*, 'Beowulf and Judith', New York and London 1953, pp. xxv-xxvi.

29. Once again, this idea is mentioned by Irving, op. cit., pp. 147–50.

30. I have departed here from the *ASPR* edition to the extent of making a noun, *edwenden*, from what might be a verb, *edwendan*. The case for this (fairly unimportant) change is put by Klaeber in his note to the passage cited, op. cit., p. 139.

31. In *The Anglo-Saxon Dictionary*, Ed. J. Bosworth and T. W. Toller, London 1898 (with supplement by Toller 1921), *wlencu* is given in several contexts. In prose it is generally unfavourable, being used even for the stubbornness of a strayed animal; it can also mean 'pomp' or 'wealth', no doubt because connected with the attitudes which prosperity engenders. These uses only show up the strangeness of the favourable poetic contexts. The word is illuminated by its use

to translate the Psalms' *abundantia,* and by its collocations with *orsorgnesse* [carelessness] and *geogoðe* [youth].

32. *Guthlac,* lines 206–9. The devils complain that St Guthlac has done them the greatest of harms, *siððan he for wlence on westenne beorgas bræce . . .* [once he in his daring disturbed the mounds in the wilderness . . .].

33. There is a very thorough article by B. J. Timmer, '*Wyrd* in Anglo-Saxon Prose and Poetry', *Neophil.* 26 (1941), 24–33, 213–28. This marks the word's transitions of meaning very clearly. However, Timmer never questions that the 'outlook on life of the Germanic peoples was fatalistic' in some unrecorded era; more far-reaching is the discussion of the word in *The Wanderer,* Ed. T. P. Dunning and A. J. Bliss, London 1969, pp. 71–4. See also A. H. Roper, 'Boethius and the Three Fates of *Beowulf* ', *PQ* 41 (1962), 386–400.

34. It has been pointed out that even the metaphor of the 'weaving of fate' is not as passive and deterministic a one as we might think, see R. B. Onians, *The Origins of European Thought,* Cambridge 1954, pp. 347–57.

35. The attempt to relate this speech closely to Beowulf leads insidiously to arguments that the hero is meant to be condemned, or seen as increasingly weak and sinful, as for instance in H. L. Rogers, 'Beowulf's Three Great Fights', *RES NS* 6 (1955), 339–55. There is a more cautious statement by A. G. Brodeur, *The Art of Beowulf,* pp. 212–15.

36. E. B. Irving jr, op. cit., p. 147.

37. There is a fine summary of learned Christian material similar to Hrothgar's 'sermon' in Margaret E. Goldsmith's *The Mode and Meaning of Beowulf,* London 1970, pp. 183–209. See also R. E. Kaske, '*Sapientia et Fortitudo* as the Controlling Theme of *Beowulf* ', *SP* 55 (1958), 423–56, an attractive and judicious article, but one reminiscent of Curtius (see note 21).

38. The parallels with *Christ* (lines 660ff.) and *Daniel* (lines 488ff.) are discussed by Goldsmith, loc. cit., and Klaeber in his edition of *Beowulf,* pp. cx–cxiii. The passages in the other poems mentioned are *Guthlac* 495–504, *Gifts* 18–29, *Judgement* 73–80, and Proem to *Boethius* 3–10.

39. E. Auerbach, *Mimesis,* trans. Willard Trask, Princeton 1953, pp. 1–20.

40. This is suggested by R. E. Kaske, 'Weohstan's Sword', *MLN* 75 (1960), 465–8. Kaske sees the whole episode as a multiple contrast between the claims of kinship and a retainer's duties, an interpretation both true and attractive, but expressed more schematically than might have been possible for the poet himself.

41. Lines 2202–6 and 2379–96.

42. In *The Digressions in Beowulf,* Oxford 1950, Adrien Bonjour argues that the existence of the sword should remind us of probable future conflict between Wiglaf and Eanmund's brother, now apparently king of the Swedes. This is possible, but far removed from the situation of Beowulf and Wiglaf at the time.

43. Lines 212–16.

44. J. R. R. Tolkien, 'Beowulf: the Monsters and the Critics', p. 259.

45. There has not been much attempt to relate these strikingly detached 'nuggets' of story to the poem, perhaps because their thematic rather than narrative connection is so strikingly obvious. Klaeber's edition, for example, contains some remarks about legendary parallels, but no more.

46. A view rather like the last of these possibilities has been expressed by M. E. Goldsmith, op. cit., pp. 222–41, though she argues that the corruption is one inevitable for all humanity.

47. The essentially critical view seems to underly the work of Goldsmith and Rogers noted above, while few people would care now to put forward a reading of unmixed praise—though such a reaction would be natural enough. A 'mixed' view has been put most notably by J. R. R. Tolkien, op. cit., and more recently

by E. G. Stanley, '*Hæthenra Hyht* in *Beowulf*', in *Studies in Old English Literature in Honor of A. G. Brodeur*, Ed. S. B. Greenfield, Oregon 1963, pp. 136–51.

48. For this aspect of the poem, important but necessarily neglected in an account of the poet's *intentions*, see R. W. Chambers, *Introduction*, pp. 42–68, 451–85; and N. K. Chadwick, 'The Monsters and Beowulf', in *The Anglo-Saxons: Studies for Bruce Dickins*, Ed. P. Clemoes, London 1959, pp. 171–203.

49. The phrase comes from Gilbert Murray's *The Rise of the Greek Epic*, 4th ed. Oxford 1934, see especially pp. 242–60; though old-fashioned and with no direct bearing on *Beowulf*, this book still has illuminating conclusions about the nature of a heroic age, and of a traditional epic. A similar idea is expressed by W. P. Ker, *The Dark Ages*, London 1904, pp. 252–4.

Chapter 3
Wisdom and experience: The Old English 'elegies'

1. The word is discussed critically by B. J. Timmer, 'The Elegiac Mood in Old English Poetry', *ES* 24 (1942), 33–44.

2. All the poems prominently discussed in this chapter (with the exception of *Solomon and Saturn*) come from vol. III of *The Anglo-Saxon Poetic Records,* 'The Exeter Book', Ed. G. P. Krapp and E. van K. Dobbie, New York 1936, and many, including this one, are to be found conveniently nowhere else.

3. W. W. Lawrence, '*The Wanderer* and *The Seafarer*', *JEGP* 4 (1902), 460–80. See also B. J. Timmer, 'Heathen and Christian Elements in Old English Poetry', *Neophil.* 29 (1944), 180–5. In articles such as B. F. Huppé, '*The Wanderer*: Theme and Structure', *JEGP* 42 (1943), 516–38, these (hypothetical) differences of attitude are erected into a structural principle.

4. Nevertheless, there is a fine modern statement of this view, J. C. Pope's 'Dramatic Voices in *The Wanderer* and *The Seafarer*', included in *Franciplegius: Medieval and Linguistic Studies in Honour of F. P. Magoun*, Ed. J. B. Bessinger jr and R. P. Creed, London and New York 1965, pp. 164–93.

5. I. L. Gordon, 'Traditional Themes in *The Wanderer* and *The Seafarer*', *RES NS* 5 (1954), 1–13.

6. In this the Old English poems are unlike many classical examples—in Boethius's *De Consolatione Philosophiae,* for example, Philosophy's first action is to abuse and drive off the Muses (a passage omitted by King Alfred in his translation). For parallels between *The Wanderer* and classical consolations, see J. E. Cross, 'On the Genre of *The Wanderer*', *Neophil.* 45 (1961), 63–75.

7. The translation here is in some doubt. Is *mod* or *maga gemynd* the subject? For support of the reading given, see *The Wanderer,* Ed. T. P. Dunning and A. J. Bliss, London 1969, pp. 21–3. This edition as a whole solves many translation problems.

8. See Dunning and Bliss, op. cit., pp. 23–5.

9. The parallel has been noted also by E. G. Stanley, 'Old English Poetic Diction and the Interpretation of *The Wanderer, The Seafarer,* and *The Penitent's Prayer*', *Anglia* 73 (1955), 413–66. Further discussion of symbolism in the 'elegies' appears in Edward B. Irving jr, 'Image and Meaning in the Elegies', in *Old English Poetry: Fifteen Essays,* Ed. R. P. Creed, Providence 1967, pp. 153–66.

10. See Dunning and Bliss, op. cit., p. 42.

11. This argument is by J. C. Pope, in his article on 'Dramatic Voices' already cited.

12. P. Clemoes, '*Mens absentia cogitans* in *The Seafarer* and *The Wanderer*', in *Medieval Literature and Civilisation: Studies in Memory of G. N. Garmonsway,* Ed. D. A. Pearsall and R. A. Waldron, London 1969, pp. 62–77.

13. The phrase 'exaltation of undefeated will' comes from J. R. R. Tolkien, 'Beowulf: the Monsters and the Critics', p. 259.

14. Such a genre may seem curiously sophisticated for this period. Yet the end of the Old Norse *Guðrunarhvöt* implies poetry designed to cure grief in a rather similar way. The existence of such genres in other primitive or early cultures is vouched for by G. Thomson, *Studies in Ancient Greek Society: The Prehistoric Aegean*, London 1949, pp. 435–62, and (much more obscurely) by C. Lévi-Strauss, *Structural Anthropology*, trans. C. Jacobson and B. G. Schoepf, New York 1963, pp. 186–205.

15. N. K. Chadwick and V. Zhirmunsky, *Oral Epics of Central Asia*, London 1969, pp. 181, 229.

16. See the discussion in *The Poetical Dialogues of Solomon and Saturn*, Ed. R. J. Menner, London and New York 1941, pp. 6–7.

17. Bede, *Historia Ecclesiastica* II 13.

18. In the manuscript these few lines are found *before* the second dialogue, and are printed in this position in the *Anglo-Saxon Poetic Records* vol. VI; but Menner argues that they have been misplaced from the end, op. cit., pp. 10–12.

19. For instance, two of Odin's valkyries are called 'Chain' and 'Fetter'; even in quite prosaic sagas there is a fear of sudden paralysis; the first *Merseburg Proverb* (an Old High German charm), runs roughly as follows: 'Once there were women seated here and there on the ground, some binding a captive, some hindering a host, some picking at fetters: "Escape from the fetters, escape from the foes."' For discussion of this latter, see J. K. Bostock, *A Handbook on O. H. G. Literature*, Oxford 1955, pp. 16–32; for the whole question of bondage, see R. B. Onians, *The Origins of European Thought*, 2nd ed., Cambridge 1954, pp. 352–8.

20. The young man's 'despairing mind' is mentioned in *The Wanderer* lines 15–16; for the mother's situation, see *Fortunes of Men* 1–9 (and *Maxims* I 22–5?), and note Hrothgar's retrospective remarks in *Beowulf* 942–6.

21. See the interesting arguments of F. Anne Payne, *King Alfred and Boethius*, Madison 1968, especially pp. 15–21; but the whole book is most remarkable for its demonstration of a coherent philosophy informing Alfred's many changes from his author. At several points this philosophy shows remarkable resemblance to the conclusions drawn (in my view) from Old English verse. See pp. 181–2 above.

22. It occurs frequently in *Genesis* and *Christ and Satan*, and is used to end victoriously debates with devils in *Guthlac* 665–84, *Elene* 766–71, and *Andreas* 1376–85. See pp. 125 and 130 above.

23. This is urged by Morton W. Bloomfield, 'Understanding Old English Poetry', *Annuale Mediaevale* 9 (1968), 5–25.

24. Erich Heller, *The Disinherited Mind*, Edinburgh 1961 (Pelican ed.), p. 16.

25. See Dunning and Bliss, op. cit., pp. 23–5, for argument that lines 53–5 of *The Wanderer* do refer to the sea-birds.

26. J. E. Cross, 'On the Allegory in *The Seafarer*—Illustrative Notes', *Medium Aevum* 28 (1959), 104–6.

27. D. Whitelock, 'The Interpretation of *The Seafarer*', In *Early Cultures of N.W. Europe (H. M. Chadwick Memorial Studies)*, Cambridge 1950, pp. 261–72.

28. For discussion, and some good examples, see P. L. Henry, *The Early English and Celtic Lyric*, London 1966, pp. 24, 67–8, and elsewhere. But too easy identification of the different traditions is strongly condemned by H. Pilch, 'The Elegiac Genre in Old English and Early Welsh Poetry', *Zeitschrift für celtische Philologie*, 29 (1964), 209–24.

29. The reading here varies from that given in the *ASPR* edition of the *Exeter Book*, where a new sentence is printed from *Forþon* in line 64. I have followed the reading of *The Seafarer*, Ed. I. L. Gordon, London 1959. There is now little

doubt that Old English poetic sentences were longer and better organised than early editors thought, and that repeated words such as *forþon . . . forþon* or *þa . . . þa* were used to signal clause-boundaries rather than sentence ones.

30. G. V. Smithers, 'The Meaning of *The Seafarer* and *The Wanderer*', *Medium Aevum* 26 (1957), 137–53, and 28 (1959), 1–22.

31. This is discussed by E. G. Stanley, op. cit.—an article which defies summary or paraphrase.

32. As we can see from Beowulf himself, or from *Guthlac* 495ff., or *The Wanderer* 64–5.

33. See S. B. Greenfield, 'Attitudes and Values in *The Seafarer*', *SP* 51 (1954). 15–20.

34. The most prominent pieces in what has been a very extended discussion are perhaps A. C. Bouman, *Patterns in Old English and Old Icelandic Literature*, Leiden 1962, chs 3 and 4; R. C. Bambas, 'Another View of the Old English *Wife's Lament*', *JEGP* 62 (1963), 303–9; and R. P. Fitzgerald, '*The Wife's Lament* and "The Search for the Lost Husband"', *JEGP* 62 (1963), 769–77. But at least seven other recent, precise interpretations of these poems could be cited.

35. Again, this may seem a far-fetched and sophisticated explanation for this period. Still, it is suggested also by the remarks of E. G. Stanley, op. cit., to the effect that in Old English moods may instigate rather than follow familiar scenes, as one might gather by comparing *The Wanderer*, say, with that simpler poem *The Ruin*. Similarly, a wish to portray a 'frozen mind' could precede, and would certainly lead to, such a situation as the one guessed at behind *The Wife's Lament*. One might compare the vague personal situation behind *The Wanderer*, which we are certainly not meant to dissect, and which serves its purpose if it justifies the thoughts of the imagined speaker; in this as in the 'women's poems' it is the dramatic but loosely-visualised present situation which is important.

36. Alain Renoir, '*Wulf and Eadwacer*: a Non-interpretation', in the *Studies in Honour of Magoun* already cited, pp. 147–63. This is a fine article, and, as its name suggests, one reacting to the many over-precise and over-literal arguments which had appeared just before.

37. The best analysis of these repetitions is to be found in R. D. Stevick, 'Formal Aspects of *The Wife's Lament*', *JEGP* 59 (1960), 21–5.

38. This is one of the points which have led some to argue that the 'wife' must be masculine, see R. C. Bambas, op. cit.—though if one starts from the premise that 'Old English secular poetry reflects the limited attitudes and interests of a primitive warrior culture', many Old English poems become hard to read!

39. It is important to realise (a) that *þæs* and *þisses* are in the genitive case and so not precisely the grammatical subjects and (b) that *mæg* does not mean 'may'—a word too weakly hopeful.

40. Probably this is a false translation of *be wurman*, but all others involve considerable argument, to discuss which would distract from the point being made here. For analysis, see *Deor*, Ed. K. Malone, 3rd ed., London 1961, pp. 6–7, and *Seven Old English Poems*, Ed. J. C. Pope, New York 1966, pp. 91–6.

41. Again, see Malone, op. cit., pp. 4–6.

42. It is not clear whether this refers to Theodric the Ostrogoth or Theodric the Frank. The latter is proposed by Malone and accepted by Pope in the editions cited.

43. By Norman E. Eliason, '*Deor*—a Begging Poem?', in the volume of *Studies for Garmonsway* already cited, pp. 55–61. In this and in an earlier article, 'Two Old English *Scop* poems', *PMLA* 81 (1966), 185–92, Professor Eliason develops the argument that *Deor* and *Widsith* are the 'advertisements' of professional minstrels.

44. This is even more obvious if, as seems likely, lines 28–34 are to be read as one

sentence, 'If a sorrowful man sits and grows gloomy . . . he can then reflect. . . .'

45. Morton W. Bloomfield, 'The Form of *Deor*', *PMLA* 79 (1964), 534–41—an excellent article.

Chapter 4
Language and style

1. These are edited by E. van K. Dobbie as vol. VI of *The Anglo-Saxon Poetic Records*, 'The Anglo-Saxon Minor Poems', London and New York 1942.

2. Edited together by G. P. Krapp as vol. V of *The Anglo-Saxon Poetic Records*, London and New York 1932.

3. This date is based on the style of handwriting, almost the only evidence for many of our poetic manuscripts.

4. K. Sisam, *Studies in the History of Old English Literature*, Oxford 1953, p. 118. I have relied heavily on this work, especially during the first section of this chapter.

5. Some suggestions as to its connections before 1050 are given by Dunning and Bliss in their edition of *The Wanderer* already cited, pp. 1–2.

6. *The Dream of the Rood*, Ed. B. Dickins and A. S. C. Ross, 4th ed., London 1954, p. 13.

7. A. Campbell, *Old English Grammar*, Oxford 1959, p. 10.

8. See A. Campbell, op. cit., p. 186.

9. G. Sarrazin, 'Zur Chronologie und Verfasserfrage Angelsächsischer Dichtungen', *Englische Studien* 38 (1907), 145–95. Other tests of date, and other results, are conveniently summarised by Klaeber in his edition of *Beowulf*, pp. cviii–cix.

10. D. Whitelock, *The Audience of Beowulf*, Oxford 1951, pp. 19–33.

11. The correspondence is not quite as close as it appears; the word *furður* has been added to *Beowulf* (here defective), as a result of comparison with *Maldon*. However, the emendation is reasonable, and could be right.

12. Repeated words are in bold type; words of the same grammatical type or expressing similar ideas are in italics.

13. *Christ and Satan*, Ed. M. D. Clubb, New Haven 1925, pp. xxiv–xlii.

14. *Andreas and The Fates of the Apostles*, Ed. G. P. Krapp, New York and London 1906, p. lvii.

15. C. Schaar, *Critical Studies in the Cynewulf Group*, Lund 1949, pp. 235–309.

16. See Milman Parry, 'Studies in the Epic Technique of oral Verse-Making. I: Homer and Homeric Style', *HSCP* 41 (1930), 73–147, and 'II: The Homeric Language as the Language of an Oral Poetry', *HSCP* 43 (1932), 1–50; A. B. Lord, *The Singer of Tales*, Cambridge, Mass. 1960; F. P. Magoun, 'The Oral-formulaic Character of Anglo-Saxon Narrative Poetry', *Speculum* 28 (1953), 446–67. The book by Lord is probably the best and fullest guide for anyone wishing to pursue the subject fully, even though for most of the time it has little to do with English poetry.

17. Parry, 'Homer and Homeric Style', p. 80.

18. See, for instance, U. Bellugi and R. Brown, 'Three processes in the Child's Acquisition of Syntax', *Harvard Educational Review*, 34 (1964), 133–51.

19. The word is taken from H. L. Rogers, 'The Crypto-Psychological Character of the Oral Formula', *ES* 47 (1966), 89–102. Though largely condemnatory, this article is useful for its detailed criticism of Parry's much-quoted definition of the formula. It is certainly true that the cases of Greek and Old English epic are so far apart that they resist almost any summary joint definition.

20. *The Odyssey*, Book VIII, trans. Robert Fitzgerald, London 1962.

21. See R. E. Diamond, 'Theme as Ornament in Anglo-Saxon Poetry', *PMLA*

76 (1961), 461–8. The author is clearly aware of the points I make, and has written other useful articles on this general subject; I wish to suggest only that the method employed in such studies has yielded its results, and is unlikely to produce any more.

22. In many ways the oral-formulaic theory exemplifies a 'paradigm situation' as defined by Thomas S. Kuhn in *The Structure of Scientific Revolutions,* Chicago 1962. In other words, before its arrival conventional thinking about Old English poetry was aware of a problem, engaged in the attempt to solve it by increasing refinement of method, but fundamentally on the wrong track. As soon as the theory was developed, the well-established problem (the *Parallelstellen*) was solved; but at the same time many others were created, whose appearance has given opportunity for much well-founded criticism and complaint. Nevertheless, the subject can never be exactly the same again.

23. C. Schaar, 'On a new theory of Old English poetic diction', *Neophil.* 40 (1956), 301–5.

24. Lord, *The Singer of Tales,* p. 129.

25. F. P. Magoun, 'Bede's story of Cædman: the Case-history of an Anglo-Saxon oral Singer', *Speculum* 30 (1955), 49–63.

26. See, respectively, R. D. Stevick, *The Diction of the Anglo-Saxon Metrical Psalms,* The Hague 1963, and Larry D. Benson, 'The Literary Character of Anglo-Saxon Formulaic Poetry', *PMLA* 81 (1966), 334–41. Neither author is generally favourable to any strict form of the oral-formulaic theory.

27. Jackson J. Campbell, 'Learned Rhetoric in Old English Poetry', *MP* 63 (1966), 189–201.

28. See D. H. Green, *The Carolingian Lord: semantic studies on four Old High German words,* Cambridge 1965, esp. pp. 265–9.

29. The same argument is given by R. F. Lawrence, 'The Formulaic Theory and its Application to English Alliterative Poetry', in *Essays on Style and Language,* Ed. R. Fowler, London 1966, pp. 166–83. This article is valuable also for its review of earlier critical material.

30. Sisam, *Studies,* p. 34.

31. *The Penguin Book of Modern Verse Translation,* Ed. G. Steiner, London 1966, p. 21.

32. *Beowulf,* trans. D. Wright, London 1957, p. 22 (Penguin Classics ed.).

33. See W. Whallon, 'The Diction of *Beowulf*', *PMLA* 76 (1961), 309–19. This is an extremely useful article; but the suggestion made, that Old English poetry must have been relatively underdeveloped, is answered by Whallon's own later article, 'Formulas for Heroes in *The Iliad* and *Beowulf*', *MP* 63 (1965), 95–104.

34. E. G. Stanley, in the article already cited on 'Poetic Diction and the Interpretation of *The Wanderer* etc.', esp. pp. 433–6.

35. There is a modern *Concordance to Beowulf,* Ed. Jess B. Bessinger jr, Ithaca 1969, and a concordance to the whole of Old English poetry is said to be under way. On the other hand, fully itemised glossaries are now less common than they were; it was one of the strong points of the old 'Albion' series, which produced editions of *Andreas, Christ,* and *The Riddles.* These have been used extensively, along with Klaeber's *Beowulf,* for confirmatory analysis of the points in this chapter.

36. The system was stated by Sievers in his *Altgermanische Metrik,* Halle 1893. A useful modern rehandling of it appears in B. M. H. Strang, *A History of English,* London 1970, pp. 323–33; while many readers will find C. S. Lewis's 'The Alliterative Metre' invaluable, not least for the author's own modern English examples. The essay is to be found most readily in C. S. Lewis, *Rehabilitations and other essays,* London 1939, or reprinted in *Essential Articles for the Study of Old English Poetry,* Ed. J. B. Bessinger and S. J. Kahrl, Hamden, Conn. 1968.

37. J. C. Pope, *The Rhythm of Beowulf*, rev. ed., New Haven 1966. A major point of his argument is that rhythm was marked by pauses as well as by speech, more obvious in recitation to the harp than in unaccompanied reading. An alternative and practical form of scansion is set out by R. P. Creed, 'A New Approach to the Rhythm of *Beowulf*', *PMLA* 81 (1966), 23–33.

38. L. Fakundiny, 'The Art of Old English Verse Composition' *RES NS* 21 (1970), 129–42 and 257–66.

39. This has not been discussed recently with regard to Old English. Marie Borroff's *Sir Gawain and the Green Knight: a stylistic and metrical study*, New Haven 1962, gives a fine account of the idea with reference to Middle English, see esp. pp. 52–90. The information given here has been checked against the poems with full glossaries mentioned in note 35, as well as *Beowulf*. The picture remains much the same, though there are one or two interesting particular divergences.

40. See R. Quirk, 'Poetic Language and Old English Metre', in *Early English and Norse Studies presented to Hugh Smith*, Ed. A. Brown and P. Foote, London 1963, pp. 150–71.

41. 57 lines collected from nine of the longer poems gave the following words as most frequently linked in alliteration with *flod*—(some variant of) *feor* [far]: 6 times; *folde* [earth]: 6 times; *fyr, feorh, fæþm* [fire, life, embrace]: 5 times each; *fealo* [grey]: 4 times; *fær* [danger] and *fæge* [doomed]: 3 each. No other single word occurred as frequently as four times, though variants of *faran, ferian, frefran* [to travel, transport, comfort] occurred three times each, as did the noun *folc* [people] and the adjective *famig* [foamy]. The words listed thus account for 52 of the 93 cases of alliteration with *flod* in these 57 lines. Only 17 words occurred once only. I need hardly add that this distribution is very obviously not a random one; moreover no similar feature can be found by looking up 'flood' in, say, a concordance to Milton, though the language of *Paradise Lost* has been thought repetitive by literary standards.

42. The line is oddly reminiscent of an image twice repeated in the twelfth-century poem, Layamon's *Brut—Vðen þer urnen, al-se tunes þer burnen* [Waves ran by like burning towns]. The simile has been much praised; but perhaps the rhyme was responsible for it, as with the alliteration in Old English!

43. *Exeter Book*, Ed. Krapp and Dobbie, pp. 220–3. The poem describes Christ's resurrection and the Harrowing of Hell.

44. See Frederic G. Cassidy, 'How Free was the Anglo-Saxon Scop?', in *Studies for Magoun*, pp. 75–85. The root source of his statement is unpublished.

45. A. J. Bliss, *RES NS* 21 (1970), on p. 71.

46. The term comes from Adeline C. Bartlett, *The Larger Rhetorical Patterns in Anglo-Saxon Poetry*, New York, 1935. The book also provides many examples.

47. C. Brett, 'Notes on Old and Middle English', *MLR* 22 (1927), 260.

48. See the article by E. A. Nida in the collection *On Translation*, Ed. R. A. Brower, Cambridge, Mass. 1959, pp. 11–31. The collection also contains a most valuable article by R. Jakobson.

49. *The Battle of Maldon and other Old English Poems*, trans. K. Crossley-Holland and Ed. B. Mitchell, London 1965.

50. *Beowulf*, trans. D. Wright, London 1957 (Penguin Classics).

51. For instance, Richard Hamer, *A Choice of Anglo-Saxon Verse*, London 1970; E. Talbot Donaldson's *Beowulf*, London 1967; and see J. R. R. Tolkien's Preface to the translation of *Beowulf* by J. R. Clark Hall, as revised by C. L. Wrenn, London 1950.

52. J. R. R. Tolkien, 'The Homecoming of Beorhtnoth Beorhthelm's Son', *Essays & Studies* 38 (1953), 1–18. In this two speakers, the sober and experienced Tidwald [Time-Ruler], and the young and sensitive Torhthelm [Bright-Helmet], debate the results of the battle. The latter is presented as misled by the superficial

qualities of Old English verse; the former perhaps appreciates the deeper and more melancholy ones. Tolkien's own alliterative verse, here and elsewhere, is of course the product of a very full response to the meaning, vocabulary and syntax of Old English poetry.

53. The poem exists in a Northumbrian version, given here, and a 'translated' West Saxon one, which also makes slight verbal changes to some of the compounds. See *Three Northumbrian Poems,* Ed. A. H. Smith, rev. ed., London 1968.

Chapter 5
The fight for truth: Non-Cynewulfian saints' lives

1. The word is taken from E. G. Stanley, *'Beowulf',* in *Continuations and Beginnings,* Ed. E. G. Stanley, London 1966, p. 137.

2. This is suggested by the editor of the two Latin lives, Franz Blatt, in *Die lateinischen Bearbeitungen der Acta Andreae et Matthiae apud anthropophagos,* Giessen and Copenhagen 1930, p. 1. One of the Old English prose versions is to be found conveniently edited and translated in *The Blickling Homilies,* Ed. R. Morris, London 1880 (*EETS OS* 58), pp. 228–49.

3. The two arguments against this assumption are either that all three genitives, *wira . . . landes . . . beaga,* are dependent on *gespann,* or else that *Næbbe* for once takes an implied genitive, 'I do not have (anything) of land or twisted rings'. Neither is entirely satisfactory. However, it is possible that the phrase has been loosely borrowed from formulaic tradition in general, not from one (unimportant) passage of *Beowulf* in particular.

4. The root meaning of the hypothetical verb *scerwan* appears to be 'to grant'. *Meoduscerwen,* 'a granting of mead', therefore has a heavily ironic force in describing the flood; but *ealuscerwen,* 'a granting of ale', makes little sense of the scene outside Heorot. Hence the arguments that it means 'a deprivation of ale', 'a granting of something bitter', etc.

5. The phrase is quoted by G. P. Krapp in his edition of *Andreas and The Fates of the Apostles,* Boston, Mass. 1906, p. li. The assumption that *Beowulf* influenced *Andreas* heavily is made by Fr. Klaeber and C. L. Wrenn, among others, in their editions of *Beowulf* already cited.

6. L. J. Peters, 'The relationship of the Old English *Andreas* to *Beowulf',* *PMLA* 66 (1951), 844–63.

7. D. Whitelock, 'Anglo-Saxon Poetry and the Historian', *Trans. Royal Hist. Soc.* 31 (1949), 75–94.

8. R. Woolf, 'Saints' Lives', in *Continuations and Beginnings,* pp. 37–66.

9. Claes Schaar, *Critical Studies in the Cynewulf Group,* Lund 1949, pp. 161–3. Although I disagree with Schaar here and on p. 93 above, his work has been more useful than that of almost any other scholar. His attempts to distinguish Cynewulfian from non-Cynewulfian texts are especially valuable in pointing out repeated stylistic habits (like the use of *sippan*-clauses).

10. K. R. Brooks suggests this in his edition of *Andreas and The Fates of the Apostles,* Oxford 1961, p. 80.

11. See D. K. Crowne, 'The Hero on the beach: an example of composition by theme in Anglo-Saxon Poetry', *NM* 61 (1960), 362–72; Alain Renoir, 'Oral-formulaic theme survival: a possible instance in the *Nibelungenlied',* *NM* 65 (1964), 70–5; D. K. Fry, 'The Hero on the beach in *Finnsburh',* *NM* 67 (1966), 27–31; and D. K. Fry, 'The Heroine on the beach in *Judith',* *NM* 68 (1967), 168–84.

12. See S. B. Greenfield, 'The Formulaic Expression of the Theme of "Exile" in Anglo-Saxon Poetry', *Speculum* 30 (1955), 200–6; G. Clark, 'The Traveller recognises his Goal; a Theme in Anglo-Saxon Poetry', *JEGP* 64 (1965), 645–59;

and a more negative view, Adrien Bonjour, '*Beowulf* and the Beasts of Battle', *PMLA* 72 (1957), 563–73.

13. Line references are, respectively: *Elene* 426ff., *Judith* 83–94, *Maldon* 175–80, *Juliana* 695ff., *Andreas* 1164–7 and 1602–6.

14. Again, line references respectively: *Andreas* 454–8, *Genesis* 723ff., *Beowulf* 728ff., *Judith* 21–7, *Maldon* 146–8.

15. It could be compared with the speech of Ælfwine in *Maldon* 212–17.

16. Extracts are given in *Judith*, Ed. B. J. Timmer, 2nd ed., London 1961, pp. 14–16.

17. This milieu has been suggested for *Beowulf* by Larry D. Benson, 'The Pagan Coloring of *Beowulf*', in *Old English Poetry*, Ed. R. P. Creed, Providence 1967, pp. 193–213. For information about the missionary effort, see W. Levison, *England and the Continent in the Eighth Century*, Oxford 1946; translated texts to do with this work are available in *The Anglo-Saxon Missionaries in Germany*, Ed. C. H. Talbot, London 1954.

18. See the remarks of G. P. Krapp and E. van K. Dobbie in their edition of *The Exeter Book*, pp. xxx–xxxi.

19. The connection of this work with Felix is discussed by B. P. Kurtz, 'From St. Anthony to St. Guthlac: a study in biography', *Univ. of California Publications in Modern Philology* 12, 2 (1925–6), 103–46. The best treatment of English saints' lives as a whole is T. Wolpers, *Die Englische Heiligenlegende des Mittelalters*, Tübingen 1964. See also H. Delehaye, *The Legends of the Saints*, trans. D. Attwater, London 1962.

20. Evidence for this theory is given by C. W. Jones, *Saints' Lives and Chronicles in Early England*, New York, 1947, pp. 57–64. This most entertaining work also gives a translation of Felix's *Vita sancti Guthlaci*. Other translations may be found in C. Albertson, *Anglo-Saxon Saints and Heroes*, New York 1967.

21. The problem is realised, but slightly skirted, in *Anglo-Saxon Poetry*, trans. R. K. Gordon, rev. ed., London 1954, p. 256; the 'and', for instance, becomes 'and yet', and there are further changes.

22. See again Jones, *Saints' Lives and Chronicles*, footnotes to pp. 125–7.

23. R. Woolf, 'Saints' Lives', op. cit., p. 58.

24. The interest of the poet of *Guthlac A* in points of doctrinal detail is well indicated by L. K. Shook in two articles, 'The Burial Mound in *Guthlac A*', *MP* 58 (1960), 1–10; and 'The Prologue of the Old English *Guthlac A*', *Med. Stud.* 23 (1961), 294–304.

Chapter 6
Poetry and the Bible: The Junius Manuscript

1. *The Old English Heptateuch, Ælfric's Treatise on the Old and New Testament, and his Preface to Genesis*, Ed. S. J. Crawford, London 1922 (*EETS OS* 160), pp. 74–5.

2. *Heptateuch*, Ed. Crawford, pages 76–80.

3. The Old English Preface to the First Series of *Catholic Homilies*, Ed. B. Thorpe, London 1844, pp. 2–3.

4. The existence of a Greek translation from the Hebrew was rationalised, for example, by the legend that the seventy translators who worked on it independently found their versions identical and needing no revision, a story repeated by Augustine himself in his *De Doctrina Christiana* Book II, ch. 15. Admittedly, other Old English translations of the Bible did exist without any justification of that type, but such confidence was rare: see *The Cambridge History of the Bible* vol. II, Ed. G. W. H. Lampe, Cambridge 1969, pp. 338–491.

5. The most influential statement of this view is B. F. Huppé's *Doctrine and*

Poetry, New York 1959, but this has been echoed by several articles applying similar techniques; see for example J. E. Cross and S. I. Tucker, 'Allegorical Tradition and the Old English *Exodus*', *Neophil.* 44 (1960), 122–7, or T. D. Hill, 'Figural Narrative in *Andreas:* the Conversion of the Mermedonians', *NM* 70 (1969), 261–73.

6. There is a modern translation of this text in the 'Ancient Christian Writers' series, *The First Catechetical Instruction,* Ed. J. P. Christopher, Maryland 1946, esp. pp. 61–5.

7. See M. M. Larès, 'Echos d'un rite Hierosolymitain dans un manuscrit du haut Moyen Age Anglais', *Revue de l'histoire des Religions* 165 (1964), 13–47. It has also been suggested, by G. C. Thornley, 'The Accents and Points of Manuscript Junius XI' *TPS* (1953), 178–205, that the manuscript's hitherto obscure accent markings indicate that it was meant to be sung according to the modes of the 'liturgical recitative'—again implying a formal ecclesiastical use for the poems.

8. The text of the Bible available to the Anglo-Saxons may not always have been the same as the Latin Vulgate, since standardisation was still not complete; but no variant readings explain these poems' deviations. It would seem presumptuous to offer my own translation of the Latin Bible in place of the familiar Authorised Version.

9. See the notes to lines 280ff., in E. B. Irving jr's edition of *Exodus*, New Haven 1953.

10. E. B. Irving, op. cit., p. 84.

11. See the homily for Shrove Sunday in the first Series of the *Catholic Homilies,* Ed. Thorpe, pp. 152–65.

12. Bede, *In Genesim* (*CCSL* CXVIII A), Turnholt 1967, pp. 187–9.

13. E. Auerbach, *Mimesis,* trans. Willard Trask, p. 101. One might add that any commentator would of course *deny* this remark fiercely, asserting that the events must have happened, and that any other suggestion would overthrow the truth of Scripture. Nevertheless, anyone who reads much allegorical commentary soon becomes aware that for long periods the commentator's eyes are well 'off the object', and that the motives or feelings of the characters involved have only secondary interest, if even that. Milton's contrast of 'shadowy types' and 'truth', in *Paradise Lost* Book 12, bears witness to a similar realisation, as does his irritated denial, in Book 5, of 'mist, the common gloss Of Theologians'.

14. In his edition of *Exodus* already cited, Irving makes out a good case for inverting the order of lines 516–48 and 549–90; see pp. 11–12.

15. See, for example, G. T. Shepherd's article on 'Scriptural Poetry' in *Continuations and Beginnings,* p. 31.

16. These are listed by J. W. Tyrer, *Historical Survey of Holy Week,* London 1932, pp. 156–7, and are referred to also, with much other information, by R. T. Farrell in his interesting articles, 'The Unity of Old English *Daniel*' *RES NS* 18 (1967), 117–35, and 'A Reading of Old English *Exodus*' *RES NS* 20 (1969), 401–17. The most pertinent Biblical references (other than those on which the three poems are based) are Genesis xxvii, Deuteronomy xxxi–xxxii, Joshua iii–iv, 2 Chronicles xxxiv–xxxv, Ezekiel xxxvii, though, as Tyrer says, these would not necessarily all be found together in the same service.

17. The awareness of allegory breaks through, for instance, in lines 94–106, where the poet seems to identify the pillars of fire and cloud guiding the Israelites with the Holy Ghost showing Christians the 'way of life' [*lifweg*]. He also makes a fairly consistent distinction between the Israelites as 'seamen' and the Egyptians as belonging to the land, which might suggest some metaphor of the Christian as pilgrim and seafarer. But these suggestions are never developed quite unmistakably, and in his edition Irving can often find literal as well as allegorical explanations for particular lines or scenes. And in many places the poet's brevity

causes doubt, as for example in the speech of Moses already quoted on p. 139. When Moses calls the pursuing Egyptians *deade feðan* [dead troops], does this mean 'men who are spiritually dead, sinners trying to involve others in their sin', or just 'men already as good as dead'?

18. The priority of *Daniel* is confidently asserted in Klaeber's edition of *Beowulf,* pp. cx–cxi. Nowadays, however, few would agree that Hrothgar's sermon has been 'adapted—not entirely successfully—to the subject in hand'.

19. This question is dealt with very fully in R. T. Farrell's article already mentioned. Farrell makes a reasonable case for the integrity of the poem by indicating the many difficulties already present at this point in Biblical texts.

20. This point is slightly missed by those who equate *Azarias* with *Daniel* 279–361, as for instance in the *ASPR* edition of 'The Junius Manuscript'.

21. See the references given in the *ASPR* edition of 'The Junius Manuscript', pp. xxv–xxvi.

22. In *Doctrine and Poetry,* pp. 131–210, B. F. Huppé makes as much as he can of such points, but the only other very obvious borrowing from commentary, apart from the two mentioned, is the explanation (lines 1446–8) of why the raven did not return to the Ark, again a point of simply factual interest.

23. The process is well-described in B. J. Timmer's edition of *The Later Genesis,* Oxford 1948, pp. 48–54. Timmer concludes that the translator, as well as the original poet, was a Continental Saxon, and this may well be true, though to avoid ambiguity I have referred to the 'Old English translator'.

24. An interesting book on the relations of the various literatures of N.W. Europe, Old English, Old Saxon and Old Norse, is W. P. Lehmann's *The Development of Germanic Verse Form,* Austin, Texas 1956.

25. Milton knew Junius, who published the first edition of *Genesis* and the other three poems in 1655, twelve years before the appearance of *Paradise Lost.* The possibilities of influence are well reviewed, but rejected, by Timmer, op. cit., pp. 60–6.

26. For a good, short history of the growth of this legend, see J. M. Evans, *Paradise Lost and the Genesis Tradition,* Oxford 1968, a book I have used considerably, especially its chapter on 'The Heroic Treatments', pp. 142–67. Though I agree with Evans' conclusions, I feel that the changes made in *Genesis B* are rather more typical of Old English narrative and rather less a product of individual art than he implies.

27. The most obvious quotation from St. Paul is 1 Cor. xv, 21–2. For an account of Augustine's views, see Evans, op. cit., pp. 92–9.

28. Avitus and other Latin poets of the Dark Ages are connected with both Milton and *Genesis B* by Evans, op. cit., pp. 107–42. See also E. S. Duckett, *Latin Writers of the Fifth Century,* New York 1930, for a discussion with ample (translated) quotations.

29. Ælfric's translation of Alcuin was edited by G. E. MacLean in *Anglia* 6 (1883), 425–73, and 7 (1884), 1–59. To this negative evidence of omission one might add his plain statement that the tree of knowledge was not itself fatal, in Ælfric's *Exameron,* Ed. S. J. Crawford (*BAP* vol. 10), Hamburg 1921, p. 66.

30. Evans argues this, op. cit., p. 166, and connects the poem's viewpoint with reaction against the Saxon monk Gottschalk's very rigorous views on predestination, condemned officially in 848 and 849. For an account of the controversy, see M. J. W. Laistner, *Thought and Letters in Western Europe: A.D. 500–900,* London 1931, pp. 242–6.

31. This is marked off from the other three poems not only stylistically, but by handwriting (see p. 81), and by the fact that it ends with the comment *Finit Liber II.* Though the end of *Daniel* is lost, it is probable that the first three poems together constituted *Liber I,* and were therefore seen in some way as a unit.

Though he did not connect the other poems with Easter Week or Holy Saturday, M. D. Clubb suggested, in his edition of *Christ and Satan*, New Haven 1925, that the poem was based on a homily for Easter Sunday, a fact which might account for its incorporation in this manuscript. It has been suggested that *Christ and Satan* echoes *Genesis B* deliberately, by Jean I. Young, 'Two Notes on the *Later Genesis*', in *The Anglo-Saxons*, Ed. P. Clemoes, London 1959, pp. 204–11.

32. Irving's edition of *Exodus*, p. 15.

33. William James, *The Will to Believe and other essays*, New York and London 1897, p. 66.

34. The phrase comes from J. R. R. Tolkien, '*Beowulf*: the Monsters and the Critics', pp. 247–8.

35. B. Smalley, *The Study of the Bible in the Middle Ages*, 2nd ed., Oxford 1952, pp. 369–70.

Chapter 7
Poetry and the individual: Cynewulf

1. The evidence for Cynewulf's date and nationality rests on two facts: (a) the alternative spellings of his name, and the non-appearance of the common Northern form Cyniwulf; and (b) imperfect rhymes such as *miht: þeaht* or *onwreah: fah* in one section of *Elene*. In an Anglian dialect these would have been, more neatly, *mæht: þæht* and *onwrah: fah*. These and other facts are discussed by K. Sisam, *Studies in the History of Old English Literature*, pp. 1–28. Probably Cynewulf was a West Mercian from around 800–50.

2. W. P. Lehmann, *The Development of Germanic Verse Form*, p. 136. Otfrid's work is usually dated *c.* 865–870, i.e. about a generation after Cynewulf.

3. *Juliana*, Ed. Rosemary Woolf, London 1955, p. 19.

4. The exception is *Juliana*, where the runes, to tell the truth, make little apparent sense. For fuller discussions of the runes and 'signatures', see Sisam, loc. cit.; and R. W. V. Elliott, *Runes: an Introduction*, 2nd ed., Manchester 1963; and 'Cynewulf's Runes in *Crist*' and *Elene*, *ES* 34 (1953), 49–57, 193–204.

5. Edited in vol. VI of *The Anglo-Saxon Poetic Records*, 'The Minor Poems', pp. 28–30.

6. These suggestions are made by A. S. Cook in his edition of *The Christ of Cynewulf*, Boston 1909, pages 151–63. They are largely accepted by R. K. Gordon and C. W. Kennedy in their translations of the poem, respectively in *Anglo-Saxon Poetry*, pp. 141–8, and *The Poems of Cynewulf*, New York and London 1910, pp. 166–78.

7. It is not very clear what Cynewulf means here. Possibly he is using the sea as a symbol of the transitoriness of life, with the meaning: 'all our wealth has gone; even while it was here it was never secure.'

8. Especially by S. K. Das, *Cynewulf and the Cynewulf Canon*, Calcutta 1942, and Claes Schaar, *Critical Studies in the Cynewulf Group*. See their conclusions on pp. 236–7 and 323–6 respectively.

9. *Anglo-Saxon Poetic Records* vol. III, 'The Exeter Book', p. xxvi.

10. This can be found in J-P. Migne's *Patrologia Latina* vol. 76, Paris 1849, columns 1213–19. Cynewulf picks up his source at the start of the ninth paragraph.

11. As usual, some have thought the situation so unclear as to demand re-arrangement or additions somewhere, see Cook's edition of the *Christ*, pp. 129–31.

12. There is a separate edition and translation of them by Jackson J. Campbell, *The Advent Lyrics of the Exeter Book*, Princeton 1959.

13. Robert B. Burlin, *The Old English Advent: a typological commentary*, New Haven 1968.

14. This has been noted by Rosemary Woolf, 'Doctrinal Influences on *The Dream of the Rood*', *Medium Aevum* 27 (1958), 137–53, and also in Professor P. Clemoes' inaugural lecture, *Rhythm and Cosmic Order in Old English Christian Literature*, Cambridge 1970.

15. These and other deliberate ambiguities have been set out, among others, by L. H. Leiter, '*The Dream of the Rood:* Patterns of Transformation', in *Old English Poetry*, Ed. R. P. Creed, pp. 93–127; F. Patten, 'Structure and Meaning in *The Dream of the Rood*', *ES* 49 (1968), 385–401; and M. J. Swanton, 'Ambiguity and Anticipation in *The Dream of the Rood*', *NM* 70 (1969), 407–25.

16. The phrase comes from the end of the *Advent* poem, where it refers to the duality of Christ's nature; but the verb *wrixlan* [to change or vary] is used to describe the creation of poetry in *Beowulf* 874 and the Exeter *Maxims* 4. It seems a good phrase to describe the characteristic activity of Old English poets.

17. The *Doomsday* poem has been praised, by G. T. Shepherd in his article on 'Scriptural Poetry' in *Continuations and Beginnings*, p. 20, but in terms which show sufficiently its difference from the *Ascension*. One might note that the *Advent* also has long and complex structures; but if one looks, say, at lines 261–74, the comparative repetitiousness and slight clumsiness becomes apparent.

18. K. Sisam, *Studies*, p. 17.

19. This conclusion may seem less rash if one considers the work now being done on that other Old English 'classic', the prose-writer Ælfric. There is no doubt about his massively erudite Latinity. Still, in his inaugural lecture already mentioned, Professor Clemoes notes the origin of Ælfric's very characteristic rhythmic prose in native vernacular poetry; he too made equal use of two literary cultures.

20. See the *Acta Sanctorum*, produced by the Bollandist Society from 1643 onwards, and reprinted in Brussels from 1965 onwards. Legends at least closely similar to *Elene* and *Juliana* are to be found respectively under May 4th (pp. 445–8) and February 16th (pp. 873–7).

21. C. Schaar, *Critical Studies*, p. 29. The point is taken up with more energy by C. W. Kennedy, *The Earliest English Poetry*, London 1943, p. 210.

22. P. O. E. Gradon makes the charge that Cynewulf deviated little from his source in her edition of *Elene*, London 1958, p. 20. Against this, see Robert Stepsis and Richard Rand, 'Contrast and Conversion in Cynewulf's *Elene*', *NM* 70 (1969), 273–82. This article shows in detail Cynewulf's thematic additions of light and darkness, burial and discovery. It does not, however, remark on the similarity of these to parts of *Andreas, Judith, Juliana* or indeed *Beowulf*, so that the assumption that the idea was original with Cynewulf may be a little over-stated. A recent and thorough article is J. Gardner, 'Cynewulf's *Elene*: Sources and Structure', *Neophil.* 54 (1970), 65–76.

23. Of course Cynewulf was wrong here. The date of Constantine's victory at the Milvian Bridge was A.D. 312. He took the false date from his source.

24. K. Sisam, *Studies*, p. 24.

25. For informative discussions of this concept, deeply rooted in the Christian breakdown of classical levels of style, see E. Auerbach, *Literary Language and its Public,* trans. R. Manheim, London 1965, especially the chapters on 'Sermo Humilis' and 'Latin Prose in the Early Middle Ages'.

26. The quotations are from the emended text provided by S.R.T.O. d'Ardenne in her edition of *Þe Liflade ant te Passiun of Seinte Iuliene*, London 1961 (*EETS* 248). The legend can be strongly recommended for sheer verve if for nothing else.

Chapter 8
The decline: King Alfred and after

1. Dating Old English poems is notoriously difficult and uncertain, but virtually no one now thinks of *Beowulf* as post-825; the Junius poems are generally thought to be earlier; Cynewulf is not likely to be after 850, while *Andreas* and *Guthlac* are put close to or before him. The single long exception is one tending to prove the rule—*Genesis B* may be dated around 900, but of course is probably not the work of an Anglo-Saxon. Short poems are obviously harder to place, and some of the 'elegies', for instance, are probably early tenth-century works.

2. The poem appears to be mentioned in Symeon's *Historia Dunelmensis Ecclesiae,* around 1109, and refers to St Cuthbert's body as within the town, which it was not before 1104. But this traditional argument is not quite certain; see H. S. Offler, 'The Date of Durham *(Carmen de Situ Dunelmi)*', *JEGP* 61 (1962), 591–4. This suggests that the poem could be fifty or sixty years earlier.

3. Cecily Clark's edition of *The Peterborough Chronicle 1070–1154,* 2nd ed., Oxford 1970, has some interesting remarks on this general topic, esp. pp. xlii-xlv. It looks as if the Peterborough chronicler had been trained to write West Saxon, but did not write it naturally, making some revealing mistakes. The very rapid dissolution of Old English makes it quite likely that the West Saxon we know was a formalised literary language not closely related to the spoken one, and therefore requiring to be taught. Once the 'schools' disappeared, the tradition went too. Of course this must have made the composition of poetry even harder. See C. L. Wrenn, 'Standard Old English', reprinted in *Word and Symbol,* London 1967, pp. 57–77; F. P. Magoun, 'Colloquial Old and Middle English', *Harvard Studies and Notes in Philology and Literature* 14 (1937), 167–73; and also Aldo Ricci, 'The Anglo-Saxon 11th Century Crisis', *RES* 5 (1929), 1–11.

4. This is true of one of the manuscripts. The other (now lost) had *strong. Stronge* could be a copyist's error rather than the poet's; but this would only postpone the situation described for a generation or so.

5. *Asser's Life of King Alfred,* Ed. W. H. Stevenson, Oxford 1904, new impression with supplement by D. Whitelock, 1959, ch. 23.

6. D. Whitelock, in the edition cited above, defends the work from the charge of being a late forgery, and extends the defence in *The Genuine Asser,* Stenton Lecture for 1967, Reading.

7. Quoted from vol. V of the *Anglo-Saxon Poetic Records,* 'The Paris Psalter and the Metres of Boethius', Ed. G. P. Krapp, New York and London 1932. References are to sections, and lines within the section.

8. Quoted from W. J. Sedgefield, *King Alfred's Old English Version of Boethius,* Oxford 1899. Contractions have been expanded.

9. Larry D. Benson, 'The Literary Character of Anglo-Saxon Formulaic Poetry', *PMLA* 81 (1966), 334–41.

10. F. Anne Payne, *King Alfred and Boethius,* Madison, Wisconsin 1968.

11. ibid., p. 74.

12. ibid., p. 104.

13. Marjorie Daunt, 'Old English Verse and English Speech Rhythm', *TPS* (1946), 56–72. There is no doubt that the article is generally right, but is too often glibly and carelessly quoted as an excuse for not considering the special features of the verse.

14. A. McIntosh, 'Wulfstan's Prose', *PBA* 35 (1949), 109–42.

15. Quoted from *Sweet's Anglo-Saxon Reader* (XVI), 15th ed. revised by D. Whitelock, Oxford 1967.

16. Quoted from G. I. Needham's edition of *Ælfric: Lives of Three English Saints,* London 1966.

17. The 'sharing' of poetry is properly stressed by B. M. H. Strang, *A History of English,* London 1970, p. 330, though her assumption that this form of society was destroyed by the Conquest leaves several problems unanswered.

18. These are found conveniently in vol. VI of the *Anglo-Saxon Poetic Records,* 'The Minor Poems', though the editors, as they admit, have omitted several pieces that could be called verse.

19. Milton was especially annoyed by it, mentioning the battle in Book Five of his *History of Britain,* and adding, 'to describe which, the *Saxon* Annalist wont to be sober and succinct, whether the same or another writer, now labouring under the weight of his Argument, and overcharg'd, runs on a sudden into such extravagant fansies and metaphors, as bear him quite beside the scope of being understood'.

20. An article by W. F. Bolton, ' "Variation" in *The Battle of Brunanburh*', *RES NS* 19 (1968), 363–72, seeks to analyse the poem's structure at greater length.

21. One feature that may be a mark of late date is the large number of second half-lines of A type, often intensive 'tags' or obvious noun-variations, the easiest phrases of all to make up and throw in. A. Campbell notes this in his edition of *The Battle of Brunanburh,* London 1938, pp. 30–3, but assumes it to be deliberate (as it may be, in that poem).

22. Compare A. B. Lord's descriptions of the late stages of a tradition in *The Singer of Tales,* pp. 43–5 and 124–38.

23. The last piece in the *Chronicle* that might be called verse comes under 1104, but there are several in the ten or twenty years after the Conquest.

24. E. B. Irving, 'The Heroic Style in *The Battle of Maldon*', *SP* 58 (1961), 457–67.

25. The last quotation is from E. D. Laborde, 'The Style of *The Battle of Maldon*', *MLR* 19 (1924), 401–17; the idea that *Maldon* is a 'popular' poem can be found, for instance, in R. M. Wilson, *Early Middle English Literature,* London 1939, pp. 14–16. Though this last view is now unfashionable, it does recognise that an explanation is needed for the partial survival of Old English poetic vocabulary up to the twelfth century and beyond.

SELECTED BIBLIOGRAPHY

(The discussion of Old English literature has been carried on to a very large extent through articles in learned journals, which generally present single points or views. Where relevant, many of these have been referred to above, in the Notes. However, except where they are of primary importance, or immediate utility, articles have not been listed a second time here.)

1. EDITIONS

The six volumes of *The Anglo-Saxon Poetic Records*, Ed. G. P. Krapp and E. van K. Dobbie, New York and London 1931–54, have been used throughout this book for the sake of conformity. However, there are many editions of single poems which will be much more useful to students. The 'Methuen's Old English Library' series, printed in London, includes: *Waldere*, Ed. F. Norman (2nd ed. 1949); *The Dream of the Rood*, Ed. B. Dickins and A. S. C. Ross (rev. ed. 1954); *Juliana*, Ed. R. Woolf (1955); *The Battle of Maldon*, Ed. E. V. Gordon (rev. ed. 1957); *Elene*, Ed. P. O. E. Gradon (1958); *Judith*, Ed. B. J. Timmer (2nd ed. 1961); *Deor*, Ed. K. Malone (3rd ed. 1961); *The Seafarer*, Ed. I. L. Gordon (1966); *Three Northumbrian Poems*, Ed. A. H. Smith (rev. ed. 1968); *The Wanderer*, Ed. T. P. Dunning and A. J. Bliss (1969). Manchester University Press has published R. F. Leslie's editions of *Three Old English Elegies* (1961) and *The Wanderer* (1966), as well as N. F. Blake's *The Phoenix* (1964) and M. J. Swanton's *The Dream of the Rood* (1970). In addition, there are good single editions of: *The Later Genesis*, Ed. B. J. Timmer, Oxford 1948; *Exodus*, Ed. E. B. Irving jr, New Haven 1953; *Andreas and The Fates of the Apostles*, Ed. K. R. Brooks, Oxford 1961; *Christ*, Ed. A. S. Cook, Boston 1909; *The Advent Lyrics of the Exeter Book*, Ed. Jackson J. Campbell, Princeton 1959; *The Riddles of the Exeter Book*, Ed. F. Tupper, Boston 1910; *Gnomic Poetry in Anglo-Saxon*, Ed. Blanche C. Williams, New York 1914; *Brunanburh*, Ed. A. Campbell, London 1938; and *The Poetical Dialogues of Solomon and Saturn*, Ed. R. J. Menner, New York, 1941. Fr. Klaeber's edition of *Beowulf*, 3rd ed., Boston 1950, is invaluable. Recent collections include J. C. Pope's *Seven Old English Poems*, New York 1966; and B. F. Huppé's *The Web of Words*, Albany 1970, an edition of *The Dream of the Rood, Judith,* and two meditative poems, with translation and commentary.

2. TRANSLATIONS

Many Old English poems have been translated repeatedly. The most convenient collections are R. K. Gordon's *Anglo-Saxon Poetry*, rev. ed., London 1954 (Everyman Library); and C. W. Kennedy's *The Poems of Cynewulf* and *The Cædmon Poems*, London 1910 and 1916 respectively. Since Kennedy interprets 'Cynewulf' and 'Cædmon' very widely, these two volumes are a guide to the bulk of the religious poetry. More modern works include: *The Anglo-Saxon Riddles of the Exeter Book*, trans. P. F. Baum, Durham, N. C. 1963; *Beowulf*, trans. E. T. Donaldson, London 1967; and *A Choice of Anglo-Saxon Verse*, Ed. and trans. R. Hamer, London 1970.

3. INTERPRETATION AND CRITICISM

(a) General

Essential Articles for the Study of Old English Poetry, Ed. J. B. Bessinger jr. and S. J. Kahrl, Hamden, Connecticut 1968. (The best collection available)
Old English Poetry: fifteen essays, Ed. R. P. Creed, Providence 1967.
J. E. Cross, 'The Old English Period', in *The Middle Ages* (Sphere History of Literature vol. I), Ed. W. F. Bolton, London 1970, pp. 12–66.
S. B. Greenfield, *A Critical History of Old English Literature*, New York 1965
N. D. Isaacs, *Structural Principles in Old English Poetry*, Knoxville 1968
Continuations and Beginnings, Ed. E. G. Stanley, London 1966
Old English Literature: twenty-two analytical essays, Ed. M. Stevens and J. Mandel, Lincoln, Nebraska 1968
C. L. Wrenn, *A Study of Old English Literature*, London 1967

Several important articles are to be found in collections presented to scholars, for instance N. K. Chadwick's contribution to *The Anglo-Saxons: Studies for Bruce Dickins*, Ed. P. Clemoes, London 1959; the essays by G. N. Garmonsway, Alain Renoir, and J. C. Pope in *Franciplegius: Medieval and Linguistic Studies in Honour of F. P. Magoun*, Ed. J. B. Bessinger jr and R. P. Creed, New York and London 1965; and those by Bessinger, E. G. Stanley, R. Woolf and others in *Studies in Old English Literature in Honor of A. G. Brodeur*, Ed. S. B. Greenfield, Eugene, Oregon 1963. Many of the contributions to this latter volume may also be found in *CL* 14 (1962).

(b) Heroic poetry

Beowulf and its Analogues, Ed. and trans. G. N. Garmonsway and Jacqueline Simpson, London and New York 1968
The Beowulf Poet, Ed. D. K. Fry, New Jersey 1968 (20th Century Views series)
W. F. Bolton, 'Byrhtnoth in the Wilderness', *MLR* 64 (1969), 481–90
A. Bonjour, *The Digressions in Beowulf*, Oxford 1950
——, *Twelve Beowulf Papers 1940–60*, Neuchatel and Geneva 1962
A. G. Brodeur, *The Art of Beowulf*, Berkeley and Los Angeles 1959
R. W. Chambers, *Beowulf: an Introduction*, 3rd ed. with supplement by C. L. Wrenn, Cambridge 1959
G. Clark, '*The Battle of Maldon*: a heroic poem', *Speculum* 43 (1968), 52–71
R. Girvan, *Beowulf and the Seventh Century*, rev. ed. with supplement by R. Bruce-Mitford, London 1971
M. E. Goldsmith, *The Mode and Meaning of Beowulf*, London 1970
E. B. Irving jr, *A Reading of Beowulf*, New Haven 1968

W. W. Lawrence, *Beowulf and Epic Tradition*, 2nd ed., New York 1961
L. E. Nicholson, *An Anthology of Beowulf Criticism*, Notre Dame 1963. (Includes important articles by J. R. R. Tolkien and R. E. Kaske)
K. Sisam, *The Structure of Beowulf*, Oxford 1965
G. V. Smithers, *The Making of Beowulf*, Durham 1961. (Inaugural lecture)
D. Whitelock, *The Audience of Beowulf*, Oxford 1951

(c) *Wisdom poetry*

Morton W. Bloomfield, 'The Form of *Deor*', *PMLA* 79 (1964), 534–41; 'Understanding Old English Poetry', *Annuale Medievale* 9 (1968), 5–25
P. Clemoes, '*Mens absentia cogitans* in *The Wanderer* and *The Seafarer*', in *Medieval Literature and Civilisation: studies in memory of G. N. Garmonsway*, Ed. D. A. Pearsall and R. A. Waldron, London 1969
J. E. Cross, 'On the Genre of *The Wanderer*', *Neophil.* 45 (1961), 63–75
P. L. Henry, *The Early English and Celtic Lyric*, London 1966
E. G. Stanley, 'Old English Poetic Diction and the Interpretation of *The Wanderer*, *The Seafarer*, and *The Penitent's Prayer*', *Anglia* 73 (1955), 413–66
R. D. Stevick, 'Formal Aspects of *The Wife's Lament*', *JEGP* 59 (1960), 21–5

(d) *Religious literature*

Robert B. Burlin, *The Old English Advent: a typological commentary*, New Haven 1968
J. M. Evans, *Paradise Lost and the Genesis Tradition*, Oxford 1968
B. F. Huppé, *Doctrine and Poetry*, New York 1959
C. W. Jones, *Saints' Lives and Chronicles in Early England*, New York 1947
B. Raw, '*The Dream of the Rood* and its connections with Early Christian Art', *Medium Aevum* 39 (1970), 239–56
J. F. Vickrey, 'The Vision of Eve in *Genesis B*', *Speculum* 44 (1969), 86–102
R. Woolf, 'The Devil in Old English Poetry', *RES NS* 4 (1953), 1–12; 'Doctrinal Influences on *The Dream of the Rood*', *Medium Aevum* 27 (1958), 137–53

(e) *Language and style*

Larry D. Benson, 'The Literary Character of Anglo-Saxon Formulaic Poetry', *PMLA* 81 (1966), 334–41
A. J. Bliss, *The Metre of Beowulf*, Oxford 1958
A. Campbell, 'The Old English Epic Style', in *English and Medieval Studies presented to J. R. R. Tolkien*, Ed. N. Davis and C. L. Wrenn, London 1963
P. Clemoes, *Rhythm and Cosmic Order in Old English Christian Literature*, Cambridge 1970. (Inaugural lecture)
W. P. Lehmann, *The Development of Germanic Verse Form*, Austin, Texas 1956
A. B. Lord, *The Singer of Tales*, Cambridge, Mass. 1960
J. C. Pope, *The Rhythm of Beowulf*, 2nd ed., New Haven, 1966
R. Quirk, 'Poetic Language and Old English Metre', in *Early English and Norse Studies presented to A. H. Smith*, Ed. A. Brown and P. Foote, London 1963
Claes Schaar, *Critical Studies in the Cynewulf Group*, Lund 1949
W. Whallon, 'The Diction of Beowulf', *PMLA* 76 (1961), 309–19

(f) *Miscellaneous*

In this section I have added a few books which are suggestive rather than utilitarian. In different ways, F. Anne Payne, *King Alfred and Boethius*, Madison, Wisc. 1968, and *Honour and Shame: the values of Mediterranean society*,

Ed. J. G. Peristiany, London 1965, are useful in helping one to understand how ideas may be formed and disseminated in non-industrial societies. There is a good description of the ramifications of wisdom literature in N. K. Chadwick's *Poetry and Prophecy,* Cambridge 1952. The limits of reliability to be expected from non-literate peoples are discussed in Jan Vansina's *Oral Tradition: a study in historical methodology,* London 1965, in which examples are drawn mainly from modern Africa. Some of the puzzles of the 'figural' view may be cleared up by G. W. H. Lampe and K. J. Woolcombe, *Essays on Typology,* London 1957. Students faced with the problem of translating Old into Modern English will find several useful contributions in the collection *On Translation,* Ed. R. A. Brower, Cambridge, Mass. 1959

(g) *Recent additions*

While this book has been in press, a certain amount of new critical material has appeared, for the most part along well-established lines. Thomas D. Hill, 'Notes on the Old English *Maxims* I and II', *NQ* 215 (1970), 445–7, remarks on the influence of Old Testament wisdom literature, while R. E. Kaske, '*Beowulf* and the Book of Enoch', *Speculum* 46 (1971), 421–31, observes traces of the Apocrypha. In 'The *Micel Wundor* of *Genesis B*', *SP* 68 (1971), 245–54, John F. Vickrey continues to argue for the orthodoxy of that poem, suggesting an alternative translation for the speech quoted on p. 151 above. In '*The Wanderer* 65b–72: the Passions of the Mind and the Cardinal Virtues', *Neophil.* 55 (1971), 73–88, F. N. M. Diekstra urges yet once more that this poem finds its inspiration in 'Latin-Christian literature'. Alvin A. Lee's book *The Guest-Hall of Eden,* New Haven and London 1972, follows the same general tradition but deserves commendation for its wide range, as does Jackson J. Campbell's 'Schematic Technique in *Judith*', *ELH* 38 (1971), 155–72, an article which notes both symbolic and narrative features in that poem. Milton McC. Gatch's *Loyalties and Traditions: Man and his World in Old English Literature,* New York 1971, offers a broad historical and literary coverage. In conclusion, the *Philological Essays in Honour of H. D. Meritt,* Ed. James L. Rosier, Paris and The Hague 1970, include not only pieces by Rosier, J. C. Pope, and Alistair Campbell, but also G. V. Smithers' interesting study of the concept of fate, 'Destiny and the Heroic Warrior in *Beowulf*', pp. 62–81.

INDEX

Main references are italicised